1 'I've earned a good deal of butter to my bread in my time;
but I should have enjoyed it more if it had been better spread.'

Barry Anthony is a historian with a particular interest in the Victorian and Edwardian period. He has written extensively about popular culture and entertainment, co-authoring, with Richard Brown, a groundbreaking study of the early British cinema, *A Victorian Film Enterprise*.

THE KING'S JESTER

The Life of Dan Leno, Victorian Comic Genius

BARRY ANTHONY

I.B. TAURIS

LONDON · NEW YORK

Published in 2010 by I.B.Tauris & Co Ltd
6 Salem Road, London W2 4BU
175 Fifth Avenue, New York NY 10010
www.ibtauris.com

Distributed in the United States and Canada Exclusively by Palgrave Macmillan
175 Fifth Avenue, New York NY 10010

ISBN: 978 1 84885 430 7

A full CIP record for this book is available from the British Library
A full CIP record is available from the Library of Congress

Library of Congress Catalog Card Number: available

Typeset in Modern Extended by Artform, Oxfordshire
Printed and bound in the UK by CPI Antony Rowe, Chippenham
from camera-ready copy edited and supplied by the author with the assistance of Alan Mauro

CONTENTS

ILLUSTRATIONS

FOREWORD

I'd dreamt the dream again and again. It was a regularly recurring one which I'd first had when I was fifteen and last had forty years ago. It *was* a dream – not a nightmare. It was quite ordinary. I'd make my way around a high-ceilinged Victorian house, through the rooms, down steps into a garden (lit by tiny lanterns) and finally (the dream always ended this way) I would go down into a cellar where I would be surrounded by images of myself. That was the only slightly disturbing part.

I never told anyone about it. It wasn't sensational or even vaguely interesting till, in the early sixties, I had a phone call from two actor friends. They'd moved into a new flat and thought I'd like to see it.

So one Sunday morning myself and my first wife, Ann, drove to Brixton to have a look. We turned into Ackerman Road and halfway down I said, 'Stop! This is the house I've dreamed about for years.' I dashed up the front steps and pushed past our friends. 'Don't say a word about these rooms I'll tell you exactly what they're like.' I did and described them perfectly before we went in.

Now I started to get over excited and burbled on about the magically-lit garden and the cellar full of Roy Hudd clones. The garden wasn't lit and there was no way down into the cellar. The only time I was in the house and didn't end up in the cellar was when I was in the *actual* house. Slightly shaky I asked why they wanted me to see the place. 'This house,' they explained, 'once belonged to the Victorian comedian, Dan Leno, so, knowing how keen you are on music hall, we thought you'd like to see it.' 'I've seen it dozens of times before,' I said and told them about the recurring dream. They, and my wife, were as intrigued as I was. That was all there was to it.

We came away with me determined to find out more about Mr Leno.

He was quite simply the most popular music hall and pantomime comedian of his day. That he was loved and admired by countless thousands is proven by the turn out for his funeral. A three and a half-mile route lined with people, standing three deep, all the way. My Gran used to say whenever it rained it was the angels crying with laughter at Dan.

Audiences of his time (1860–1904) are so often thought of as people whose humour was of the most basic kind. Dan Leno's wasn't. As you will read in the following pages his thinking was highly inventive, off the wall, fantastical and totally original. So much for the Victorians only appreciating the obvious.

Barry Anthony has learned so much more than I about the great little clown who became The King's Jester. He has brought it all together in this fascinating and, so well documented, story of his life and times.

Let me just tidy up the parts of my recurring dream I didn't understand, I discovered he was one of the first to have fairy lights in his garden and, being a dancer (he was the Champion Clog-Dancer of the World in 1880) he could easily have rehearsed in front of mirrors.

I have to tell you I am not in the least bit psychic. If anything I'm ultra sceptical. I told about my dream on television many years ago and the response was amazing. Letters and memories from people who had seen, and never forgotten, Dan. There was correspondence from mediums too. Apparently he was always popping up in their seances and they all assured me that he was a benign influence. The only thing so many of them advised was for me not to go to where he was buried. I was living just round the corner from that very spot.

Just a couple of years ago The Grand Order of Water Rats had the Leno grave refurbished and, as a King Rat, I was asked to be at the graveside for a short service of remembrance. I declined the invitation.

Roy Hudd OBE
President of The British Music Hall Society

ACKNOWLEDGEMENTS

First and foremost I would like to thank Tony Barker without whose assistance this book would not have been possible. As editor of *Music Hall* and producer of several CD compilations of historic recordings Tony has been a mainstay of music hall studies for many years. I would also like to acknowledge the help and encouragement provided by comedy expert Glenn Mitchell; the co-editors of *Music Hall Studies* Richard Anthony Baker and Max Tyler; and early film historians the late John Barnes and his brother Bill, Richard Brown, Stephen Herbert and Tony Fletcher. Others to have given valuable advice have been Pat and Malcolm Crisp; Pamela Dodsworth; Lydia and Tony Galvin; Bill Greenwell; Tony Lidington (presenter of the one man show *Dan Leno: The King's Jester*); Fred Mead; Cliff Reynolds and Stephen Roud. I would also like to thank Alan Mauro and Peter Barnes for their help in preparing this book and Roy Hudd for contributing such an excellent foreword. Finally my thanks go to my wife Jean and my daughters Madeleine and Elizabeth for supplying round-the-clock support and for sharing their home with Dan for such a very long time.

Tony Barker supplied illustrations 6, 8, 9, 13, 14, 20, 22, 25 and 39; Fred Mead illustration 38; Cliff Reynolds illustrations 28 and 35. The remainder are from the author's collection.

1

PRELUDE

The Gaumont movie camera clattered into action. It had been a good morning for filming, the low November sun throwing trees and buildings into sharp relief. But now, at midday, a cold wind began to blow, with heavily-banked rain clouds filling the sky. Despite the sudden change in the weather the scene was still full of sombre interest. Dark, dense crowds stood respectfully watching the long procession of carriages slowly depart from Clapham Park. The hearse was pulled by six black horses, plumed and with ornate trappings. Beside, as pallbearers, walked some of the most famous stars of the British music hall.

Londoners had turned out in their thousands to bid farewell to an old and cherished friend. There were few people, from King Edward downward, who did not spare a thought for Dan Leno on the day of his funeral. Some had known him by other names – 'Little George, the Infant Wonder'; one of 'The Brothers Leno'; 'Young Leno'; 'Dan Patrick, Irish Comedian'; even 'Pongo', the most mischievous of stage monkeys. For the previous 20 years, however, the nation's leading comedian had been almost universally referred to as 'Dan'.

Alongside the elaborate floral tributes, from celebrities such as the actor Sir Henry Irving and the opera diva Nellie Melba, were more humble offerings from those who had known him in earlier years. There were wreathes from his brother, Harry Galvin, with whom he had danced as a boy in the 1860s; from Bradley Truman, a comedian he had shared the bill with in the 1870s; from King Ohmy and other proprietors of Northern music halls where he had made his earliest successes. And from his uncle and life-long friend Johnny Danvers, there was an allusion to his seemingly endless supply of nervous energy, a cushion of flowers bearing the words 'Rest, Dan, Rest.'

After a service at the Church of the Ascension, Balham Hill, the cortège moved on, its progress impeded by a multitude of mourners. Such was the congestion that shops closed their doors and the Clapham tramcars suspended their services. Street hawkers did a brisk trade in 'In Memoriam' cards, decorated with a photo of the departed comedian and bearing a few lines of doggerel verse. Despite a decade of entertaining

privileged audiences in the spectacular pantomimes presented at the
Theatre Royal, Drury Lane, Dan was still seen by millions of the working classes as their principal representative. It was a culture that had
seen many changes since his childhood days in the slums of London and
Liverpool, and one which was to alter even more radically within the
next few decades. During his final years Dan had become a major figure
in the fledgling film and recording industries. As one of the earliest
superstars of a new, mass media age he had also become the first of many
performers to suffer the negative consequences of unlimited fame and a
life lived almost entirely in the public gaze.

By the time the carriages reached Tooting Cemetery it was three in
the afternoon, too dark for the Gaumont cameraman to secure any
further 'animated photographs'. A notice attached to the gates announced that the interment was to be held in private, but Dan's audience, always reluctant to let him take his leave, crushed against the gates
until their heavy chains gave way. Gradually the crowd filed past the
simple stone cross, its base bearing the inscription 'Here Sleeps the King
of Laughter-Makers'. They were paying their last respects not only to
the comedian Dan Leno, but to the many characters he had created.
There was the blustering recruiting sergeant with so many medals that
he had become knock-kneed under their weight; the ice-cream seller
whose sweetheart left him for another because 'she liked his raspberry
better'; the harassed mother who stopped to exchange a few words before rushing 'off to buy milk for the twins'. And above all there was Mrs
Kelly, the infamous gossip and busybody whose strategic position at the
street corner allowed her to keep an eagle eye on what things had happened and what were about to take place.

2

AN INCONVENIENCE

London during the mid-nineteenth century was a city bursting at the seams. The end of the Napoleonic wars in 1815 had caused a general increase in population, added to which rural poverty and the lure of regular employment resulted in a vast influx of migrants into the capital. London's heavy clay soil provided the raw material for London's growth. Brickfields and kilns multiplied on the fringes of the city, their distinctive yellow bricks being laid one on the other to build streets of new houses, railway stations, churches and chapels, public houses and music halls. At the ancient centre of London a maze of courts and alleys harboured a seething population of labourers, street traders, bricklayers, beggars, prostitutes and, sometimes, comic singers – all desperately struggling to keep body and soul together. Male life expectancy over the whole of London hovered around the mid-30s, but in the densely-packed central area the inhabitants might expect substantially less. The old graveyards were so choked with burials that extensive new necropolises were created in the outer, less congested suburbs.

George Wild Galvin, later to become famous as Dan Leno, joined the three and a half million inhabitants of London on 20 December 1860. Amid such crowds and turmoil his birth was unremarkable. 'Everybody – mark this – everybody has to be born, one way or another,' he wrote in a spoof autobiography, 'you have to go through this inconvenience.' Dan's comments emphasised the ordinariness of being born. It was a matter of fact, commonplace sort of thing, like catching a cold or stubbing one's toe. But it was unavoidable – 'birth comes to us all sooner or later.'[1]

That other inescapable inconvenience caught up with Dan only 43 years later. Despite its brevity, his life ended at an appropriate time. His career as a music-hall comedian was played out against a background of an evolving entertainment business. To provide diversions for a rapidly multiplying population, music halls had grown larger, attempting to balance the intimacy of their public-house origins with the constant requirement to increase audience capacity. The industrialisation of music halls continued with the establishment of limited companies and syndicates, which attempted to impose a degree of standardisation and centralised control. Being by definition 'variety', music hall proved difficult to regulate, but economic factors were eventually to win the day. A few weeks after Dan's death a gigantic 'palace of variety', the London Coliseum, opened in central London. Its enormous stage and immense auditorium dictated that entertainments should be excessive in scale and effect – the antithesis of Dan's miniature, reflective style of performance. His death drew the curtain on a form of entertainment that still bore traces of its 'free and easy' tavern-concert ancestry, while the Coliseum heralded an age of spectacular but impersonal showmanship.

Unlike *Sunset Boulevard*'s Norma Desmond, Dan stayed small, the music hall got big. He achieved his success by being diminutive in both a physical and intellectual sense. On stage he stuttered and stumbled, struggling to convey the intricacies, and inconveniences of everyday life. His characters were born losers: careworn charwomen, weary waiters and harassed husbands who fought a futile battle to preserve a tiny vestige of dignity and self respect. He had rubbed shoulders with most of the characters he portrayed: some were based on friends and family, others came about through chance encounters in cheap lodging houses, pubs and local shops.

2   Eve Place, *c.* 1870

Dan was born at 6 Eve Place situated in Somers Town, a sprawling slum that lay on the sloping ground between central London and Camden Town. The Place was a single row of nine dilapidated cottages, 'two up, two down' dwellings with little room to accommodate their numerous occupants. The 1861 census, taken when Dan was four months old, shows a total of 51 residents of The Place. A wide range of occupations was recorded; a gold-chain maker, two labourers, a laundress, a butcher's boy, three errand boys, a jeweller, a grocer's assistant, a railway carman, an 'express' van driver, a coal porter and a French polisher. Dan's parents, John and Louisa Galvin, were described as 'comedian' and 'vocalist', with George listed as the youngest of four children. John and Louisa were not the only music-hall performers living in Eve Place – no. 3 was occupied by Benjamin Mills, 'author and vocalist', and his wife Elizabeth, 'vocalist'. Ben had been a well-known comic singer for over 20 years, and written songs for one of the most famous early music-hall performers, J.W. 'Jacky' Sharp.

Louisa's antecedents are obscure. She was born in about 1831, probably in Worthing, a small seaside town close to the Sussex coastal resort of Brighton. Her father, named on her two marriage certificates as Richard Dutton, was a 'painter', not of houses, but an 'artist'. At the birth of her brother James in Carey Street, Westminster, in July 1840, Richard was described as a 'gentleman', but when the census was taken in April 1841 Louisa, her young brother, three sisters and mother were living in John Street, Waterloo. The reason for her father's disappearance may well have been health related – the same census recorded a 45-year-old actor named Richard Dutton as a patient at the Middlesex Pauper Lunatic Asylum. John Galvin's origins are clearer. Born in 1826, he was recorded on the 1841 census as living with his family in Wild Street, in the notorious central London 'rookery' of St Giles. His father, Maurice Galvin, was a labourer, born in about 1791, almost certainly in Ireland. A later census shows that John's mother, Frances, was born in Northamptonshire in about 1801. Like John, his sisters Mary and Frances and brother Michael were all born in London. Wild Street itself was to possess a special significance for John Galvin, not only providing him with his early home but supplying him and Louisa with their stage noms-de-plume, 'Mr and Mrs Johnny Wild', and his son with an unusual middle name.

John and Louisa were married at St John's Church, Waterloo, on 2 January 1850. St John's is an imposing and elegant neo-classical building that still stands at the south side of Waterloo Bridge facing the railway terminus. When John and Louisa married, the church was relatively new, one of a number constructed in the 1820s to minister to the spiritual needs of Lambeth's mushrooming population. Waterloo Station was an even more recent addition to the south-east London landscape, the first train – the Southampton Mail – having arrived there on 13 July 1848. The Galvins gave nearby Ann Street as their address when registering the wedding, but they were soon to leave London for a number of years. At about this time the older Galvin family appears to have met with disaster. The 1851 census records Frances, widowed and working as a charwoman, living with 14-year-old Michael in new, crowded lodgings in St Giles.

The Galvins' movements throughout the 1850s can be traced through the births of their children. The eldest, John, was born in Dublin in 1851, and a girl, Frances Elizabeth, in Liverpool in 1852. At this time John, like his father, was a labourer, but by the birth of Henry Michael in Salford, Lancashire, in 1854 he had become a commercial traveller. Despite John's roving occupation the family appear to have settled in Salford for some time, Maurice Danvers Galvin being born there in 1855. By 1859 when Louisa Mary was born the family had returned to London, where John and Louisa pursued careers as music-hall performers.

Before moving to Eve Place the Galvins had occupied lodgings in Gloster Buildings, White Cross Street, St Luke's, a slum area situated between Old Street and the Barbican. White Cross Street was famous, or infamous, for a massive street market that sold leather goods, clothes, household items and, perhaps of some interest to John and Louisa, cheap literature and street ballads. Tradition links Mr and Mrs Johnny Wild with the Rotunda, a predominately working-class hall close to Black-friars Bridge, Southwark, but there were scores of similar establishments in which they might have performed. It is almost certain that they appeared in the vicinity of John's childhood home in Wild Street. Concert rooms abounded in the area, with the Middlesex Music Hall, opened in 1851, standing just a few yards away in Drury Lane. Despite some attempts to elevate standards and to provide a more family-orientated entertainment most halls still reeked of their tavern origins. Many, like the Middlesex, which was built onto the Old Mogul Saloon, were still part of the pubs that had engendered them, and it was common practice to offer admission through a refreshment ticket or token which could be redeemed at the bar for alcohol.

G. M. W. Reynolds described the 'Old Mo' during the 1850s as:

> [A] large room holding several hundred persons: concerts and performances every night: frequented by all kinds of people: great numbers of dissolute livery servants meet here: also young apprentices and their girls. The landlord keeps it as respectable as he can.[2]

The proprietor of the Black Bull, in Windmill Street, Haymarket, had no such interest in maintaining respectability:

Music and dancing at this place: singing to a piano accompaniment. Most of the men frequenting are cross coves, thimble-men, or swell-mobsmen: the females are women of the town. A great many juveniles visit this house, young thieves with their girls. The waiter is a comic fellow, sings comic songs, is on good terms with everybody and sips of everybody's brandy-and-water with the most condescending friendship: always calling for 'ladies and gentlemen to give their orders'. The songs sung at this place are not indecent, mostly humorous.[3]

One such a humorous song from music hall's early days suggests that the entertainers, like the entertainment, were frequently fuelled by drink:

> In a garret I show'd my nob [head]
> In Earl Street, Seven Dials,
> My father was a snob [shoemaker],
> My mother dealt in *wials*;
> But my mind took higher flights,
> I hated low-life things!
> Made friends with a cove wot writes,
> Now I'm the chap what sings.
>
> Chorus: Tol de rol, etc.
> When at singing I made a start,
> Some said my voice was fine;
> I tried a serious part,
> But turned to the comic line;
> I found out that that was best,
> Some fun it always brings –
> To the room it gives a zest,
> And it suits the cove wot sings.
>
> To a concert, ball or rout,
> At night I'm asked to go;
> With my new toggery, I go out,
> And I cut no *dirty show*;
> Goes up to the music, all right,
> At the women I sheep's eyes flings,
> Gets my lush free all the night,
> Because I'm the cove wot sings …
>
> While strolling t'other night,
> I dropped in a house, d'ye see?
> The landlord so polite,

Insisted on treating me;
I called for a glass of port,
When *half-a-bottle* he brings;
'How much to pay, landlord?' said I –
'Nothing of the sort,' says he,
'You're a cove wot sings ...'[4]

Drink wrecked the careers of both great and small. The irrepressible
Jacky Sharp died at the age of 38 in Dover workhouse. W.G. Ross, whose
compelling song about a condemned murderer, 'Sam Hall', gripped audiences during the late 1840s, slipped down the theatrical ladder to end
his days as a ragged and bloated extra. The foremost comedian of the
1850s, Sam Cowell, died aged 44 in 1864, after a recuperative stay in
Somerset during which he consumed a bottle of brandy a day. Although
alcohol was always readily available, salaries were not inflated. Among
the lesser lights of the profession it was often difficult to make a living
wage. A vocalist interviewed by Henry Mayhew in 1850 explained how
much could be earned at the smaller halls:

Now, my wife, my daughter, and I might take 25s. a week by
open-air singing. Concert singing is extra, and the best payment is
a crown per head a night for low-priced concerts. The inferior vocalists get 4s., 3s., 2s.6d., and some as low as 2s. Very many who
sing at the concerts have received a high musical education, but
the profession is so overstocked that excellent singers are compelled to take poor engagements.[5]

The same vocalist commented on the morals of music-hall singers and
the content of their songs:

The better sort of cheap concert singers . . . were a well-conducted
body of people, often struggling for a very poor maintenance, the
women rarely being improper characters. But now . . . John Bull's
taste is inclined to the brutal and filthy. Some of the 'character
songs' such as 'Sam Hall', 'Jack Sheppard', and others, are so in-
delicate that a respectable man ought not to take his wife and
daughters to see them. The men who sing character songs are the
worst class of singers, both as regard to character and skill, they
are generally loose fellows; some are what is called fancy men;
persons supported, wholly or partly, by women of the town.[6]

Most of the halls in which John and Louisa appeared were built to a similar pattern. A long room filled with benches or chairs and tables faced a
small stage, sometimes an open platform, at the side of which sat a genial

master of ceremonies, the chairman. Many halls had a single balcony extending around three sides of the auditorium, supported by ornately decorated cast-iron columns. Food and drink were consumed by the audience, while a single pianist or small band battled to make themselves heard over the general hubbub. Despite gas lighting, the overall scene was rendered hazy by tobacco smoke billowing from scores of pipes and cigars.

There is scant record of the Galvins' professional engagements during the 1850s. The names 'Mr and Mrs J. Wild – Characteristic Vocalists' were on the opening bill of Byrne's Mammoth Concert Hall and City Tavern, Dublin, on Easter Monday 1856,[7] and they also featured in advertisements for entertainments at Wilton's Music Hall, Whitechapel, in the summer of 1857.[8] The fullest account of their movements at a particular time is provided by an advertisement placed in the theatrical newspaper *The Era* by the couple's agent, Ambrose Maynard. The issue for the week commencing 20 March 1859 informed the public that 'Mr and Mrs J. Wild, the legitimate COMIC DUET SINGERS will commence engagements at Mr D. Barnard's Railway Station [concert hall], Chatham, March 28; Mr Gordon's Theatre Tavern, Southampton, April 28; and Mr Phillip's, Commercial Road, May 23, for two months.'

It is not easy to estimate the degree of success that Mr and Mrs Johnny Wild achieved. Following John's death Louisa went on to become a respected performer, and there is no reason to suppose that John was any less talented. Their home at Eve Place perhaps provides a clue. Somers Town was undoubtedly one of London's worst districts, but the Galvins appear to have occupied a rare pocket of respectability. Some undesirable features of the neighbourhood were unavoidable. Damp from the Fleet River and the Regent's Canal was all pervasive, as were the foul smells created by bone-boilers, soap manufacturers and knackers' yards, and on a far greater scale by the Imperial Gasworks and King's Cross railway station. But Eve Place was not chronically overcrowded in comparison to its neighbours, and on the whole its residents were honest merchants and semi-professionals. If anything John and Louisa were beginning to go up in the world.

Back in the 1820s, when Charles Dickens lived in a Georgian house in the Polygon, Somers Town, the area still retained many pastoral aspects, but already a number of bottle-shaped kilns had begun to produce bricks for London's increasing building requirements. By the start of the 1860s all signs of rurality had long departed. John Hollingshead, a crusading journalist later to become manager of London's famous Gaiety Theatre, recorded his impressions after visiting the district during the early months of 1861. One of the streets nearest to Eve Place appeared to be at the heart of the slum:

Dustbins are unknown in that portion of the old town named
Cambridge Crescent, and the usual public privies are another
rarity. The tiles on the huts are broken off. The interiors represent
the lowest condition of poverty and filth; the yards often contain
clothes-lines, on which were a few wet sole-skins, used by brewers,
are drying for sale; the children are barefooted and ragged; the
women seem to know no better way of closing a hole in a dirty
garment than with a pin or a bit of string; donkeys roam about the
place as clean and well housed as their masters; and under the
rough flooring you can often see the rough uncovered earth. The
whole population of this district may be six thousand or seven
thousand and the rents vary from one shilling and sixpence to
three shillings a week for a room.[9]

Hollingshead's description of the area often dwelt on surreal aspects of
the urban landscape, much as Dan was later to do in his comic monologues:

It is filled with courts and alleys; it puts forward a gin-palace built
in the true Seven Dials' style, even to a clock in the wall near the
roof; and it is crowded with cheap china-shops, cheap clothiers,
and cheap haberdashers. Its side streets have a smoky, worn-out
appearance; the gas lamps project jauntily from the walls, the iron
posts at the end lean towards each other as if for mutual support;
every street door is open; no house is without patched windows;
and every passage is full of children. Back views of dingy public-
houses make the scene more dismal; and wherever there is a butcher's shop it contrives to look like a cat's-meat warehouse.[10]

Although situated at the centre of an area of dense housing Eve Place
contrived to stand apart from the rest of Somers Town. It was separated
from its neighbors in Cambridge Crescent by the Old St Pancras Burial
Ground and the St Giles Parochial Cemetery, adjacent graveyards whose
tightly packed gravestones gave only a limited idea of the overall
number of burials that they contained. Monuments to the writers Mary
Wollstonecraft and William Godwin, the artist John Flaxman and the
antiquarian Sir John Soane were conspicuous, but space was at such a
premium that coffins were frequently stacked on top of each other in the
waterlogged soil. Eve Place was largely hidden from the busy Old St
Pancras Road by Adam and Eve Terrace and the Adam and Eve public
house. Alongside the Place stood the Old St Pancras Church, its parish
duties long since relinquished in favour of a far grander edifice in the
nearby Euston Road. And some way further to the north loomed the

baleful presence of the St Pancras Workhouse, described by Hollingshead as a 'stately pauper palace'.

There was an historical and spiritual dimension to this curiously isolated row of houses that few would have appreciated. The church was
reputedly one of the first in Britain, according to some sources built
alongside a Roman camp in the fourth century. Although the present
building can only be dated to the late Saxon or Norman period, its
dedication to one of the earliest saints venerated in Britain suggests an
earlier existence. Pancras, a 14-year-old orphan martyred during the
reign of the emperor Diocletian, became a patron saint of children,
appropriately for an area occupied by so many young people. But Chris-
tianity may have replaced an earlier religion in the area, for close to the
church stood a holy well, one of several sacred springs that lay along the
course of the Fleet River on its journey from Hampstead Heath into
central London.

Before the advent of the nineteenth century's dust heaps and stinking
ditches, a little Eden had existed in the form of the Adam and Eve Tea
Gardens. From the late 1600s the resort had offered bucolic pleasures for
London city dwellers; tree-lined walks, scented arbours and a herd of
cows providing fresh milk for syllabubs. When patrons grew tired of such
rustic pursuits, a 'long room' was available to provide indoor entertainments. As the character of the area steadily deteriorated the gardens lost
their popularity, and a portion of them was taken over by the cemetery
in 1803. By 1860 only the Adam and Eve pub, providing a tavern sing-
song and the use of a tatty bowling green, remained to bear witness to an
Arcadian past.

Dan would certainly have benefited from St Pancras's protection
shortly before and after his birth. During the early part of her pregnancy
Louisa lost her two youngest children, Louisa Mary to 'debility and consumption' on 2 April 1860, and Maurice Danvers to a 'remittent fever' on
12 May. The double tragedy may have been the cause of the family
moving from White Cross Street to Eve Place. Around the time of Dan's
birth the weather became bitterly cold, the freezing conditions continuing to the end of January 1861. Most outdoor work ceased, causing the
streets of London to be filled with unemployed bricklayers, labourers
and dockers begging for coppers. In the East End mounted police proved
incapable of protecting baker's shops and eating houses from hungry
mobs, while the workhouse system and local centres of poor relief could
not cope with the demands made on them. Fuel and provisions were
scarce, and like all workers depending on the general public for employment variety performers would have found their income drastically reduced. As entertainers of a primarily working-class audience Dan's family
would often suffer during economic depressions over the next 20 years.

Dan moved from Somers Town at an early age, taking with him only the vaguest recollection of Eve Place. For many years afterwards he thought that his birth date was January 1861 and that his birth place was Eve Court, both misconceptions included in the light-hearted 'auto-biography' *Dan Leno: Hys Booke*:

> That was in the year 1861, on the 32nd of Danuary, and it oc-curred in Eve Court, King's Cross, London. London is a large vil-lage on the Thames where the principal industries carried on are music-halls and the confidence trick. It is a curious fact that the place where I was born is now covered by St Pancras Station, and it's rather aggravating to know that somewhere underneath that station there's a little property belonging to me that I can't get at.[11]

In fact, Eve Place stood to the north of St Pancras Station and, although the construction of the Midland Railway's lines, platforms and Gilbert Scott's gigantic neo-Gothic hotel were completely to alter the nature of the district, it was not demolished until the 1870s. Shortly before Eve Place and much of the adjoining area were swept away, a local photog-rapher took several photographs of the locality, including two existing images of Dan's birthplace. Although much of Somers Town was to be-come a railway goods depot, the immediate surroundings of Old St Pan-cras Church were converted into public gardens which retained many original monuments and gravestones.

The dead as well as the living had to be evicted from their accom-modation to make room for the coming of the railway. In 1865 the novel-ist Thomas Hardy, then employed as an assistant architect, supervised the disinterment of several hundred bodies and their reburial in a mass grave nearby. His feelings about the grotesque jumble of human re-mains, broken coffins and displaced gravestones were expressed in the poem 'The Levelled Churchyard':

> Where we are huddled none can trace
> And if our names remain
> They pave some path or p-ing place
> Where we have never lain.[12]

Where the Galvin family were huddled for the first five years of Dan's life is similarly difficult to trace. His music-hall debut took place in London when he was three or four years old, but by this time the family had already resumed their nomadic lifestyle. In June 1862 they appeared for three weeks at the Surrey Music Hall, Sheffield, before moving on to engagements in Manchester, Glasgow and Northampton.[13] When they appeared at the Royal Oak Concert Hall, Salford, in April 1863[14] they were accompanied by their son – not Dan, but John or Henry, who were already seasoned performers.

3

THE INFANT WONDER

Dan's future may have been uncertain, but his occupation was fixed from an early age. It is likely that all the Galvin children became entertainers to help supplement their parent's earnings. Henry, in particular, was a good dancer and had probably made his stage debut long before Dan took to the boards. But any contributions that the younger Galvins were able to make were suddenly rendered inconsequential by the sudden death of their father.

In the absence of a firm date of death for John Galvin it is impossible to say whether he was present at his youngest child's first appearance on the stage. Dan's debut occurred, probably in 1864, at the Royal Cosmotheca, a small music hall situated in Paddington, West London. Such rough and ready 'penny gaffs' were to become familiar to Dan during his future travels around the United Kingdom. It had been assembled in a few days, a wooden structure built over a stable yard in Bell Street, off the Edgware Road. Fixtures and fittings were rudimentary and the audience, comprising mainly Irish labourers and the itinerant street traders known as costermongers, were quick to show enthusiasm or displeasure. The music-hall critic H. Chance Newton visited the hall in his youth:

> The Cosmotheka [sic] shows were always of a most mixed kind, and the language of 'kind friends in front' was often anything but kind. When, however, audience were specially pleased to approve of an artiste's efforts, they would often mark their appreciation by showering pennies on the stage.[1]

Family legend has it that Dan was billed as 'Little George – the Infant Wonder, Contortionist and Posturer'. His costume consisted of tights fashioned from a pair of his mother's stockings fastened round the neck with a garter, while his performance consisted of a few acrobatic tricks and dances. Perhaps some pennies were thrown, but Dan's perception was that a neutral stand-off took place between him and his first audience: 'I didn't sing or patter, but mostly looked at the audience, and wondered what they were wasting their time there for, and I didn't get very good money for that.'[2]

The prices at the 'Cosmo' reflected the relative poverty of its patrons. Fourpence secured the best seat in the house, while one penny allowed basic admission. To maximise the use of the building its proprietor Joseph Adolphus Cave had introduced the novel concept of presenting two shows nightly.

Within a short time an accident brought an end to Dan's posturing career. His brother Henry taught him some new dances and together they made their debut as a double act in about 1865. Dan recalled:

> I made my first appearance with my brother at a music-hall in the north of London. We danced on a stage that was surrounded with mirrors, and I remember that when we had finished we got so confused that we could not find the right exit, and banged our-selves against the glass with such force that we both suddenly sat down. The audience thought this was part of the turn, and showed its appreciation of it so much that we had to go on and do it again.[3]

The family's precarious situation was resolved when Louisa met a new and supportive partner, William Grant. Will, another performer, was six years younger than Louisa, but full of confidence and resourcefulness. His failings, a flaming temper and an aggressive disposition, were largely attributable to heavy drinking. Dan's biographer J. Hickory Wood wrote:

> It must be confessed that Dan's step-father was a strong man with a weakness: he had a great fondness for alcohol, and his chief ex-cuse for flying to it was grief. He seems to have been a man of catholic sympathies, for it is stated that a colliery explosion in South Wales, a wreck in the North Sea, or an eruption of Mount Vesuvius were just as likely to upset him and send him to the bottle for consolation as any personal bereavement. Failing all else, he had been known to plunge himself deeply into woe through reading obituary notices in the daily papers and refuse to be com-forted except in his own peculiar manner.[4]

Will was a larger than-life character and it is difficult not to see in Dan's numerous anecdotes about his 'dad', reflections of some of Charles Dickens' most colourful creations. William Grant combined the opti-mism of a Wilkins Micawber with the ingenuity and loquaciousness of a Vincent Crummles and the harmful predilections of a Newman Noggs. Along with a new paternal presence Will provided Dan with one special gift which was to become of supreme importance to his future career, the mysteriously evocative stage-name 'Leno'. Resonant of an exotic clown from the *Commedia dell'Arte* or a brooding hero in a Gothic romance, the name's derivation is obscure. The writings and poetry of the political radical John Bedford Leno may well have appealed to Will's inde pendence of spirit, while he would certainly have been aware of 'leno' as a form of open-work fabric that was extensively manufactured in the north of England. Or, more prosaically, he may just have adopted an unusual-sounding name. In the late 1850s Will had appeared under his own name as an actor in Charles Kean's company at the Princess's Theatre, London, but by the end of 1859 he had adopted 'Leno' to pursue a career as a pantomime performer.[5]

Like John Galvin, Will was a Londoner. He was born in Soho in 1837, the son of Alexander Grant from Inverness in Scotland. In 1861 he was living with his family at 79 Berwick Street, when his profession was given as 'assistant leather case maker', his father being a master in that trade. Will and Louisa gave their addresses as 4 and 5 Diana Place, close to the Euston Road, when their marriage banns were published in February 1865, but they were not actually married until 7 March 1866, when the ceremony took place at St John's Church in the centre of Liverpool. They had travelled north the previous year, although some of Louisa's older children may have remained with John's brother, Michael, in the St Pancras area. Louisa had relations in the north of England, for Dan's uncle or cousin, Johnny Danvers, was born in Sheffield in 1860.

'Mr and Mrs Leno – Comic Duettists' opened at James Bayliss's Milton Colosseum Concert Hall, Cowcaddens Cross, Glasgow, on 28 August 1865. By the end of the year they had made their way to Liverpool, a crowded and chaotic city that was to be their base for some years to come. The first traceable record of the Lenos appearing in the city occurs with the start of a pantomime on 18 December: *Fortunatus; or, The Magic Wishing Cap* was presented at the Royal Colosseum, locally known as the 'Colly', in Paradise Street. A massive audience attended the opening performance:

> Every part of the house was densely packed; in the pit people were completely jammed together, and occasionally an unlucky wight, seeking escape from the pressure or to secure a better place, was sent over the heads of his neighbours to a somewhat more uncomfortable one. So great was the demand for accommodation that hundreds of persons were unable to gain admission to the house.[6]

Louisa appeared as the principal boy, Fortunatus, while, according to the theatrical historian R.J. Broadbent, Dan played a 'juvenile clown'. Will appeared as 'Ursa Major Bruin, the Great Bear' and as the Clown in the concluding Harlequinade: 'There is no lack of fun in the harlequinade, a considerable amount of new and ultra-comic business being introduced. Mr Leno is a very good clown, and his funnyisms evoked many a peal of laughter.'[7]

The cast of the pantomime might have had to work a little harder to make their audience forget the theatre's unusual surroundings, for a small graveyard had been inherited from the Colosseum's previous existence as a Unitarian Chapel. Twelve years later the theatre was the scene of a major disaster when 37 people were crushed to death following a false fire alarm.

On 18 July 1866 'Mr and Mrs Leno, the Great, Sensational, Dramatic and Comic Duettists' and 'The Brothers Leno, Lancashire Clog, Boot and Pump Dancers' appeared at the opening of the Cambridge Music Hall, Mill Street, in the Toxteth Park area of Liverpool. With walls and ceiling painted with allegorical representations of 'Science', 'Music', 'Night', 'Morning' and 'The Seasons', and boasting a small orchestra, the Cambridge appears to have been considerably more respectable than some of its neighbouring entertainments.

It was not long before the names of 'Mr and Mrs Leno' and 'The Brothers Leno' were prominently displayed on music-hall posters throughout Liverpool and the surrounding area. The mid-1860s were years desperately in need of entertainment. During the period 1863–66 over 5,000 Liverpudlians died of typhus fever. In addition, a cotton blockade imposed during the American Civil War had caused a widespread economic depression affecting both the port of Liverpool and the mill towns of Lancashire. But there were still opportunities for industrious performers. Behind the dockside, lined with tall sailing ships, and amid the hillside jumble of churches, warehouses and taverns were situated seven theatres, 13 music halls and scores of singing rooms. Some places of entertainment had an extremely poor reputation. Broadbent described a singing room in the Williamson Square area, a 'long, narrow apartment in a filthy state' reached by ascending a flight of 'very rickety stairs'. A low stage, faced rows of benches set at each side of the auditorium, allowing the waiters room to serve patrons who had already imbibed excessive amounts of alcohol. The performers, struggling to make an impression on the rowdy audience, were constantly interrupted by foreign sailors 'audibly kissing the bare-necked, lightly dressed girls' who had them 'in tow'.[8]

Occasionally the family left Liverpool to fulfil engagements. A tattered handbill recovered from below the balcony floor of the Britannia Music Hall, Glasgow, announces:

Mr and Mrs Leno. The Unrivalled Comic Duettists, Burlesque Actors, Dancers, etc. Owing to their great success they are engaged to appear at this establishment in 1867... Brothers Leno. The popular Great Little Dancers. Last Week of their Engagement.[9]

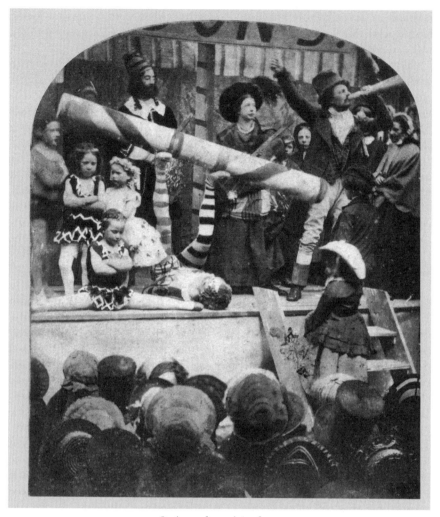

3   An early variety show

The family remained closely linked with the Cambridge Music Hall. After returning from an engagement at Holder's Concert Hall, Birmingham, the Brothers Leno made an early appearance there in December 1866, sharing an archetypal variety bill with a *serio comique* (a female singer and dancer) a comic vocalist, a gymnast, a ballad vocalist, a comedian, a black-face performer and an Irish comedian, 'E.D. Davies – The Dublin Boy.'[10] Other popular halls to engage the Lenos were the St James's Hall, Lime Street, where 'Master George and Henry Leno, American Breakdown Dancers' appeared in April 1867;[11] the New Adelphi Theatre, Christian Street, in May 1867, supporting 'the celebrated equestrian actor James Harwood in Marzeppa';[12] and the Alhambra, Manchester Street, where the quartet were recorded as making 'a great hit' in October 1868.[13]

In December 1867 the family returned to Scotland, where Dan was to achieve one of his earliest individual successes. The pantomime *Little Red Riding Hood* was produced from 23 December at the three-thousand-seat Exchange Rooms, Paisley:

> The pantomime at this establishment has proved a great success, and crowded audiences have enthusiastically shown their appreciation of the excellent holiday entertainment provided for them. *Little Red Riding Hood; or, Harlequin and the Good Woman Who Lived in the Wood* is the title of Mr George's new venture, and he has carried out the story with much drollery. The principal characters in the Opening are well supported by Mrs G. H. George, Mrs Leno, Miss Annie Anderson, Mr J. C. Barr, Young Leno (as the Wolf), and Mr A. Cummock. The fun of the Harlequinade is fast and furious: Mr J. Keith, is Harlequin, Miss Lizzie Robertson Columbine, Mr Leno Clown, and Mr Barr Pantaloon, who are all worthy of much praise for their untiring exertions.[14]

Over the next four decades Dan was to witness many changes in the traditional Christmas entertainment. When he first appeared pantomimes were still largely performed as in the days of England's greatest clown, Joseph Grimaldi, opening with a dramatised fairy tale and concluding with a Harlequinade during which Harlequin, Columbine and Clown performed a succession of startling tricks. The two halves of the production were linked by the spectacular 'Transformation Scene', in which the protagonists of the 'Opening' were metamorphosed into the anarchistic characters of the Harlequinade. During a short life, but a long career, Dan became one of the most experienced and knowledgeable pantomime performers, absorbing the advice and reminiscences of older pantomimists and becoming thoroughly familiar with all types of arcane stage machinery. As a child, like Grimaldi, he was sometimes called upon to play an animal, a piece of casting that brought with it a certain degree of high-spirited licence. Dan's attachment to his wolf costume in *Little Red Riding Hood* was such that he insisted on sleeping in it after the show.

On their return to Liverpool the Lenos appeared at the Cambridge Music Hall in February 1868.[15] They were present again at the Hall in October when it re-opened after a seasonal closure.[16] Their two-month engagement coincided with a brief appearance by one of music hall's major stars, Harry Liston (1843–1929). Young Leno would probably have observed his fellow performer with considerable interest; Harry was an excellent 'character' comedian and one of the best dancers on the halls. Born in Stockport he (like John Galvin) had been a commercial traveller before making his performing debut at the Scotia Music Hall, Glasgow, in 1863. His first appearance in London, in 1865, took place at a time when variety entertainment was undergoing wide-ranging changes. Music halls were becoming larger and more ornate, bringing with them the *Lions Comiques*, a new generation of comedians who lived up to their surroundings with an uninhibited display of flamboyance and swagger. Liston quickly became associated with such 'swell' comedians as Arthur Lloyd, George 'Champagne Charlie' Leybourne, Alfred 'The Great' Vance, 'Jolly' John Nash and 'The Great' MacDermott, all of whom celebrated the carefree life-style of 'men about town'. Like many other *Lions*, Harry also performed songs dealing with everyday life. When he appeared at the Cambridge for three nights in November 1868 he probably sung his current hits 'The Ginger-haired Swell', 'Naughty Mary Ann' and 'I'll Tell Your Wife'. He might also have encored with his most famous song 'When Johnny Comes Marching Home'.

Will Leno's status at the Cambridge was such that he was chosen to present Liston with an engraved silver goblet to commemorate his appearance at the hall.[17] Although Dan and Harry followed divergent paths over the next 30 years it is likely that they occasionally encountered each other. While continuing to play the halls, Harry created his own, socially superior, entertainment – 'Merry Moments' – with which he toured concert halls throughout the country. Many years after Louisa, Will and Dan had died Harry was still performing his act.

Liverpool was a breeding ground for music-hall talent. During Dan's stay in the second half of the decade he appeared alongside many performers who were to become major stars. Jenny Hill (1848–96), later to be hailed as music hall's leading lady, was eking out a living at the Rotunda, the Oxford and the Lenos' own Cambridge. George Chirgwin (1854–1922), whose persona as 'The White-Eyed Musical Kaffir' united traditional cockney comedian with the new black-face minstrel, was making his way as one of the Brothers Chirgwine at the Vine Concert Hall, in Great Charlotte Street. And at various establishments across the city, a well-proportioned young comedian was appearing as one of a black-face trio. Herbert Campbell was at the start of a career that was to lead to him co-starring with Dan at the most famous of English theatres, the Theatre Royal, Drury Lane.

With the excitement of Harry Liston's visit subsiding, the management of the Cambridge Music Hall looked for a fresh novelty to entice their audience. Will was on hand to suggest a pre-Christmas pantomime. It was a standing joke within the Leno family that whenever bookings or Will's inspiration flagged, his first response was to mount a pantomime. *Harlequin Rapscallion: or, the Good Fairy of the Shamrock Dell* was written by him, and he also appeared as Clown. The Irish theme implied by the title was reinforced by the presence of a well known comedian, J.C. 'Paddy' Phillips, often billed as 'The Original Tipperary Cuckoo'. At the end of November Will was given a reward for his efforts in the form of a benefit evening. *The Era*, which had already observed that the production abounded in 'witticism and pungent comments', noted that 'he in conjunction with the other funny and dancing spirits was much applauded'.[18]

A short time later the Lenos sailed to Ireland to appear in another pantomime. It was during the run of *Old King Humpy; or, Harlequin Emerald Isle and Katty of Killarney* at the Monster Saloon, in Crampton Court, Dublin, that Dan received a few words of praise from one of the most eminent of Victorians.[19] Charles Dickens was presenting a series of readings from his novels when he encountered the Lenos in Belfast in January 1869. Always an astute judge of theatrical talent, the great writer congratulated Dan after seeing him perform. 'Good little man,' he said 'you'll make headway.'[20]

Dickens died within the year, but his approval was to have a lasting effect on Dan's self-esteem and, possibly, on the development of his comedy. The famous impersonator of Dickensian characters, Bransby Williams, linked the comedian and the novelist:

> I once heard that great comedian Arthur Roberts say that Charles Dickens had the key of the street, and wrote of the people, and that therefore the people understood. So I think Dan Leno held the key of the street; he was domestic and simple and once more, be it noted, all great things are simple.[21]

The key, it seems, was presented with a reassuring pat on the head, a personal imprimatur from the creator of some of the most memorable characters in English fiction. Dan's later songs and monologues were to be peopled with comic creations that could easily have flitted in and out of Dickens's novels – Lucy Jaggs, Dr McFabback, Mr Pipkins, Mrs Snaggles, Michael Miclemac, Sergeant Smirks, Mary Ann McCoff, and many others who were never afforded the luxury of a name.

Dan's career as a solo singer appears to have commenced in 1869. Henry left the troupe at about this time, possibly to rejoin other family members still living in London. Lacking a partner, Dan amplified his part of the act by adding singing and patter to his already accomplished dancing skills. Given the large concentration of Irish immigrants in the Liverpool area and the family's own Irish connections, it was predictable that he should become 'The Great Little Leno, the Quintessence of Irish Comedians.'[22]

Despite an obvious talent for comic singing, dancing remained the mainstay of Dan's performance. In November 1869 he received one of his first music-hall reviews, while appearing at the Argyle, Birkenhead, a ship-building area just across the river Mersey from Liverpool. 'Young Leno' was reported to be 'a juvenile, but clever dancer'.[23] The owner of the Argyle Music Hall, Dennis Grannell, must have been impressed by the Lenos, for they were re-engaged in December.[24] In the same month they appeared at Grannell's newly opened Rotunda Music Hall, an imposing building that dominated the junction of Scotland Road and Stanley Road, in Liverpool. The Lenos had previously performed at the Rotunda while it was still a pub offering 'Free and Easy' concerts, but the new, first-floor hall was far more impressive, with a balcony and stage boxes. 'The Pre-eminently Popular Place of Entertainment in Liverpool' also offered two billiard rooms and eight American bowling alleys.[25]

Will was entrusted with writing and arranging the Rotunda's first pantomime. Starting late, in January 1870, *Jack the Giant Killer; or, Harlequin Grim Gosling, or the Good Fairy Queen of the Golden Pine Grove* provided Dan with an opportunity to demonstrate his all-round talents.[26] The Lenos featured in the variety entertainment that preceded the pantomime, and later Louisa played Princess Madeline and Dan appeared as the giant-killer himself. 'Paddy' Phillips took the parts of Giant Rusty Fusty and Pantaloon, playing alongside Will in his familiar role of Clown. The two old colleagues sometimes extended the fun of the Harlequinade into the audience area of the Rotunda. Dan recalled that 'Paddy' and his step-father developed an acrobatic trick of tumbling into the inner recesses of one the boxes adjoining the stage, a process that was repeated several times during the course of the pantomime. As their visits to the dark interior of the box grew more extended, it was discovered that a party of 'toffs' were plying the convivial comedians with free liquor.

Another recollection of the Rotunda pantomime was that the Leno's landlady at the time was a Mrs Kelly. The name, if not the personality, was to become the centrepiece of Dan's most celebrated comic routine. It is possible that the landlady was connected to a certain Miss Kate Kelly, who played Fairy Mayflower in the pantomime, although the name was hardly an unusual one in Liverpool. At the conclusion of the pantomime Grannell acknowledged Dan's 'fine alto singing' by presenting him with a silver medal.[27]

Towards the end of the 1860s the Leno family could reasonably anticipate a bright future. Louisa and Will had built a considerable reputation in Liverpool, and Dan had received a commendation from Charles Dickens. Once, while fulfilling an engagement in Rochdale, funds were sufficiently healthy for Louisa to purchase the boys matching black corduroy knickerbocker-suits with gilt buttons. Disaster struck on the first occasion that Henry and Dan wore their Sunday best. An alluring plank connecting a barge to a canal bank gave way under their weight and they were forced to dry their new suits at a nearby brick kiln. The garments shrunk, causing the brothers to be scolded and sent to bed without their evening meal.[28] It was not long, however, before the entire family went without dinner on a regular and prolonged basis. Bookings grew hard to secure and the Lenos were compelled to travel widely in search of work. Shortly before the start of these 'nightmare years' Dan obtained an impromptu engagement at the holiday resort of New Brighton, a short ferry-trip across the Mersey. He recounted the event to the novelist and playwright George R. Sims:

I have good reason to remember Egg and Ham Terrace. [an row of cheap restaurants facing the beach] It was there that I made what was practically my first public appearance as an entertainer.

I had gone across from Liverpool one Easter Monday. I was a very small boy, very hard up, and very hungry, and I looked at the good things in the windows of the eating-houses with longing eyes.

Presently I passed a 'restaurant' which was packed with people putting away the shilling dinner vigorously.

There was a piano inside, and one of the customers was trying to sing a song. But he couldn't sing for nuts.

Then an idea came to me. The proprietor was standing at the door looking up and down the parade with an eye for likely customers. I went up to him and said, 'Governor, do you want somebody to sing songs for 'em? – I can.'

'Can you?' he said 'Well, come in, and if you're all right I'll give you a bob to sing till three o'clock and a hot dinner when you've finished.' I went in and struck up, and all the people stared at me, I was such a bit of a boy.

But I sang a comic song and did a bit of a dance at the end, and they banged the tables and nearly shouted the roof off – I'd fairly hit 'em!

I expected the proprietor to come and congratulate me, but he took me on one side and said: 'Very good, my boy – but you make 'em too noisy. You see, my missus is lying dead upstairs, and it jars a bit on me.'

Of course I was very sorry and said I'd sing something quieter. So I started a sentimental ballad.

It didn't go at all, and all the customers began to get up and go. Then the proprietor came to me again.

'Look hear, my boy,' he said, 'you'd better give 'em one of the comic ones again. After all, she can't hear!'[29]

Dan was to travel much further afield and perform for far less reward over the next five years.

4

NIGHTMARE YEARS

Dan, or 'Young George' as he was then billed, had his childhood torn from him during the early 1870s. Like some cosmic transformation scene a catastrophic change of circumstances robbed the Leno family of what small degree of security they had achieved, leaving them to chase elusive and poorly paid engagements throughout the north of England and the Midlands. Often appearing before audiences that 'just managed to reach vanishing point',[1] their everyday existence became a continual battle against the demons of poverty, hunger and illness. It was probably no coincidence that the family did not start to pull out of their 'nightmare years' until Dan reached early manhood. The reasons for the decline in their fortunes are not clear. Dan attributed their reverses to a piece of theatrical legislation which prohibited dramatic performance on the music-hall stage, but Louisa's health, Will's temperament or a general change in popular taste may all have contributed to the situation. Dan left his own account of some of the troubles that the family encountered during the mid-1870s:

My father and mother once held good positions on the stage, considering the condition of theatres and halls in those days …

When pantomime was out of season they appeared together and were billed as 'Sensational Duettists'. My mother had a beautiful voice, and my father supplied the comedy. 'Sensational Duets' were a big feature, and brought in six or seven pounds a week, until stopped by the Lord Chamberlain as being of the nature of stage plays. As a matter of fact, there was no more acting in them than is connected with the ordinary duet. They were generally in two scenes. In the first, for example, a sailor would say good-bye to his sweetheart. After a quick change, the second scene would display the poor sailor returned from battle with a patch over his eye, his arm in a sling, and a wooden leg. The sweetheart at first recoiled from her battered lover, but true love prevailed, and then the sailor owned to a trick – off came the patch, sling and wooden leg, they had only been assumed to try the affections of his lass, and Jack would bring the duet to a close by pouring bags of guineas into her lap …

After the authorities put a stop to the 'Sensational Duets' bad luck set solidly in, and remained with us. We were frequently out of engagements, and those we had turned unremunerative. All our savings vanished, things went from bad to worse, until it seemed impossible for us to get deeper into the mire of misfortune.

I am not naturally superstitious, but I have heard that rats are unlucky, and I can certainly date the commencement of our troubles to the time when I first sang a song called 'Pity the Poor Italian Boy', in which I utilised as an embellishment, a couple of live white rats. These creatures played about on me and ran on the stage, always coming to my call.

I remember my original rendering of this song vividly. We had engaged a hall in Sleaford, Lincolnshire, having been taken to that part of the country by a manager who engaged us at Yarmouth. The man left us in the lurch, and, after we had paid in advance for the hall at Sleaford, we were absolutely penniless. We billed our-selves with the posters left behind by our departed impresario, having first cut off the old headings. These posters could not have been attractive, for, when we opened the door, the only people present were one lady and her two children. She wanted three six-penny seats and tendered half-a-crown. There was not a farthing of change in the treasury. But my father was a man of many ex-pedients, and he held hard on to the half-crown. 'Step inside, madam,' he said, 'and I will bring you the shilling change.' The lady sat in the centre of the stalls, father went out, broke into the coin, and returned. After giving our patron her change, our bank consisted of one-and-fourpence.

The lady and her children formed the entire audience. We waited and waited, with the doors wide open; but nobody entered. The lady became fidgety, and wanted to know when the performance would commence. There was no help for it; we had to make a start. 'Go on and sing your new song,' said my father.

He accompanied me on the flageolet. He was not a first-class play-er, he could not read music, and had no idea of key. But, to use a professional term, he could 'fluff through' my accompaniment, provided I was prepared to sing in any key he happened to strike.

Under these conditions I commenced 'Pity the Poor Italian Boy' to a beggarly array of empty benches, save for the mother and her children sitting in the centre like an oasis in the desert. I believe I was a great success in the opening verse and chorus, and I anticipated greater triumphs when I let my rats loose from their box. I thought they would have a great effect. They did. Directly the lady and her children saw them, they broke into frightened screams, gathered up their skirts and things, and fled out of the theatre for their lives.

The day after this fiasco, we tramped twenty miles through the snow, with nothing to eat, and without a penny in the world. My mother was taken ill, and we had to leave her with some kind people at an inn, while my father and I went tramping on in the hope of picking up a bare living.

It was about this period that somebody, seeing the state we were in, asked us, 'why don't you go to Sutton-in-Ashfield; you're sure to make pounds; there's the cattle fair on.'

We went. It was a walk of fifteen miles, and I was obliged to trudge there in my dancing clogs. I arrived with blood blisters on my heels. The first place we struck was a public-house filled with people. I sang, I exhibited my dancing and my rats, and my father also 'obliged'. We collected – one penny!

At the next try we fared even worse. We received nothing; not a rap, not a bite. And that was the tale of the whole day.

Evening came, we were hungry, thirsty and dead tired. But at last we seemed in luck. In one inn we found a large company, and asked for permission to sing them a song or two. This was readily granted and we thought we were doing well, for my father made them laugh, and my dancing was applauded. Then my father made the unlucky suggestion 'Sing them the "Italian Boy".' Oh, that unlucky song! I went behind a door to 'make up' for the ditty – to colour my face, put on a wig, a cap, a velveteen jacket, and so on. Father meanwhile, was pattering. But a suspicious voice interrupted him.

'What's the boy doing?'

'He is about to sing you a new song, "Pity the Poor Italian Boy".'

'But he's not an Italian boy!' was the startling suggestion.

'No certainly not. But he is just dressing up to impersonate one.'

'We don't want any impersonating here. It's a fraud!'
Father was thunderstruck.

'Don't you understand? He merely pretends to be an Italian. It's
an impersonation.'

'Yes, it's an impersonation,' they replied, 'and we don't hold with
it. It's a fraud to pass the boy off as an Italian, and we want no
impostors here. Get out!'

The story is scarcely credible, but we were turned out there and
then. Imagine our feelings as we turned our backs on the town for
our return walk of fifteen miles! Yet scarcely had we started when
we experienced a wonderful stroke of luck. We found a shilling in
the road. I remember seeing it lying there, edge upwards between
two stones. I think it was the most welcome sum of money I have
ever seen. It stayed our hunger and our thirst.

Like lions refreshed we entered an inn on the road and found a
kind of sing-song in progress. Some of the company noted my
clogs. 'Can the boy dance?' they asked. 'Yes,' they were told.

'We've got a lad who'll dance him for two shillings.'

'Done,' cried my father; 'for two shillings.' He had not a red-cent
in his pocket. But he had a cart-load of nerve.

I was helped on the table. But my opponent objected to my clogs.
He danced in naked feet, and I must do the same. My father would
have backed me to dance on my head. So my clogs were removed,
and, with aching, blistered feet, I danced to the accompaniment of
my father's uncertain flageolet till the room rang with applause.
The battle was already won, but my rival wanted a run for his
money. He leaped on the table, commenced a few steps, slipped on
some spilled beer, and toppled over into the arms of his backer.
There was no doubt about my victory, and we went off proudly
with the two shillings I had won…

We tried to keep my mother in ignorance of the fact that we were
singing in public-houses. We always left her behind, as her health

was so bad, when we explored a fresh town, and gave her to understand that we were fulfilling ordinary engagements. But she often wondered how it was that so many managers failed to pay us. At length, we had to break out with the solid truth. She had plenty of pluck; perhaps she had suspected the facts of the case all along. Anyhow, she resolved to accompany me, hoping that her still beautiful voice would bring better luck.

I stood by her side in the saloon of an inn in Clay Cross, where the landlord was very good to me. She was singing a ballad. As she finished, there was clapping of hands, and then one huge, drunken fellow approached and insulted her – insulted my mother. I was only a bit of a boy, about fourteen, but I lifted a pewter pot and hit the man across the head with it. He went down like a log. They hurried me out of the house, and out of the town, for my life was not safe after that.

In Yarmouth, before we commenced that terrible tour, I had seen two men stabbed by foreign sailors, and one of these gentry, not having sufficient pluck to stab me, compromised matters by pouring a kettle of boiling water over my legs.

But let me be done with those six years of nightmare. When I sit down to think of them I shudder. No man ever fared worse, for we were days together without food, always without money, and walking, walking all the while.[2]

Dan's estimation that the period of extreme hardship extended over six years seems excessive, although given the severity of the family's situation, such an exaggeration is understandable. Dates are few and far between for the Lenos' travels during the 1870s. In August 1870 they had journeyed as far as Portsmouth, in Hampshire, to appear at the South of England Music Hall. When the census was taken in April 1871 Louisa, Will and Dan were lodging with a barrel-maker in Preston, Lancashire. By the autumn of 1871 they had crossed to Ireland, playing at the Great Strand Music Hall, Dublin. Their stay in Ireland's capital appears to have been prolonged, with further engagements at St Patrick's Music Hall in March 1872, the Harp in April[3] and the City Music Hall in August.[4] At some stage they travelled to Germany, and it was perhaps on their return from the continent that they arrived in Yarmouth at the start of the 'terrible tour'.

Dan's account of the 'nightmare years' is supported by the recollections of Arthur Stevens, who met the family early in 1875. He encountered them near the village of Kelham, in Nottinghamshire, just after they had played at four tavern music-halls in Leicester, followed by a week in Sutton-in-Ashfield. The engagements could not have been very profitable for they were walking 20 miles to their next booking in Newark. Arthur treated the family to bread and cheese at a local inn, and some days later dropped in to watch young George perform:

> During the week he stayed at Newark, I was a frequent visitor to the new White Hart and saw the lad give several performances. He sang and danced with exceptional ability for one so young and, during his show, a variegated rat ran round him, perched upon his shoulder or found a resting place in the outside pocket of his costume. The Australian or variegated rat was then quite a novelty in this country and hence it added an extra effort to what was in itself a very smart and attractive turn.[5]

The familiar 'Good Old Days' tag frequently attached to modern representations of Victorian music hall is resoundingly inappropriate for the situation that prevailed in Northern variety theatres in the 1870s and 1880s. Times were extremely hard, and managers tried every possible ruse to attract audiences. At the Star Music Hall, Sunderland, 'Signor' George Durland, who featured in many of Dan's anecdotes, provided free soup for his patrons. On one occasion, when the occupants of the gallery barracked an unpopular act, the Signor threatened to impose his ultimate sanction: 'Silence up there!' he thundered, pointing dramatically towards his cauldron-carrying attendants, 'Silence! Or I'll stop your soup.'[6] Free food was also a lure for Saturday-night audiences at the Monster Saloon, Dublin, where the highlight of the evening's performance was a scramble to secure a joint of meat placed tantalisingly at the top of a greasy pole.[7] Dan's first major clog-dancing prize was a small purse of silver and a large leg of mutton.

By the end of the 1870s Dan's rapidly improving skills as an entertainer resulted in the Lenos re-establishing themselves as a popular music-hall act. A fellow performer, Bradley Truman, recalled Dan's progress:

> I first met Leno at the People's Music Hall in Oldham in 1876. At that time he was simply assisting his step father and mother in a triple turn. His step-father was an old pantomimist whom I knew very well. At that time, of course, there was nothing like the salaries of the present paid, and Dan and his parents suffered much from poverty ... I don't think he was exceptionally clever. He was very nimble on his feet, and sang a couple of patter songs. But to tell you the truth, he was a stripling, and I didn't heed him much.

The second time was at the People's Concert Hall, Manchester, in 1878. Dan was still traveling with his father and mother, but was giving a separate turn on his own … Well, he had improved wonderfully in the two years since first I met him. He sang better, giving two songs and a step-dance. There were plenty of men in Manchester who were clever with their clogs. There was Tom Ward, Robson and other well-known step-dancers, but not one could dance better, if as well, as Dan, and he had the advantage of youth.[8]

To coincide with his burgeoning career as a solo performer 'Young George' was given a new name, Dan Patrick, a suitably Hibernian-sounding soubriquet for an entertainer specialising in Irish comic songs. The name may have been in part homage to Dan Lowrey, the owner of the Malakoff Music Hall, Liverpool, where the Leno family frequently performed. Universally known as 'Dan Himself', Lowrey was an old-style Irish comedian who wore a swallow-tailed coat and knee-length breeches. It was Will's tippling pal 'Paddy' Phillips who, according to Dan, became the first Irish comic to adopt full-length trousers. By the late 1870s the lessons learned from 'Dan Himself' and 'The Original Tipperary Cuckoo' had been augmented by the tuition of 'The Solid Man', an eccentric Irish-American called Willie John Ashcroft. Dan's indebtedness to Willie John appears to have been profound. The older performer was an outstanding dancer and a skilful character comedian with the ability to 'people the stage with the persons of whom he was singing'.[9] In future years Dan was also to become famous for conveying his own imaginary world to an entire audience.

Dan's talent as a comedian was becoming widely recognised. On 23 October 1878 the family troupe opened at the Oak Farm Music Hall, Crewe: 'Among the artists who claim special attention are Mr and Mrs Leno (comic duettists) [and] Dan Patrick Leno (champion clog, pump and big boot dancer), who brings down the house with roars of laughter …'[10] Seven months later Dan triumphed over wet and gloomy weather to entertain Bristol audiences at the Great Annual Fetes held in the open air at the Zoological Gardens, Clifton: 'Dan Patrick, the Irish Comedian, raised a continuous roar by his grotesque antics.'[11]

A prerequisite of any Irish comedian worth his shamrock was the ability to perform a lively jig, and in this Dan Patrick excelled. Irish step-dancing was closely related to the esoteric art of Lancashire clog-dancing. Originating with the employees of the northern textile mills who kept warm by tapping their wooden-soled footwear to the rhythms of the power looms, clog dancing reached a peak of popularity in Lancashire during the mid-nineteenth century. Each town and village had its own champion, and competitions were frequently held at local music halls. As with Irish dancing the upper part of the body played little part, contestants being judged on the frequency and complexity of taps created by heel and toe movements. Frequently, a strange air of anonymity was created by the judges sitting, out of sight of the contestant, below the stage. It was an eerily mechanical process, an appropriate product of an industrial age.

Dan was proud of his own abilities. He later wrote:

> When a man has been initiated into the first part of his business, there are two things for him to work for – 'time' and 'elevation'. Although I say it myself, I had the gift. I had wonderful time and perfect elevation ... I can do three hundred taps with my feet in eight bars of music, and that cannot be done with the fingers.[12]

He was always happy to provide a technical explanation of his dancing, although such intricacies as 'rolling', 'kicking', 'taps', 'twizzles' and 'shuffles' usually proved baffling to his non-Northern acquaintances.

If clog dancing required a methodical and relentless discipline, Dan found an outlet for his spontaneous self in a series of short sketches devised by his step-father. Acted by Dan, Will, Louisa and any of the other performers who increasingly began to appear with the Leno troupe, the sketches drew heavily on the slapstick comedy of Christmas pantomimes. Strictly speaking, they fell foul of the legislation prohibiting dramatic representation on the music-hall stage, but it appears that the Lord Chamberlain had few spies in England's industrial heartland.

Plots were simple and the humour basic. In *Pongo the Monkey* a 'New Burlesque and Pantomimical Sketch' presented at Pullan's Theatre of Varieties, Brunswick Place, Bradford, during the week commencing 20 May 1878, Dan was given the opportunity to relive his happy childhood experience of dressing as a wild animal. As an escaped monkey he chased the rest of the cast around the stage, leaping onto the kitchen table and belabouring Will with a roll of brown paper. In *Torpedo Bill* he played the son of a washerwoman and a cobbler, who drove his parents to distraction by inventing a series of catastrophic and explosive devices. It was in a sketch performed at Signor Durland's Star Music Hall that Dan discovered that melodramatic acting was one of the few areas in which he did not excel. From his hiding place beneath a table he was meant to overhear a plot hatched by a band of murderous Italian brigands. To establish his presence Dan was called upon to peep out from beneath the tablecloth, a dramatic device that completely misfired when the audience was reduced to helpless laughter.[13]

At times Dan found an able partner in Johnny Danvers, a talented singer and dancer who drifted in and out of the Leno troupe in the late 1870s and early 1880s. It has not been possible to establish Johnny's exact relationship with Dan – alternatively given as cousin or uncle – but it seems likely that their grandmothers were sisters.[14] Johnny was born John Danvers Harold just seven days before Dan, the son of John Danvers Harold, a 'Professor of Music', and Elizabeth Harold, née Mallinson. He had known Dan since perambulator days, and like him had made his stage debut at a similarly early age. Johnny was born in Sheffield, but by the time of his father's death in 1868 the family had moved to Glasgow.[15] By 1881 Lizzie Harold and her two sons had returned to Sheffield, where the census recorded them as living at 38 Allen Street. When not appearing on stage Johnny was following the trade of 'silver plater'.

Johnny and Dan remained the closest of friends throughout their lives, sharing a host of memories, some of which were distressing, many amusing and others, for teenage boys, downright embarrassing. Their struggle to keep up appearances often led to ludicrous situations. An all-enveloping ulster raincoat was employed by members of the family to hide their shabby clothes and, in some cases, lack of them. The garment appears to have fitted Johnny best, or perhaps he had the greatest need of its protection. During an engagement in Coventry Dan and Johnny became friendly with two girls, 'walking out' during their free afternoons. Eventually, Johnny's appearance in the inevitable ulster prompted one of the young women to ask why he always wore it. 'Well,' explained Dan 'it's this way. That ulster was given him by his grandmother, and he's so fond of the old lady that he can't bear to wear anything else.'[16] The raincoat was worn one blazing August day when Johnny went to Victoria Station, Manchester, to welcome Dan, who was returning from an engagement. Dan left a thumbnail sketch of their meeting, with a cheeky urchin calling 'Say, governor, is it cold?'

Shared laughter provided Dan and Johnny with a resilient defence against the harsh realities of their lives. Dan's recollections of his own early childhood often dwelt on the privations he had endured, whereas memories involving Johnny usually had a strong element of humour about them. In his later stage-routines Dan seemed to talk to an old friend who, like Johnny, readily grasped most, if not all, of his allusions. He was intimate and confidential, referring to third parties as if they were mutual acquaintances, discussing places that were located in a readily comprehended, alternative reality. A sense of commonality was fostered by reference to everyday objects. 'Four-half', 'shandy-gaff', 'bloaters', 'bluchers', 'mustard plasters', 'tally bills', 'four-pound loaves', 'winkles', 'whelks' and 'grid-irons' were just a few of a collection of exemplars that provided familiar, but somehow esoteric, furnishings to an imagined area in which comedian and audience interacted.

A small, but powerful symbol of Victorian society, the copper coin, was at the centre of an anecdote which demonstrated Dan's growing independence and self confidence. The year was 1877 and the family had been without engagements for 19 weeks. Dan had set out from Manchester on yet another long walk in search of employment. When he reached Hyde, on the outskirts of the city, he discovered that a 'Free and Easy' concert was to be held at the Railway Tavern. A kind-hearted landlord invited him to share a family dinner, and later Dan sang and danced at the inn for most of the evening. He collected one pound 18 shillings, mainly in halfpennies and pennies, a substantial amount of money and a heavy weight to carry home. After sleeping on the pub floor, he set off next morning, bearing his evening's earnings. Almost immediately he encountered a family of beggars singing by the roadside. It is hardly surprising that he identified with their plight. Dan probably needed Johnny to restrain his impulsive nature, but, left to his own judgement, he decided that generosity was in order. Three fistfuls of hard-earned coppers were swiftly handed to the struggling family. 'I don't think I ever walked six miles as lightly and easily as I did after that,' he recollected.[17]

5

MONARCH IN WOODEN SHOES

'Isn't it Leno? Right, see how I'll play for you.' A whispered voice from Will's past assured Dan's future. Messrs Melrose and Richards, 'grotesque performers', had been granted a benefit at Sherwood's 'Free and Easy', in Wakefield, West Yorkshire, the highlight of the evening to be a clog-dancing competition. The Lenos must have looked more than usually down at heel, for Dan entered under an assumed name. But Jack Richards, an excellent violinist, recognised him and spoke encouragingly to the young dancer as he tuned his fiddle. With Richards playing like an 'angel', Dan was easily victorious in the first major clog-dancing contest of his career.[1]

It seems that other familiar faces began to re-appear at the dawn of the new decade. At Christmas 1879 the Leno Quartet were appearing at the Star Music Hall, Manchester, with 'Dan Patrick' listed separately on the bill. Will had also devised a 'spectacular ballet' entitled *The Wicklow Wedding* in which he appeared with Dan, Louisa, the misses Payce and Mayfield, Jim Keefe (probably the James Keith who had appeared with the family back in 1868) and H. Leno.[2] It is reasonable to suppose that that 'H. Leno' was Henry making a brief re-appearance with the family troupe; by 1881, when the census recorded him as living at 4 Little George Street, Westminster, he had quit the troupe to pursue the lowly occupation of 'labourer'. Although moving away from his mother and younger brother, Henry was still close to another member of the family, his older brother John, who was living at number 25 in the same street. Henry did not entirely lose his connection with the entertainment business. Following Dan's London success he advertised: 'Clog dancing taught by H. Wild, Brother and Tutor of Dan Leno, J.H. Haslam, etc., 13 Windmill Street, Tottenham Court Road.'[3] When the 1891 census was taken, he was recorded as a 'Teacher of Dancing' at 31 Berwick Street, Soho, close to Will's childhood home.

Despite his outstanding natural talent Dan had to practise continually. George Belmont, a clog dancer who went on to become one of music hall's most flamboyant impresarios, remembered appearing with the Lenos at the Theatre Royal, Rotherham, at Easter 1881. On the

Friday following the Bank Holiday an audience of two had their money refunded and 'the company adjourned to an adjacent hostelry for refreshments.' Belmont remembered that Dan was 'practising two to three hours a day at his clog-dancing.'[4]

The competition to establish 'The Champion Clog Dancer of the World' held at the Princess's Palace, Leeds, during Whit Week 1880, was, as might be expected, open to all comers. But the barely hidden agenda was to match two local favourites, Tom Robson and Tom Ward, against each other. Rivalries were intense in the world of clog dancing, sharpened and embittered by side wagers and general betting on the outcome of the contest. Dan was venturing into a lion's den when he allowed his name to be put forward for the competition. The Lenos were appearing at Templeton's Varieties, Halifax, for the week commencing 10 May 1880[5] when a comic singer, Frank Belton, suggested to Will that his step-son might stand a reasonable chance in the following week's contest. At first Leno senior was doubtful. Eventually, when he allowed Belton to enter Dan's name, a misunderstanding led to 'Dan', from 'Dan Patrick', being coupled with the family name 'Leno'. Posters for the Princess's Palace printed the name 'Dan Leno' for the first time, in error.

The famous comedian Arthur Lloyd topped the bill at the Princess's, with heats of the clog-dancing contest forming part of each evening's programme throughout the week. Ward was successful against Jess Juba on Monday, with Dan trouncing F. Doyle on Tuesday. On the Friday Ward and Dan both won. Finally, on Saturday 22 May Dan scraped home when Ward made a mistake towards the end of his series of set steps. The victory was a complete shock to most of the audience, many of whom had backed Ward to win. The two Toms were furious – it was a severe blow to their pockets as well as their pride, for whoever won could make extensive capital from their 'world champion' status, and from the exhibition of the prize 44½-ounce silver belt. At a time when a leg of mutton and a purse of silver were considered a suitable prize for winning a clog-dancing contest, the belt, valued at £50, and an accompanying purse of 15 gold sovereigns, conferred extraordinary distinction on their recipient. The belt was a gleaming symbol of success, a precious artefact to be jealously protected.

The ill-feeling between the Ward and Leno camps was evident in two long adverts that appeared in the theatrical press:

Talent Without Gas. Dan Leno Champion Clog Dancer of the World. English Irish Comedian and Pantomimist. I, Dan Leno, never Challenged any Man in my life, but when the contest was open to the World I thought I would stand my chance, and, after dancing Seven of the best Dancers in the Profession, I am proud to say I won the laurels and the Dancers acknowledged they were fairly beaten. I have to thank the judges, Mr Wood, [proprietor of the Princess's Palace] and all connected with it, for the honourable manner in which it was carried out. I am appearing every evening at the PRINCESS'S PALACE, LEEDS, till further notice, wearing the magnificent Champion Belt; also the funny Leno [sic] in their screaming Burlesques. Forty minutes roars of laughter, six curtain calls Nightly.[6]

Tom Ward was not a step slower in presenting his own take on the contest:

Mr Tom Ward, Great Variety Performer, acknowledged by the Judges in the late Dancing Contest to be the Greatest Dancer ever they saw in all their lives for original steps and execution. Challenge to the World – I will dance Dan Leno, or any of the competitors who fancy themselves, for £50 or £100 a side, to dance on a stage with boards laid down for the express purpose, and have a competent Man to play, such as Mr T. Firth, Mechanics, Hull; or Mr P. Conroy of the Star, Manchester, to who I offered £5 to play to me in the above Contest, but was objected to. If Dan Leno will dance me any time before Six Months I will wager him £50 to £40 or £100 to £80, for the Championship and the Belt ...[7]

Having at first been sceptical about Dan's chances of winning the competition, Will was now wholehearted in his exploitation of the victory. The family had experienced too many setbacks to allow such an opportunity to slip through their fingers. At subsequent engagements a major feature was Dan's reprise of his championship-winning dance and a triumphant exhibition of the heavy belt. The trophy must have looked even more massive on Dan's waist, for he was painfully thin and his adult height had settled at five feet three inches. The Leno troupe provided a varied entertainment to support Dan's singing and dancing. *The Era*'s review of their act at the People's Music Hall, Oldham, in June 1880 suggests that their musical accomplishments had grown substantially since the days of Will's uncertain flageolet 'fluffing'. Danvers and Clarence (possibly Johnny performing with a partner) gave 'an exciting performance with broadswords', while the 'clever performances by the Leno family on the harp, guitar, ocarina, banjo, concertina, etc, forded a rare treat'.[8]

Dan now headed music-hall bills, his fame expressed in effulgent language. On his reappearance in Scotland in September 1880, the Britannia, Glasgow, announced:

First appearance in Scotland of the Conquering Hero,
Mr Dan Leno!
Champion Clog Dancer of the World.
He will nightly appear in his Champion Clog Dance.[9]

Three weeks later Dan was still at the Britannia:

Re-engagement for one week longer, by universal
Request of Dan Leno,
Champion Dancer of the World.

Despite the popularity that he had achieved under his new name, 'Dan Patrick' still appeared on the same bill, listed as a member of the Leno Comic Trio 'in their really Funny Entertainments, Songs, Dances'.[10]

Challenges and counter-challenges were furiously exchanged after the Princess's Palace contest. In April 1881 Thomas Burton, a friend of the Lenos, announced that Dan would defend the title at a contest to be held at his People's Concert Hall, Manchester, starting on 11 July. Almost immediately, J.H. Wood declared that he would organise a new championship competition. After an acrimonious debate Dan consented to take part in Wood's contest, to be held at Cooke's Royal Circus, Manchester, over the course of Whit week. Four finalists – Doyle, Ward, J.H. Haslam and Dan – battled against each other on Saturday, 11 June, before an audience that at times was in a state of near riot. The decision to award the contest to Ward prompted the furious Lenos to condemn the management of the event, the competence of the judges and the behaviour of the winner's supporters, who they described as 'a few roughs of Ancoats'.[11] Ward retaliated with a personal attack on Dan's parents published in *The Era*:

I am sorry for the cruel injustice to Dan Leno. No doubt he feels his defeat very acutely. He speaks of the roughs from Ancoats, who aided me in wrestling from him the Championship. He does not mention the crowds of ragged sympathisers who nightly shouted for the boy who had shown them his double shuffle on the cellar-flaps of Manchester, while his guardians drank pints of four-penny at adjacent beer-houses.[12]

Although Dan bitterly resented his defeat, possession of the trophy for a year had been long enough to establish him as a provincial star. At the Steam Clock, Birmingham, he was described as 'one of the very best concert hall artistes ... not only a good comedian, vocalist and pantomimist, but an excellent clog dancer'.[13] His success was such that he started to place his 'card', an advertisement listing his forthcoming engagements

and latest reviews, in the professional press. One of the first appeared in
The Era of 30 July 1881:

> Dan Leno. The first and only Champion Clog Dancer of the World
> making one of the most brilliant successes ever known in Birming-
> ham in conjunction with his Father and Mother in their Screaming
> Burlesques, – Performed for R.G. Goldsmith, Esq.'s Benefit and
> was engaged on the spot. At liberty for Pantomime, Three Parts
> and Clown and Harlequin.[14]

While Dan consolidated his position, a number of friendly managers and
music-hall proprietors combined their efforts to promote a new championship contest. In January 1882 a glowing testimonial was received
from the proprietor of the Peoples' Palace Music Hall, Rock Street, Oldham:

> Dan Leno and his father and mother are three of the oldest and
> most valued artists on my books. I prophesised that Dan, would
> be a great man some day, and my words have come true. Dan, is
> not tied to his clogs for a living; he is a comedian in every sense of
> the word. Author and Scenic Artist, and as a dancer he has beat
> the world. I, William Jeffereys, will back this Little Wonder to
> Dance any man under the sun for Five Hundred Pounds of my
> own money.[15]

Dan's backer, William Jeffereys, was known to members of 'The Profession' simply as 'Jef'. Born in Nottingham in about 1829 he had been a
confectioner before turning to music-hall management, an occupation
that he pursued in his own eccentric fashion. A well-known foible of Jef's
was to pay performers, according to their status, in packets of shillings,
pennies and farthings. Every Sunday he was to be found at Joe Taff's
bar, in Manchester, puffing on a long churchwarden pipe as he negotiated terms with his artists. It was probably at this inn, much frequented
by performers, that Jef and Will plotted Dan's clog-dancing strategies.
The canny proprietor appears to have been a good friend to the Lenos,
but, as a self-proclaimed prophet, there is no doubt that he foresaw a pile
of assorted coinage to be made by promoting the young dancer.

A volatile situation finally exploded when Tom Ward and Dan found
themselves on the same bill at the Parthenon Music Hall, Liverpool, in
April 1882. Ward was angered to the point of incoherence by Dan's im-
provisational style of dancing and by the behaviour of his supporters:

> The dissatisfied ex-Champion's corner lot, including the pot-house
> devourers have had a financial treat to a nightly exhibition of the

Champion's legitimate both-legs-alike style, without skipping all over the shop.[16]

An indignant retort was immediately issued:

Mr Ward said in last week's Era that he placed upon the stage £20 to dance Dan Leno, but that is not true. He only put down £10, but would not say on what conditions. But at Ward's Benefit Night Dan put £20 of his own money and conditions, but Ward would not cover Dan's money or dance him, to the great dissatisfaction of his friends. Ward also stated that he will not give up the Belt, as he did not receive the Six Week's Engagement at £10 per Week. Now Dan, might have kept the Belt on the same plea, for Dan never got £60 for the Six Weeks' Engagement.

When Whit-Week arrives that Belt becomes public property. It was very bad of Mr W. to call the audience a lot of roughs and pothouse companions of Dan's, when he knows that Dan never tasted intoxicating drinks in his life. The Public will not countenance a barefaced injustice. Dan's wrongs, like Caesar's wounds, will speak with a thousand tongues. Mrs And Mr Leno and Dan are now fulfilling their Fourth Week at the Parthenon, making One Week before Ward came, Two Weeks with him, and One Week after he left. ALHAMBRA, HULL, Next Week, Princess's Palace, Leeds to follow.
A life untainted by vice or shame.
Living for his art alone, struggling for fame;
Using well the great gifts that Heaven may send,
All mean and paltry foes he will conquer in the end.
                                        W. Leno, Clown, Poet.[17]

Jef and Will maintained relentless pressure on Ward to dance for the belt. As the financial inducements grew larger, Dan's gibes from the stage became more impudent. In an appearance at the Scotia, Glasgow, in February 1882 he gave an impersonation of J.W. Ashcroft in his song and dance 'Muldoon, the Solid Man', and also performed a number that proclaimed 'They've done me, they've robbed me, but, thank God, I'm the Champion Still!'[18] A poster from Ohmy's Circus of Varieties, Accrington, from early 1883, states that Dan's challenge of £400 a side remained unaccepted and that 'he will nightly expose the contest in which he was not allowed to win, after beating fifteen of the best dancers in the Kingdom.'[19] The bill went on to claim that Ward had refused to dance a second time as laid down in the rules of the contest, but had contrived to purchase the belt outright. Ward had apparently received a summons

4   Champion clog dancer, 1883

to return the trophy, but unable to reach a decision the magistrate had offered him the choice of handing it back or paying ten pounds.

With Ward clearly intent on retaining the belt by any means possible, Jeffereys arranged for another to be manufactured, a magnificent gold and silver creation decorated with allegorical figures of Music and Dance, the British lion and two straight-armed Lancashire clog-dancers. The belt's central shield was soon to be engraved with Dan's name, for he triumphed in a week-long contest held at Jeffereys' People's Palace Music Hall.

Dan was exultant. His *Era* card for the week following the contest crowed over the details of his recent career:

Dan Leno. Winner of the First Silver Champion Belt and Purse of Fifteen Sovereigns at the Princess's Palace, Leeds, Whit Week 1880. Also winner of the massive gold and silver Champion Belt, valued at £50, after a Six Nights contest at Oldham, commencing Whit Monday, May 14; finished May 19th. This talented and versatile artist is at home once more, and appearing every evening at the PEOPLE'S MUSIC HALL, MANCHESTER. Money turned away Monday last.

Dan Leno is not only a Clog Dancer, but the following:-
Dan Leno, Vocal Comedian.
Dan Leno, Irish Character Actor.
Dan Leno, Dutch Impersonator.
Dan Leno, Great Sabot Dancer.
Dan Leno, Eccentric Song and Dance.
Dan Leno, Pantomimist.
Dan Leno as Pongo the Monkey.
Dan Leno as Torpedo Bill.
Dan Leno as Captain Newgate.
Dan Leno as Billy Buttons.
Dan Leno, the First and Only Champion of the World.
Dan Leno works nobody's stuff but his own.
Dan Leno copies no one.

Words of Songs and Burlesque Pantomimes by W. Leno. Music by Sam Tute, Esq., J. Sinclare, Esq., Sydney Davis, Esq., T. Richards, Esq., C. Fenwick, Esq., Newcastle, and other acknowledged musicians.

Dan Leno wishes to thank Mr Jeffereys, People's Music Hall, for the enterprising manner in which he got up the contest. He also thanks the judges for their patience and impartial judgement not forgetting Mr W. Marchant for the kind and delicate speech he made when he presented the Belt ...[20]

Ward, the proud purchaser of the original belt was unimpressed:

> Tom Ward, Great Variety Artist, Song and Dance performer and the only Champion Clog Dancer of the World. Winner and Possessor of the Champion Belt Title at Cooke's Circus, Manchester, June 11, 1881, against all comers. Proprietors and Managers will note that all so called Champion Clog Dancing Contests are futile as I possess the only Champion Belt, and all other claimants are imposters. My standing challenge since the above date has never been accepted, and although its repetition seems useless I am still open to dance any man in the world for £100 to £500 a side ...[21]

The Lenos moved on, to the People's Music Hall, Manchester, where they again received glowing reviews:

> Mr Dan Leno 'The Monarch in Wooden Shoes' amply proves his claim to the possession of the title with which he describes himself. The Leno Trio, in their sketch 'A Nobleman in Disguise' are exceedingly amusing.[22]

The family were moving on in other ways – improved negotiating powers with music-hall managers enabling them to lead an increasingly comfortable private life. Tom Ward's posturing and the politics of clog dancing became minor irritations as Dan consolidated his position as an all-round performer. At the time when Dan had been dancing his way toward the title, a young singer with the stage name Lydia Reynolds was also making steady progress in the northern music halls. The two performers were to become legally linked when they married in 1884, but not before the 'inconvenience' of the birth of their first child earlier in the year.

Lydia was born Sarah Lydia Reynolds in Birmingham on 7 November 1866, the daughter of Sarah and John Reynolds, a carpenter who specialised in stage work. It seems that Lydia made some of her earliest appearances at the Prince of Wales Theatre, Wolverhampton, where her father was employed. At the tender age of 15 she had already received a complimentary review in the theatre's early-summer pantomime *Sinbad the Sailor*: 'Miss Lydia Reynolds played Zorilda very well for a young artiste. She is well known at this theatre and with proper training will prove a clever little actress.'[23] During this stage of her career Lydia played many *travestie* roles, her cards stating that she specialised in 'Chambermaids, Boys, and Burlesque.' A step towards becoming a fully-fledged 'principal boy' occurred at Christmas 1881/82 when she played Dandini in *Cinderella* presented at the St James's Theatre, Tunstall, in Staffordshire.[24] A year later she received favourable reviews for another 'male' role, Little John, in the pantomime *Robin Hood* at the People's Opera House, Stockport.

Dan was 23 and Lydia 16 when they first met at King Ohmy's Circus of Varieties, Rochdale, in 1883. She was only just 17 when their child was conceived, probably during the run of *Dick Whittington* at the People's Opera House, Stockport, in 1884. For the Stockport pantomime Will Leno had been cast as Alderman Fitzwilliam Sloper, a traditional character reinterpreted as the incorrigible hero of the adult comic *Ally Sloper's Half Holiday*. A less than charitable observer might have detected resonances of Will himself in Ally's drunken, boastful and self-promoting behaviour, but despite – or possibly because of – such venial sins both Sloper and Leno Senior were immensely popular with their respective audiences.

Dan gave his earliest-recorded female impersonation as Mrs Fitzwilliam Sloper. There had been isolated instances of music-hall comedians adopting bonnets and skirts, but the cross-dressing tradition had evolved largely in pantomime and burlesque. Although well known 'Dame' comedians, typified by Herbert Campbell and Harry Randall, were to introduce female characterisations into their music-hall acts Dan, more than any other, gave equal weight to portrayals of both men and women. While reducing the grotesquely overblown attributes of the pantomime Dame, he began to introduce studies of women facing problems and pitfalls that would have been familiar to most female members of his audience. Close contact with three women – a middle-aged mother, a teenage bride and an infant daughter – would have provided much material and inspiration. Within two years he was appearing at music halls playing a harassed mother of lively twins, and before the end of the decade he had delineated many other memorable female characters.

In *Dick Whittington* he had a show-stopping song: 'DAN LENO has achieved the greatest success ever known in Stockport for a panto-mimist; his song of 'Sweet Black Pears' (which is a Burlesque Song and Dance) causes screams of laughter at each performance.'[25] For possibly the last time step-father and step-son appeared together in a Harlequinade. Will, of course, played the broad-comedy figure of Clown, while Dan portrayed the dashing, mercurial and amorous Harlequin.

During the early stages of her pregnancy Lydia continued to appear as a solo turn. Her card for 16 February 1884 announced that she had just concluded a successful engagement at Wigan, and was subsequently to appear at Halifax, Rochdale, Sheffield, Hull, Bury and Liverpool. *The Wigan Advertiser* considered: 'Miss Lydia Reynolds ... a *serio* of the first rank'.[26] Boosted by their joint popularity Lydia and the Lenos made ambitious new plans for 1884. During the run of *Dick Whittington* they announced their intention of becoming music-hall managers: 'W. Leno and Son have taken the Grand Varieties, Tudor Street, Sheffield, on lease to take possession March 10, 1884 …'[27]

6

LENO'S GRAND VARIETIES

The Grand Varieties, Tudor Street, was a ramshackle wood-and-brick structure, described by a contemporary journalist as 'clumsy, ungainly, and altogether unsightly'.[1] Although ill-formed the Grand was not old, having been erected in Sheffield's town centre in 1879. It had originally been built as a circus, and later served as a Christian mission, a music hall and a theatre before being destroyed, as most wooden theatre-buildings were, by fire. Appropriately, the only articles to survive the conflagration were a bible and a trunk of pantomime props.

With its factory chimneys pouring out clouds of poisonous soot Shef-field was one of the most polluted industrial cities in the world. A sul-phuric black crust obscured both ugly and attractive buildings alike. Separated from the music hall by a narrow alley was the Mechanics' Institute, a handsome nineteenth-century edifice that housed one of the first public libraries in the United Kingdom. On the northern side of Tudor Street, facing the Grand, was the tall, bleak facade of the Tudor Works, a factory specialising in silver-, nickel- and electro-plating. Adjoining the works was the Theatre Royal, a large but anonymous building that was also to be gutted by fire. Downhill and to the south of the Grand was the Music Hall, not a rival variety theatre but a concert hall, built in 1823. Alongside the Music Hall stood a Methodist chapel and a small school. And on the corner outside the Leno's own music hall, illuminated by a wall-mounted gas light, was a cast-iron public urinal.

The people who lived in the city's claustrophobic, back-to-back ter-races were predominantly employed in the iron and steel industry. There could have been few Victorian households which did not possess a selec-tion of utensils stamped with the words 'made in Sheffield'. Local music-hall audiences were notoriously unruly, not averse on occasions to throw-ing items of their own manufacture at performers who did not meet with their approval. The great cockney comedienne Marie Lloyd once linked the city's population and its products in a fiery piece of stage repartee: 'You don't like me, well I don't like you. And you know what you can do with your stainless steel knives and your scissors and your circular saws – you can stick 'em up your arse.'[2]

Such vulgarity, however well-deserved, would not have suited the Lenos when they prepared to take over the running of the Grand. Their *Era* card for 27 December 1883 announced: 'Professionals depending on songs worded with double meanings need not write.' That Dan did not intend to be tied to the Grand was indicated by the same advertisement:

> Dan Leno will continue his Professional Tour with everything new, English, Irish and Dutch impersonations and his novel and new style of Champion Clog Dance. Belt exhibited nightly Six Different, Splendid Lithographs and Posters. At Liberty March 31st.

By the early 1880s Dan had already accumulated a wealth of entertainment experience. He recalled:

> We performed everywhere and did everything. I have performed, I suppose, in every singing-room in Manchester and Liverpool. I appeared at Ben Lang's Music Hall the week after the great panic. I have sung in the Shakespeare Music Hall, in Manchester, on the site where the central station now stands ... I have sung and painted scenery for the Star Music Hall in Ancoats. At the People's Concert Hall I spent my twenty first birthday, and was there presented with my first watch and chain. I have played in comedies and dramas at the old Rotunda in Liverpool. I have even had engagements as a serious vocalist, but, of course, that was in the days before I became a genuine comic singer and mislaid my voice.[3]

Will had frequently organised his own variety entertainments. A favourite tale of Dan's, and one which reflected his lifelong sensitivity about his own social background, concerned his step-father putting together a troupe of artists for an aristocratic celebration. Despite Will's irrepressible confidence, his chosen performers were undermined by self-doubt and an excess of free beer. Like all Dan's stories there was probably a good deal of comic exaggeration. J. Hickory Wood preserved the anecdote in his biography of Dan:

> While perusing a theatrical paper one day, Mr Leno chanced to see an advertisement that interested him greatly.

> It was, in effect, that an entrepreneur was wanted, who could supply a really good high-class entertainment on the occasion of certain festivities that were to be held in honour of the coming of age of the oldest son of a certain noble lord, whose family seat was situated some twenty miles distant from Sheffield. The fee offered

was an inclusive one of fifty pounds, and all applications were to be sent to the steward of the estate. Mr Leno immediately sat down and wrote a letter to the steward that did him infinite credit.

In it he stated that he (Mr Leno) was an entrepreneur of immense experience and world-wide fame; that he was willing, for the sum mentioned, to bring down a company of London artistes, all of unrivalled ability and marvellous versatility, adding that the happy incident of this brilliant troupe being as close at hand as Sheffield was the reason that enabled him to offer the noble lord what was really the chance of a lifetime.

His company, continued Mr Leno, was high-class or nothing; but where high-class was required it was simply and absolutely everything.

He fearlessly undertook to supply any kind of high-class entertainment that the noble lord might select – Light Opera; Comic Opera; Grand Opera; Shakespearian Revival; Farce; Orchestral Concert; or Tragedy.

'But,' he somewhat artfully concluded 'if you wish to see my company at its very best, I would recommend a variety show as being our very strongest point.'

There were days of sickening suspense, but at last there came a letter from the steward to say that Mr Leno's offer had been accepted, and requesting him to bring his company down to give a variety show on the day appointed.

Then there was great joy in the house of Leno, mingled with much furbishing up of old theatrical garments, and practising of new songs and steps.

It was arranged that the company were to travel by train to a small station down the line, where they would be met by a wagonette and driven to the scene of the festivities.

This is Dan's description of the talented company that boarded the wagonette, much to the surprise of his lordship's servants, who had been led to expect something different:

1. The old man (Mr Leno) got up as the entrepreneur. Hair well oiled, to the great detriment of his coat collar; shocking bad top-

hat; and the inevitable Family Ulster with bits of an old fur boa of mother's stitched on the collar and cuffs.

2. A harmonium player, with a groggy face, carrying his harmonium.

3. A violinist who squinted.

4. A cornet player with four teeth out – the worst cornet player in the provinces.

5. A negro comedian in a velvet coat and corduroy trousers.

6. The human eel. A very fat man with a purple face through bending backwards.

7. A lady vocalist, dressed entirely in stage 'props', and wearing a hat a man had once worn when he played Romeo.

8. Johnny Danvers in patched boots.

9. Dan Leno in frayed trousers. And

10. The luggage. An old tin box with hollows all over it, and tied up with pieces of rope.

When they arrived at their destination, they found that the entertainment took the shape of a garden party; a platform was erected at the end of a lawn for their performance, and behind it stood a large marquee.

About this lawn were strolling ladies and gentlemen, all beautifully attired, and in order to reach their dressing-room, the company had to cross it in full view of the assembled guests.

They hesitated a moment; then Mr Leno boldly took the plunge, and led the way. The others followed, and the passage being safely accomplished, they were met on the other side by two flunkeys in gorgeous livery. Before them Mr Leno, temporarily overawed by their magnificence, took off his hat and bowed humbly. The flunkeys, eyeing the party disdainfully, merely pointed to the marquee, and then retired.

They entered the marquee, and were delighted to see, spread before them, a large round of beef, pickles of many varieties, and jugs of beer wherewith to wash it all down.

For a moment they gazed in silent admiration.

The human eel was the first to speak.

'Oh dear! I wish my poor wife was here!' he said; a speech that did him credit, but suggested sad memories of hungry days. But the

human eel was not a man who wasted much time over foolish and
unavailing regrets.

He heaved one sigh, and, philosophically remarking. 'Well. If she's
not here, I am,' attacked the cold beef and pickles with a certain
amount of science, and a great deal of vigour.

He showed such strong tendencies towards rapid consumption
that the rest of the company had, in self-defence, to sit down without loss of time and join in the fray.

A somewhat prolonged meal was the result; indeed it was not until
after five or six messages, each one more urgent than the last, had
been sent by the steward to know if the company was nearly ready
to begin the performance, that Mr Leno reluctantly gave the word
to desist …

The proceedings opened with a performance of the overture to
Zampa by the full orchestra. This was so distressingly bad that the
audience took it to be intentionally so, and laughed heartily at
what they, with some reason, imagined to be a burlesque of the
real thing.

The insulted orchestra retired, in high dudgeon, to the marquee,
there to console themselves with more beef and beer, and Mr Leno,
remarking that if they wanted to laugh he would give them
something to laugh at, turned on the negro comedian instead of
the lady vocalist, whose turn it should have been.

The gentleman had a large stock of jokes from which to draw –
jokes that were for the most part more distinguished for breadth
than length, and that certainly possessed the merit of being absolutely new to a fashionable audience. The effect of them was in-
stantaneous.

At the end of the first joke a distinct shiver ran through the audience; the second caused them to shuffle their feet restlessly; the
third emptied half the seats; and the fourth was never finished because Mr Leno, who knew the point of it, audibly insisted on the
performer leaving the platform before he got more than half-way
through.

The entrepreneur now felt that something must be done quickly in
order to obviate disaster, so he decided to play his trump card.

Mounting the platform, he announced to those who had bravely remained in their seats that he had much pleasure in introducing to them a most sensational novelty, none other than 'The Human Eel.'

Applause, a chord from the band, and the human eel stepped on to the platform in the bright sunlight, attired in green tights, mended, in various places, with blue worsted.

'My first feat,' said he, 'will be to bend backwards, pick up a glass from the ground with my teeth, and consume the contents as I resume my original position.'

Placing the glass on the ground, and sighing deeply, he began to bend, anxiously watched by the rest of the company.

Poor eel! He was, as stated in the bills, only a human eel after all, and, as was to be expected under existing conditions, he never got his mouth anywhere near that glass.

He struggled nobly, until – there was a sharp 'rip', the green tights yielded where the blue worsted most predominated; and the remainder of the audience retired.

In vain Mr Leno remounted the platform, and entreated them to remain and see 'the great and only Dan Leno, the greatest dancer and comedian on the stage'. They knew when they had had enough, and publicly intimated the same.

A brief period of doubt among the company as to what was advisable to do next was peremptorily settled by the steward, who informed Mr Leno that the further services of himself and the distinguished company would be dispensed with; that the wagonette was now waiting to take them back to where it had, unfortunately, found them; and that the cheque for £50 would be sent in the course of a day or two ...[4]

When the cheque failed to arrive after three days, Will decided to collect his payment in person. He discovered the lord hosting a shooting party in the grounds of his estate, but was only able to collect seven pounds 'on account'. Retiring to the village tavern to wait for a train back to Sheffield he fell in with a group of locals who, as a 'famed London actor', he felt obliged to treat. Several missed trains later he arrived home bearing with him only three of the original seven pounds. Fortunately, his lordship's cheque for the balance arrived next morning.

The Lenos were more comfortable with the working class-audiences who patronised the Grand. On the opening night, 17 March 1884, over 4,000 were reported to have paid for admission. Having been built for circus use the Grand had a semi-circular plan, the stage facing a high bank of seats with a large coal-fired stove placed ominously at the centre of the theatre. A programme for 15 September 1884, with Dan and Will Oliver topping the bill, advertised cushioned seats for one shilling; uncushioned seats for sixpence; side seats and promenade for fourpence, and gallery seats for threepence. Disorderly persons were subject to expulsion and ladies were admitted free on Thursday nights if accompanied by a gentleman.[5]

'Mr Dan Leno is a host in himself,' commented *The Era* for 22 March 1884, an allusion not only to his hospitality but to his multiplicity of talents. With competition from several other local halls, the Lenos worked hard to make their new venture a success. For Dan's benefit a series of public competitions and an enhanced variety programme were announced:

Mr Dan Leno intends to spare no expense to make this the most pleasant and enjoyable entertainment ever witnessed in Sheffield.

Look at the following Eight Grand Contests and Double Company!

Now come Leno's seasonable gifts:
200 Half-ounces of Tobacco
To the first 200 entering the Pit and Side-seats.
Every half ounce genuine.

Now come the contests:
Ten Shillings for the best Clog Dancer.
Dan Leno, judge.
Each dancer to dance six steps,
And shuffle in good clogs.
No person that has gained his living by dancing
Will be allowed to enter.

Ten Shillings to the Lady and Gentleman that can
Waltz six times round the stage the neatest.

Half a crown each
Will be given for the longest standing jump,

For the best singer of two verses of a
Comic Song,
For the best High-Kicker,
For a Sack Race,
For a Boot-Finding Contest,
For the person that can stand on the side of a barrel
And sing a verse of a song ...[6]

Two sketches were presented as part of the entertainment; *Doctor Cut 'Em Up*, in which Dan played his original part 'Dirty Billy' plus the 'Full Star Company in their latest London sensation entitled *The Collier Boy*'.[7]

Despite strenuous efforts to make Leno's Grand Varieties a going concern, the family decided to give up the lease, announcing their final day of management to be 4 October 1884. Summer trade may have not been sufficiently lucrative, or perhaps Dan may have felt the need to pursue his career in other areas. One event would have necessitated some changes in the family's lifestyle – Georgina Louisa was born in Sheffield on 2 October.

Dan was beginning to pursue a solo career. An appearance at the Royal Alhambra Music Hall, Belfast, in November, was followed by an engagement at the Parthenon, Liverpool, which extended throughout December. By this time the Leno family had settled into a new home within commuting distance of a favourite hall, the People's Palace, in Manchester. Dan's *Era* card for 3 January 1885 read:

> Just fulfilled One Month Engagement at the comfortable Part-henon, Liverpool. Monday next Trevanion's, Blackburn. Then home to People's, Manchester. My new songs a great success. Written by myself, viz 'Twins', 'Don't Lean Against a House that's Pulled Down', 'Gaffer Goliker', etc. Notice Lydia Reynolds (Mrs Dan Leno) Burlesque, Serio and Descriptive Vocalist in conjunction with the above will make two of the biggest turns on the music hall stage.

Dan had returned to 37 Egerton Road, Hulme, a southern suburb of Manchester, at least once during his Liverpool engagement. On Monday, 15 December 1884 he and Lydia were married at St George's Church, Hulme. With its ornately decorated steeple and heavy buttresses, St George's was a flamboyant example of 1820s mock-Gothic architecture, but to Lydia, Dan and their witnesses, Albert and Frances Hickman, the building was oppressive and intimidating. Dan remembered 'four little people sneaking into a big church through a back door'.[8] Back at Egerton Road Louisa prepared a wedding breakfast of 'cold meat and potatoes, topped off with wedding cake made of bread pudding.' Louisa was probably minding Georgina, while Will was almost certainly taking the opportunity to 'wet the baby's head'. It was not long before Lydia returned to the stage. Within two weeks of their marriage she appeared in *Babes in the Wood*, the 1884/85 pantomime at the Theatre Royal, St Helens.

After the Lenos' departure the Grand Varieties struggled on until 1893, when a predictable fire removed it from the local scene. It was immediately replaced by the City Theatre, which was itself demolished within six years to make way for an infinitely grander theatre, the Lyceum. This theatre, decorated with magnificent rococo plasterwork, still stands, the only Victorian building in the café-lined development now named Tudor Square. With changes in population, St George's Church fell into disrepair, and by the 1970s had become abandoned. In 2005 the deconsecrated building was given a new lease of life when it was converted into apartments. Dan and Lydia were concerned with more immediate changes at the start of 1885. Dan could either consolidate his position as a star of the northern music hall or he could accept a new challenge, taking on the very best performers in the variety profession. With national, even international, fame as the prize, the young couple's eyes became firmly fixed on London.

7

THE TALK OF LONDON

In February 1885 Dan briefly revisited his childhood haunts, playing for a week at de Frece's Circus of Varieties, Birkenhead. No doubt he cast a nostalgic glance at the scene of his juvenile success, the Argyle, although for some years past the tiny music hall had been operating as a legitimate theatre. Dan was preparing to say farewell to the Mersey. He had arranged for R.H. Stokes to act as his London agent and announced in *The Era* that he would be arriving in the capital 'shortly'; a premature statement of intent that was not to be realised for seven months. Whatever the timing, most established London performers would have been indifferent to the arrival of yet another young hopeful from the provinces. The few who had recently appeared at northern halls might have awaited his debut with interest, perhaps considering that he was a London star in the making. Dan's typically low-key interpretation of his eventual success was: 'When I first came to London there was a great demand for comic singers, and my style struck the public taste.'

Dan was about to take his place at the head of a new wave of comedians, a generation born in the 1860s who achieved stardom during the last decade of the nineteenth century. Performers such as Harry Randall, Albert Chevalier, Gus Elen, Tom Costello, Little Tich and George Robey adopted a style that differed substantially from their predecessors'. By the mid-1880s the roar of the *Lions Comiques* had dwindled to a whimper. MacDermott was running a theatrical agency; 'Jolly' John Nash, Arthur Lloyd and Harry Liston were usually touring with their concert parties; while the once effervescent George Leybourne, had staggered through his final engagements to expire a drunken wreck in 1884. The most popular London comedian of the late 1870s, Arthur Roberts, had quit music hall in 1883 for its theatrical equivalent, burlesque, leaving a small group of performers to compete for the honours of top billing. When Dan arrived in London there were many popular, but few outstanding comic singers.

Although some performers continued to celebrate the excesses of the swaggering man-about-town, most 1890s comedians depicted the lifestyle of the working and lower-middle classes. Unlike Dan, many had

other occupations before they made their way into the variety profession, frequently via amateur concerts and entertainments at local clubs.
Some had a professional or white-collar background. Randall had been
an engraver of heraldic seals; Robey a trainee engineer; Chevalier a
teacher; and Elen, everybody's ideal conception of a dyed-in-the-wool
cockney, an assistant at the Army and Navy stores. With stricter con-
trols and regulation, and with improvements in comfort and facilities,
the music hall was becoming increasingly attractive to audiences from
such areas of society. Back at the 'comfortable Parthenon' in Liverpool,
a teenage manager, Oswald Stoll, was planning even greater changes to
music-hall entertainment. Within 20 years he had revolutionised the
industry, presiding over a chain of formulaic, standardised theatres
headed by a temple of theatrical respectability, the London Coliseum.

For the moment Dan remained in the north of England, perhaps pre-
vented from leaving by contractual agreements. Prospective London
employers probably monitored Dan's progress in the theatrical press.
A *Daily Guardian* review of his appearance at the Talbot, Nottingham,
in February 1885 gave a glowing account of his dancing prowess:

> A remarkable exhibition of clog dancing by Mr Dan Leno, the
> Champion Dancer of the World, is one of the most pleasing items
> in a specially attractive entertainment at the Palace of Varieties
> this week. Apparently in clog dancing, as in so many other stage
> performances, the present day exponents have improved on the
> skills attained by their predecessors in the art, and none of them
> could claim to make such a wonderful display as that exhibited by
> Mr Dan Leno. In watching the rapidity, neatness, and precision of
> Mr Leno's movement, the spectator might imagine himself looking
> at a cunningly arranged piece of mechanism. At the end of his per-
> formance the artist is rewarded with a heavy round of applause.[1]

Harry Randall saw Dan perform at the People's Music Hall, Manchester,
early in 1885. He remembered:

> During my second week – not being required on the stage till after
> ten – I used to amuse myself in the early part of the evening by
> visiting the local theatres and music-halls, or looking in at some of
> the numerous 'sing-songs' that flourished in those days. One
> evening I paid a visit to a hall called 'The Peoples', also known as
> 'Burton's'. It was swept away years ago by the Midland Hotel.
>
> It was rather a rough sort of place, and you could get a seat for
> twopence. After listening to one or two turns; a young fellow came
> on with a large pail in his hand, and sang a song describing his

adventures in getting 'Milk for the Twins'. He struck me as being very funny and full of resource. His last item was a most wonderful exhibition of clog dancing, which must have lasted twenty minutes. I heard he had been on earlier in the evening with his mother and father – 'The Leno Family' – in a sketch, and the combined salary was eight pounds! Verily, they earned their living.[2]

Following a two-week engagement at the People's Music Hall, Dublin, where the Lenos reprised *Pongo*, Dan took his leave of audiences in Manchester, Leeds and St Helen's before heading south. Lydia probably remained to pursue her own flourishing career. Not yet 19 she too had the potential to become a major star. To encourage her, there were a large number of women making their way to the top of the variety profession, with artists such as Jenny Hill, Vesta Tilley, Bessie Bellwood, Lottie Collins, Marie Lloyd and Vesta Victoria gaining a degree of financial and social parity with their male counterparts.

Dan's initial London appearances were announced for Monday, 5 October 1885:

FORESTERS', MIDDLESEX, and GATTI'S PALACE. Leno will be in receipt of the greatest salary of any dancer that has visited London. Can only stay one month, open in Glasgow Nov. 9th for Three Weeks. Return at Christmas to Leeds for Six Weeks, one Hall only, at an increase of £18 ...[3]

The three halls selected for Dan's London debut were popular establishments, but hardly fashionable. His first appearance of the evening was arranged for 8.40 pm at the Royal Foresters' Music Hall, situated in Cambridge Road, Bethnal Green, in the heart of London's East End. Like Dan's birthplace in Somers Town the Foresters' was adjacent to the dank towpaths of the Regents Canal and the giant metal storage-tanks of an 'Imperial' gasworks. After performing at least two songs, a clog dance and a possible encore he would have hurried into a carriage, familiarly known as a 'Pro's Lot', driving through busy streets to Drury Lane, where the Middlesex stood surrounded by gin palaces and fried-fish shops. At some stage during his journey, or on arriving at the 'Old Mo' for his 9.40 turn, he would have had to change costume and apply fresh make-up. On freeing himself from the Middlesex audience, the next part of his journey was southward, down to the Strand and across the Thames to Gatti's Palace of Varieties, Westminster Bridge Road, a small hall close to the railway arches of Waterloo Station. This final appearance was scheduled for 10.40. To play three halls a night was commonplace for many performers; the record, set by Marie Kendall in 1893, was seven.

5 The Middlesex Music Hall, by Joseph Penell

The infrastructure of the capital's music-hall industry was more complex than that of even the largest provincial centres. Some 50 halls provided employment for thousands of performers, agents, musicians, dress-
ers, scene painters, limelight men, stage carpenters and scene shifters,
barmaids and waiters, front-of-house staff, song writers and composers,
theatrical journalists and illustrators, music publishers, sandwich-board
men, carriage drivers, prostitutes and a ragged army of 'supers' who
were always in attendance in the hope of picking up a job.

In 1891, F. Anstey identified four specific classes of London music
halls. At the very top was the 'aristocratic variety theatre of the West-
End' represented by the Alhambra and Empire, both situated in Leicester Square; the Pavilion and the Trocadero, Piccadilly Circus; the Royal,
High Holborn; the Oxford, Oxford Street; and the Tivoli, in the Strand.
Audiences at the 'aristocratic' variety theatres were often indifferent to
the entertainment provided:

> You pass through wide, airy corridors and down stairs, to find
> yourself in a magnificent theatre, and the stall to which you are
> shown is wide and luxuriously fitted. Smoking is universal, and a
> large proportion of the audience promenade the outer circles, or
> stand in groups before the long refreshment bars which are a

prominent feature on every tier. Most of the men are in evening dress, and in the boxes are some ladies, also in evening costume, many of them belonging to what is called good society. The women in the other parts of the house are generally pretty obvious members of a class which, so long as it behaves itself with propriety in the building, it would, whatever fanatics may say to the contrary, be neither desirable nor possible to exclude.[4]

The second category was made up of the 'smaller and less aristocratic West End halls'. These were typified by the Middlesex and the Royal Standard, Victoria. Although Anstey felt that it was 'unnecessary to describe the second class of music halls, in which neither audience nor entertainment present any characteristic features' the illustrations to his *Harper's New Monthly Magazine* article show patrons of the stalls to be respectably dressed in bowler hats and feather bonnets.

Third in Anstey's system of classification were 'the large bourgeois music halls of the less fashionable parts and in the suburbs'. Among these might be numbered the Bedford, Camden Town; the Metropolitan, Paddington; the Royal Cambridge and the Foresters' in the East End; and the South London Palace and the Canterbury, both transpontine music halls just across the river in Lambeth. Anstey wrote:

The audience is not a distinguished-looking one; there are no dress-coats and caped cloaks, no dashing toilets, to be seen here, but the vast majority are in easy circumstances and eminently respectable. You will see little family parties – father, mother and perhaps a grown-up daughter or a child or two – in the stalls. Most of them are probably regular visitors, and have the entrée here in return for exhibiting bills in their shop-windows; and these family parties all know one another as can be seen from the smiles and handshakes they exchange as they pass in and out. Then there are several girls with their sweethearts, respectable young couples employed in neighbouring workshops and factories, and a rusty old matron or two, while the fringe of the audience is made up of gay young clerks, the local 'bloods,' who have a jaunty fashion in some districts of wearing a cigar behind the ear.[5]

Anstey categorised 'the minor halls of the poor and squalid districts' as the lowest, although there were probably many 'penny-gaff' theatres that had an even worse reputation. The minor halls were located in areas whose characteristics would have been very familiar to Dan:

You must penetrate to the heart of some obscure and unsavoury region, until, in a narrow thoroughfare of small shops stocked with the most uninviting comestibles – skinned sheep's heads with a gleam of lackadaisical sentiment in their upturned eyes, pale pigs' feet, fried fish, and appalling arrangements in pastry and jam – you come upon a public house with bills in the window which inform you that it is part of the establishment of which you are in search ... You find a narrow steep staircase at the side, leading up from the street, and, half-way up, a rough pay box and barriers ... You have to force your way through a dense crowd standing packed at the back of the dress circle, and eventually stumble into a partitioned recess, fitted with rough benches, cushionless and without backs. The house is dingy and tawdry, and a kind of grimy murk is in the air; the atmosphere is something terrible, with that acrid sting to it which is so indescribably depressing to an unaccustomed sense. There is a curious absence of colour in the audience, probably due to the scarcity of the female element, the majority being youths of between seventeen and twenty.[6]

The physical arrangement of individual music halls provided a succinct mechanism for displaying class structure. From the detached comfort of the private box, through the neat terraces of stalls, to the overcrowded regions of the gallery, the music hall's seating arrangements were dictated by the purchasing power of the audience. The sensitive pricing-system also allowed potential patrons the choice of sampling entertainments at all classes of music hall. At the 'aristocratic' halls during the late 1880s, boxes might be purchased for three guineas, stalls seats for three shillings and the gallery for one shilling. The next tier of music halls charged two guineas for boxes, two shillings for stalls and sixpence for the gallery. At the 'large bourgeois music halls' admission was one guinea for boxes, one shilling for the stalls and fourpence for the privilege of squashing into the hot and noisy 'top shelf'.

Although the efforts of the temperance movement had had some effect, the bond between music halls and the sale of alcohol was hard to loosen. The tables and chairs of earlier years had been replaced by rows of theatre seats, but many were equipped with shelves on which to rest a drink. In some music halls the chairman still called for patrons to place their orders, which were then delivered by waiters who skilfully made their way around the auditorium. For those who chose to stretch their legs, conveniently placed bars provided a good view of the stage. The drinking culture that prevailed within 'The Profession' was nurtured by music-hall managers. Harry Randall remembered that at some halls salaries were paid at the bar area, with pay packets recording the deductions made for drinks during the course of the engagement.[7]

With the exception of the most basic halls, the standard of entertainment was usually high. The major difference between classes of music

hall was one of quantity rather than quality, with the top West End
halls able to offer a complete bill of ten to 15 star names, as opposed to
the two, three of four that might be found on lesser programmes. Dan's
provincial fame was such that on his London debut he was accorded star
billing, second only to Fred Coyne 'The Sterling Comedian' and the Le
Fre Trio. Advertised as 'The great Irish Comic Vocalist and present
Champion Dancer of the World', the five pounds a week of his per-hall
salary was about half of what he could command in the provinces.

H. Chance Newton was present at one of his earliest London performances:

> Never shall I forget two of his songs especially. One was called
> 'When Rafferty Raffled His Watch,' the long chorus of which con-
> tained the following graphic lines:
>
> 'The table and chairs were tumbled downstairs,
> We'd plenty of Irish and Scotch;
> And the divil's own fight there was on the night,
> When Rafferty raffled his watch.'
>
> His most startling hit that night, however, was with a screamingly
> comic ditty, in which he gave the first of his extensive gallery of
> 'funny female' impersonations. He appeared as a sort of nurse-
> maid – a cross between Dickens's two 'servant' specimens, Tilly
> Slowboy and Miggs. That Lenonian and ceaselessly dancing dam-
> sel carried a huge kitchen pail on each arm, and, breaking off into
> much extraordinary patter, periodically dashed into the startling
> refrain, 'I'm off to get milk for the twins!'[8]

Music-hall reviewers were quick to pick up on Dan's progress: 'Mr Dan
Leno has made a highly successful first appearance in London,' commented *The Entr'acte* for 12 October. Two weeks later the same periodical enthused: 'Mr Leno's Irish delineations are very praiseworthy; his
dancing is marvellously good, added to which he is adept at the art of
make up.'[9] By his third week at the Middlesex, the playbills were trum-
peting the arrival of a new star: 'The Talk of London. Dan Leno, Champion Dancer of the World and Funniest of All Vocalists.'

At this stage of his career his songs probably conformed to the usual
music-hall arrangement of a number of narrative verses linked by a
repeated chorus. His dancing, however, was of a completely new order.
Contrary to some accounts of his London debut it was enthusiastically
applauded, particularly by working-class audiences in the East End. The
artist Harry Furniss remembered Dan's dancing at an early London engagement:

Once or twice during the twelvemonth I would wander away from
the beaten track to visit haunts in the East End of London. On
these occasions I was accompanied by my male model, himself, in
a minor degree, a music hall performer, acrobat and juggler; he
was a veritable Mark Tapley. On one such excursion we found
ourselves at a Whitechapel music-hall, where the stalls were priced
sixpence, and the upper circles threepence halfpenny. The entertainment, I must admit was worth all these vast sums combined,
and one turn alone was worth a great deal more. He was a clog
dancer, a sickly-looking youth – small, delicate, insignificant
physique. His face was expressionless, he hadn't a word to say, but
he danced divinely and 'brought down the house'. He was adorned
with a wonderful belt, whether a genuine testimony to his dancing
prowess or not I cannot say – and he also wore several medals
which clicked like castanets. His name was Dan Leno.[10]

There was time for one last clog-dancing controversy. A challenge for
the World Championship came from the most unlikely area – another
nation! The Middlesex bill for the week commencing 2 November 1885
advertised Dan as 'Still the Rage ... Comic Vocalist, First and Only
Champion Dancer of the World', but also announced a new rival: 'John
Williams. A New Candidate for Championship Honours ... American
Variety Artist and Dancer, who has just come over to Compete for the
Title.'

In September, shortly before Dan arrived in London, Williams had
issued a challenge via two periodicals, *The Era* and *Sporting Life*. Dan
had quickly responded, agreeing to dance the American for any sum and
at any venue, giving his backers as W. Trevanion, Thomas Burton and
the ever-supportive William Jeffereyes. Several months went by with no
contest taking place, but eventually a match was arranged for 100
pounds a side. At the last moment however, Williams withdrew, claiming that as Dan was not prepared to put the Championship at stake 'he
saw little point in participating'. Williams forfeited his 75 pounds
deposit, and the two dancers were never pitted against each other.

As Dan prepared to return to the North to honour previously arranged engagements, Johnny Danvers set out on the reverse journey. He
had secured the role of Silly Billy in the pantomime *Robinson Crusoe* to
be held at the Surrey Theatre, Blackfriars Road, Lambeth at Christmas
1885/86. It was probably at this time that Dan and Johnny paid a visit
to the 'National Theatre', Drury Lane. Dan had never seen the Theatre
Royal, and one morning Johnny suggested that they take a stroll to look
at its exterior. From whatever direction they travelled they would have
passed through crowded streets, lined with small shops and taverns. Had
they made their way from the river they might have walked along

Holywell Street, a narrow lane running parallel to the Strand, which was the location for another of London's sacred springs and the centre of the pornographic book trade. An approach from the opposite direction would have taken them past John Galvin's childhood home in Wild Street and, in neighbouring Stanhope Street, the birthplace of Joseph Grimaldi.

Suddenly they arrived in an open space dominated by the theatre's austere regency frontage. They may have known something of the theatre's history – perhaps that it was the oldest in London, built in 1663 by the Master of the King's Revels, Thomas Killigrew. They would certainly have been aware that generations of famous actors had performed there and that it was celebrated for pantomimes unsurpassed in their grandeur. Hardly anyone in Catherine Street would have given a second glance to the slightly built young man who climbed the theatre's shallow flight of entrance steps. After kneeling briefly he returned and spoke to his colleague: 'Johnny! I shall act there some day.'[11]

8

DAME DURDEN AND MR TAMBO

The Leno family made their final appearances together during the early months of 1886. Louisa and Will had every reason to be satisfied with their tutorage, as Dan now excelled in dancing and comedy and was proving himself to be a more than capable song writer. He had inherited his maternal grandfather's artistic skills, producing attractive water-colours and large-scale stage scenery. Such talents had a literal application, for he had become particularly adept in the art of stage make-up. Above all, he was an ideal student, soaking up advice, instruction and criticism from everyone he encountered.

Dan's receptivity and retentiveness extended to chance acquaintances, particularly when they exhibited some characteristic which could be mentally logged and made use of at a later date. The anecdotes which he frequently recounted not only confirmed him as an astute student of human nature, but also demonstrated the degree of personal observation he employed in his stage comedy. One of his favourite stories concerned an exasperated porter and a barrow heavily laden with stage 'props':

A rather amusing incident occurred in connection with a Liverpool engagement. When we arrived, in order to maintain the dignity of our little company, I got some money from the manager to pay for our baggage being taken to the theatre instead of taking it ourselves. I called a man with a hand-cart, whose respectfulness touched me deeply because he was a good deal better dressed than I was. He loaded his cart with our curious assortment of baggage. There was a trick bedstead which, bundled together and tied round with rope, was not at all an object of beauty suitable for a nobleman's furniture, and an old tin tray tied in with string formed the bottom of one of the baskets, so that that when the cart was piled up with the things it looked more like a cheap eviction than the arrival of a troop of respectable professionals.

We were to open at the Adelphi Theatre in Christian Street, and we told the man to take the things to the Adelphi. He touched his cap and went, while I decided that, as I had plenty of time, I would have a walk round the town before going to the theatre, and still reach there as soon as the porter; so away I went and bought some cakes with twopence of the money that the manager had given me to pay the man with. I have a vivid recollection of these cakes, which were of an extremely obstinate nature with a speck of jam in the middle. I remember hammering one on a doorstep in order to chip a piece off, and I gave the other to some little girls, who licked off the jam and played hopscotch with the rest.

When I arrived at the theatre in about an hour's time I found no porter and no luggage. I spread myself all over the town to look for him, and you can imagine my surprise when I discovered the man with the bedstead on his back engaged in violent altercations with two liveried servants on the steps of the Adelphi Hotel in Lime Street. He insisted on putting the luggage in, and the hotel was in a state of siege. The basket, with the tin-tray false bottom, had been pitched out by the hotel people so energetically that it had fallen to pieces, and the 'props' were scattered all over the muddy street. My porter was undaunted. He had been told to put the things in the Adelphi, and he would have them in it if it killed him. It was a noble and sublime spectacle, but our belongings were being seriously depreciated. Some small boys amongst the interested crowd had found a stuffed dog which had come out of the basket, and they were playing football with it, and when I went to the rescue the poor, dumb, stuffed creature they played football with me.

At last with the dog under my arm and my clothes covered with mud, I succeeded in getting near enough to the porter to explain things. He was disappointed. I shall never forget the look on the man's face if I live to be ninety-nine. I never saw a man look with such an earnest desire to take a human life as he did, and had he raised the bedstead instead and brained me where I stood I should not have been at all surprised. I should have been sorry, but not surprised.

Well, we collected the scattered property in the face of a withering fire of criticism from the crowd, and then the porter and I, with the cart, headed a long procession marching to the theatre. Liverpool mud is very muddy indeed, and I was not happy. Even then our troubles were not ended, for when we reached Christian Street one of the wheels came off the confounded cart, and once again our poor 'props' were upset in the slimy road. For the fourteenth time our porter repeated his entire vocabulary of obscene and profane terms of general abuse and condemnation, and sent me into a cold perspiration at the fearful language he used.

And when at length I reached the theatre, tired, hungry, muddy, almost in tears, I held out my hand to reward the honest labourer for his toil. I gave him all the money I had left – *one shilling*. It was a thrilling situation. The man staggered; there was a wild glare in his eye; his breath came and went in short snorts; he clenched his fist, and – like the heroes of romance – I knew no more.[1]

Like all Dan's tales there was clearly a degree of comic embroidery, but the general accuracy of the account is confirmed by a sketch of the episode that he made on an envelope sent to Johnny.[2] The upended cart, tumbling baggage, angry porter, Dan and a crowd of onlookers are depicted above the caption 'Luggage in trouble, Lime Street, Liverpool'. With added music and a rhyming chorus, the anecdote could easily have formed the basis for the 'patter' of one of Dan's songs. Many of the ingredients of his comedy were present: misunderstanding, embarrassment, humiliation and a quirky use of language that made the listener check and re-assess what exactly was being said. Dan never performed 'The Adelphi Porter', but a handcart and a pathetic collection of possessions featured in one of his earliest London successes 'Has Anyone Seen a Moving Job?' (1888):

Has anybody seen a moving job
The one I want to find,
There's a couple of children pulling at the truck,
And the old girl shoving up behind?
We started away
At two in the afternoon
It's jolly hard luck
You want a bit of pluck,
To be always shooting the moon.

With its theme of a family absconding from their lodgings without paying the rent, the song had much in common with Marie Lloyd's 1919 hit 'Don't Dilly Dally' ('My Old Man Said Follow the Van'). But, unlike Marie's tale of a 'moonlight flit', Dan's song contained a substantial passage of dialogue. Eventually his 'songs' were to consist almost entirely of lengthy monologues with a token introductory chorus. The 'patter' section of 'Has Anyone Seen a Moving Job?' describes a scene not dissimilar to the Lime Street disaster:

I have put up with some insults today. I was walking along; some rude people said, 'Going shooting?' Now do I look like a shootist? Then a himpudent young female called me 'Pretty bird'. Now, there's no poultry about me; but I thought she might have seen my wife, so I spoke like this to her; I said, 'Have you seen three or four vans of furniture knocking about?' Then she gave me a smack in the face, and call'd a lot of people and brothers to shove me about. Of course, I couldn't 'tallyate. I'd got the mangle under one arm, and the sofa under the other.

Before returning to London at Easter 1886 Dan rejoined Louisa and Will on a tour of some familiar northern halls. Along with singing and dancing, the family produced an updated version of *The Wicklow Wedding; or, the Leprechaun's Revels*. This 'most gorgeous spectacular entertainment' was presented as a Christmas attraction at the Princess's Palace, Leeds. Dan was omnipresent on the programme; appearing in the sketch, engaging in a 'Terrific Phantom Fight' with Joe Alberto and performing his solo stage act. He was also responsible for painting the scenery, announced on the Princess's bill as being based on sketches made during his last Irish tour.[3]

The company next moved to the Star Music Hall, Bradford; then to the People's Music Hall, Manchester, and finally to the Star Music Hall, Liverpool, by which time *The Wicklow Wedding* had been expanded to five scenes – advertised as 'The Greatest Spectacle Ever Presented on Any Stage'.[4] Johnny Danvers recalled the origins of the sketch:

> Mrs Leno made most of the dresses, Dan and I painted the scenery, and the old man and I wrote the book. The whole thing was put on the stage within a fortnight. We painted scenery most of the day, wrote the book most of the night; while Dan, in the intervals of painting found time to help his mother in the making of the dresses – such as spangling tights, etc., etc.[5]

It was during a performance of *The Wicklow Wedding* that Will suffered a potentially life-threatening accident. He and Johnny were appearing, and disappearing, as leprechauns who tormented an Irishman, played by Dan. The 'old man's' fondness for alcohol was not particularly compatible with the split-second timing required for the frantic chases that took place during the sketch. Following a mistimed jump into a 'Grave trap', he was rendered unconscious with an ugly gash to his head. In response to Dan's whispered 'How's Dad?' Johnny replied that he might be 'killed', but on closer examination, it was discovered that Will was merely stunned. It was with some trepidation that the local doctor's house-maid answered the door to a stage Irishman and two bloody and bedraggled pantomime demons.[6]

Shortly before his return to London, in February 1886, Dan contributed a guinea to a collection taken on behalf of Tom Ward, who was confined to bed with a serious illness.[7] Within ten months Dan's bitter rival had died at the age of 35.[8] Arriving back in London at the beginning of March, Dan appeared at the Royal Foresters, the Metropolitan (close to the site of the Cosmotheca), the Middlesex and at one of the capital's major music halls, the Pavilion, Piccadilly Circus. Dan's re-engagement for a specially strengthened Easter programme at the 'Pav' finally established him as a fully-fledged London star. The experience was intimidating, for the bill was packed with leading comedians and the audience was unremittingly urbane. A *Punch* reviewer visited the hall at about the time of Dan's first appearance:

> There are twenty different items of amusement in the Pavilion programme, and the late gentleman who pays the highest for the privilege of coming in when he likes, may dine, if it so pleases him, in the neighbourhood say at the Café Royal, where he can have a first-rate dinner at a reasonable price, and excellent wine; and then he can talk French with the Waiters, imagine himself in Paris, with none of the risks of crossing, and with not a twentieth part of the expense – can fancy himself on the boulevards, as he buys a Gaulois or a Caricature, and saunters out into Regent Street soon after nine, so as to be at the Pavilion in time to see PAUL CINQUEVALLI, or, if he can get there a trifle earlier, and have any luck (for the programme is 'subject to alterations') he will hear Mr ARTHUR LLOYD in a highly moral temperance song ...[9]

It was a far cry from 'Signor' Durland's soup kitchen at the Star, but Dan's freshness and vitality singled him out from his fellow performers. Confirmation of his new status was provided when he was also engaged to appear on the Easter programme of the Oxford Music Hall, Oxford Street, another stronghold of the comic singer. His future was predicted on the Oxford's playbill:

> DAN LENO. First appearance at the Oxford. Eccentric and Original Comedian and Champion Dancer. A man bound to make his mark and be able to say in years to come, as so many have said before him, that his success in the Profession was due to his introduction to the public at the Oxford.

It was a more uplifting billing than that of the Oxford's principal performer: 'CHARLES GODFREY. Having recovered from his bronchial attack and tonsil cutting operation, returns with renewed vigour and fresh songs...'

Much of the impact of the 'Eccentric and Original Comedian' was attributable to his visual appearance on stage. The public, acclimatised to performers whose songs were delivered with a limited and stereotyped use of gesture, were surprised and edified by his rapidly changing features, expressive use of hands and feet and by the giant backward leaps that punctuated his 'patter' like exclamation marks. Dan's act veered from one extreme to another; frantic activity giving way to sudden stillness, garrulous monologues interspersed with spells of thoughtful silence. Although drawing on the same subject matter as many of his contemporaries his mode of expression was unique, often subverting the meaning of everyday language with a confusing mixture of colloquialisms, malapropisms and non sequiturs. Reviewers began to notice his unusual use of words:

> Mr Dan Leno, a very good comic singer, sang first of fried fish, and then of twins, the offspring of a wife who was described as by occupation 'a dressmaker's labourer'. He subsequently wins great cheering for his splendid clog dancing.[10]

Following his appearances at the Pavilion and the Oxford, Dan was engaged to play at four halls nightly: the Alhambra at 8.15, the Royal Foresters at 9.00, Deacon's at 9.55 and the Middlesex at 10.55. Such a frantic itinerary became standard practice for years to come. In an age of uncertainty, where accident, illness or a decline in popularity could mean financial ruin, performers were reluctant to turn work away. With local charities and the public workhouse representing the only forms of social security, provision for the future was left to the individual – a precarious state of affairs that led to some music-hall performers setting up their own mutual-benefit societies. But such organised attempts to provide for unemployment were poorly supported, and the theatrical press of the time frequently carried appeals on behalf of performers who had fallen on hard times. Having no desire to return to the patched boots and communal raincoat of earlier days, Dan decided to make the maximum capital out of his success. He remembered: 'I have had to work four turns at four different halls within two hours, which I believe is about the very hardest and most trying work that mortal man can do.'[11]

The comedian George Robey witnessed Dan's punishing regime:

Even in those days he was tearing from hall to hall, night after night. One would see him coming in from his brougham, still dripping with perspiration, and looking so tired! Then the moment he stepped on to the stage and heard the audience cheer, all his weariness would seem to vanish, and he would sing and dance and crack his jokes like a two year old![12]

Johnny Danvers also took up residence in London in 1886 and, like Dan, soon became a star performer in the capital's entertainment industry. Although theatrical, his employment could be seen as more of a sedentary nature than Dan's, for he had joined the famous Mohawk Minstrels, a black-face troupe who spent a good deal of their time sitting in a large half-circle, exchanging jokes. The Mohawks were closely associated with Francis, Day and Hunter, a music publisher that had originally been set up by members of the troupe to market their songs.

The rise of black-face minstrels in Britain had been largely supported by a section of society that had rejected the drink dependent and often sexually permissive nature of the music hall. Inspired by the success of American acts such as the Virginia Minstrels and the Ethopian Serenaders during the 1840s, British troupes began to provide entertainments which mixed acute sentimentality and punning humour in equal parts. Such shows were usually presented in civic buildings and local halls and often demonstrated sympathy with the aims of the temperance movement. Originally performers had dressed in ragged 'plantation' clothes, adapting black music and dances for a predominately white audience. In time stylisation and caricature led to the creation of a dandified character who sang standard ballads and told jokes that would not have been out of place in a family parlour. It was a process that initially embraced black performers such as William Henry 'Juba' Lane and the 'African Nightingale' Elizabeth Taylor Greenfield, but which eventually excluded them for their supposed lack of refinement. A small indigenous black population and a lack of knowledge about conditions in the USA resulted in British minstrel troupes and their individual performers who in style and content were totally divorced from their original inspiration.

The Mohawk Minstrels, based at the Small Agricultural Hall, Islington, were the main London rivals of the Moore and Burgess Minstrels, a troupe that had been established at St James's Hall, Piccadilly, since 1863. Soon Johnny Danvers, as 'Mr Tambo', became a leading figure in the show, sharing its comedy with 'Mr Interlocuter', Harry Hunter, and 'Mr Bones', Johnny Schofield. As with Dan, Johnny struck up a solid partnership with Johnny Schofield. Both men were excellent dancers and throughout the 1890s they entertained audiences with duets such as 'The Two Obadiahs', 'The Two Johnnies in Love' and 'We are the Sisters Gee-Up', a high kicking pastiche of sexually provocative 'sister acts'.

Amongst Johnny Danvers' solo hits were 'I'll Send You Down a Letter from the Sky', 'A Little Peach in an Orchard Grew' and 'I've Got the Ooperzootic'. The writer Shaw Desmond remembered Johnny as a skilled musician: 'Nobody could hit a tambourine like Johnny. I have seen him hit it and make sweet music out of it with nose, ears, head, feet, elbows – anything but his hand ... and how he could run it tinkling down his leg!'[13]

Dan was to perform as a 'waxi omo', the professional's slang for a black-face performer, on at least one occasion. The 'Doo-da-Day Minstrels' gave their one and only performance at the Pavilion to support manager Frank Glenister's benefit on 29 May 1899. Members of the rapidly assembled troupe included ex-minstrels such as Herbert Campbell, Eugene Stratton and Bransby Williams, and music-hall stars Harry Randall, Joe Elvin and Fred McNaughton. In an era before political correctness Stratton repeated his hit song 'The Whistling Coon' – a number he had sung over 1,000 times at the St James's Hall – while Dan obliged with 'The Funny Little Nigger'. A link with the past was provided by the appearance of G.W. 'Pony' Moore, the 79-year-old proprietor of the Moore and Burgess Minstrels. Towards the end of a selection of his famous songs, the old man slumped back in his chair with the exclamation 'I'm done.'[14] It was, more or less, the last gasp of black-face minstrelsy in Britain.

The decline in popularity of the minstrel show was remarkably rapid, coinciding almost exactly with the start of the twentieth century. Such entertainments were too thoroughly associated with the attitudes of the Victorian era to meet the requirements of a new age. As a consequence the Moore and Burgess Minstrels disbanded in 1900, while the Mohawks struggled on for a few years, before giving their final performance on 9 April 1904. It was to take the genius of Al Jolson to breathe new life into the black-face tradition with a series of Hollywood film musicals in the 1920s and 30s, followed in the 1960s by British television's 'Black and White Minstrel Show' which paid long-running but saccharine homage to its entertainment forebear.

Johnny never recaptured the triumphs of his black-face career. For a time he appeared as a music-hall solo turn, then joined the actor-manager Seymour Hicks in musical comedy. Between 1911 and 1915 he played alongside the Gilbert and Sullivan comedian Walter Passmore in a series of variety sketches, and in the early 1920s appeared in a play and a revue portraying Bruce Bairnsfather's cartoon creation, the World War I soldier 'Old Bill'.

Back in December 1886 Johnny had joined Dan for the Surrey Theatre pantomime. It was a wider reunion, for Dan was engaged with Lydia – at a joint salary of £20 a week – while another member of the cast was Johnny's wife Clara Jane, whom he had married in Sheffield the previous year. On the strength of his female impersonations Dan was cast as Dame Durden, the long suffering matriarch in *Jack and the Bean-stalk, Which Grew to the Moon; or, the Giant, Jack Frost and the Ha-Ha Balloon*. Johnny was given the role of the villainous Graball, while Lydia and Clara played Mercury and Venus.

8   THE ENTR'ACTE.   [January 15, 1887.

MR. DAN LENO.
(AS DAME DURDEN IN SURREY PANTOMIME.)

6 'Dame Durden', 1887

Although located on the unfashionable south side of the Thames, the Surrey's pantomimes were immensely popular, drawing a large portion of its audience from the local working-class public. With a gallery capable of accommodating 1,000 patrons there were many low-priced seats available. The proprietor of the theatre, George Conquest (1837–1901), had already established a London-wide reputation as a master of pantomime at the Grecian Theatre, in the East End's City Road. After taking over the Surrey in 1881 he had continued to create productions that concentrated on acrobatic comedy and elaborate special effects, rather than relying on star names and massive spectacle that typified the pantomimes presented at the Theatre Royal, Drury Lane.

Dan skipped and scampered through his role, swapping jokes and stage business with Johnny, with whom he seemed to share almost telepathic communication. Much of his humour derived from depicting an apparently modest lady of uncertain years breaking into the most indecorous gestures and unexpected movements. Although surprising it was a sympathetic portrayal. Alfred Bryan's caricature in the theatrical periodical *The Entr'acte* shows that Dan's creation was far from being a traditionally grotesque 'Dame', but a credible woman, with hair drawn back into a neat bun and wearing a practical white apron. Despite his novel approach to the role Dan had no great desire to change the way in which women were represented by men in pantomime and on the music-hall stage. For him every performance was a character study, his grasp of artistic and psychological detail adding depth to his depiction of both sexes alike. Critics were enthusiastic: 'Mr Dan Leno, as Dame Durden, is wonderfully fresh and welcome, while his step-dancing is quite a revelation. This gentleman will be certain to receive plenty of offers for next Christmas.'[15]

The characters in *Jack and the Beanstalk*, whether mortal or supernatural, were imagined to have a life of some kind, but in a novelty dance Dan introduced a creation endowed with no sentient existence, a clockwork doll. The theme of mechanical or artificial life, gently satirised in the humanoid, clockwork heroine of the ballet *Coppelia*, had been a longstanding preoccupation of the Victorians. It would have taken Charles Babbage's 'analytical engine' to calculate the number of automatons devised during the nineteenth century, ranging in complexity from children's mechanical toys to the baffling constructions of Robert Houdin and Nevil Maskelyne. Dan himself was to enjoy a degree of clockwork immortality: in the years to come his voice was captured by the newly invented wind-up gramophone, while his moving likeness was perpetuated on a hand-cranked movie viewer.

7   *Jack and the Beanstalk*, 1887

9

THE WAR BETWEEN THE SEXES

For Dan the late 1880s were years of consolidation and experiment. Although he continued to appear as a 'red-nosed' comedian he quickly dropped the drunken revels of the 'Irish' song in favour of characterisations in which ordinary women battled against male intimidation and indifference. Despite opportunities to transfer to the 'legitimate' theatre he eventually elected to remain within the music-hall environment, a decision that was to lead to difficulties when he appeared in London's leading variety theatres. Dan's working-class studies were often alien to his new audience, and he received little support from the reserved patrons of the Empire and Alhambra. But he instinctively realised that he would have to appeal to both sexes and all levels of society if he was to become more than just another popular comedian.

Of all the capital's music halls the Empire most emphatically catered for a male clientele. Many men were only present to make contact with the high-class prostitutes who patrolled the spacious promenade at the rear of the dress circle, while others congregated around the theatre's bars, keeping up an incessant chatter that made it difficult to hear the performers on stage. Those who deigned to take seats in the auditorium were generally unenthusiastic, although Anstey noted that there were at least some who were 'languidly attentive'.[1] The warmest appreciation was awarded to the short-skirted dancers in the Empire's famous ballets and to female singers who specialised in songs heavy with sexual innuendo. Dan was far more likely to be noticed by dancing and by striking comic poses than by presenting his whimsical descriptions of everyday life.

The gulf between audiences at the Empire and the more humble Middlesex, situated just a few streets apart, was demonstrated by Dan to the playwright Horace Lennard in 1889. Dan was introducing a new song at the former theatre. He cut an incongruous figure as he came on stage. Facing a large orchestra and looking into an auditorium decorated in the latest French style, Dan appeared as a middle-aged woman, dressed in a shabby bonnet and shawl, clasping a well-used shopping bag in her hands. She began to explain that she was on a mission to secure a

piece of meat for her husband's Sunday dinner. The audience knew and
cared little about the trials and tribulation of household chores. Having
probably dined excellently they would have had little understanding of
Mike's dietary requirements:

> I can do what I like with dear old Mike,
> All the days of the week but one day.
> He's as happy as you please with a bit of bread and cheese,
> But he does like his bit of meat on Sunday.

The number was met with the Empire's usual cool reception. Lennard
visited Dan in his dressing room where they discussed the reasons for the
song's failure. 'Come with me, and hear me sing it at the "Mo",' suggested the comedian, 'this audience doesn't know the type, but they'll see it
all right at the "Mo".' Set amid the cheap eating-houses of Drury Lane
the Middlesex had a close affinity with the hungry northern halls. Food
was widely consumed within the auditorium, from 'rosy-looking pork
pies at popular prices' purchased from the programme seller to the more
natural and nourishing refreshment taken by babes in arms.[2] Mike's wife
explained how she had provided her husband with various 'bits of meat'.
He had thrown the bullock's heart out of the window, but was far
happier when she cooked him an eight-penny calf's head. His favoured
Sunday dinner, however, was belly of pork, 'the waistcoat piece with the
buttons'. At this stage of the song Dan produced the very piece of meat
from his bag, throwing the audience into screams of hysterical delight.[3]

Following the 1886/87 Surrey Theatre pantomime, Dan briefly returned to the London halls before embarking on a two-month provincial
tour. At the Royal Foresters he elaborated on a theme that was to become central to his comedy: 'Mr Dan Leno sings a droll song entitled
"It's More Than a Fellow Can Stand", and appears in a very comic get-
up; and discourses on woes matrimonial, a topic that never fails to amuse
a music hall audience. His dancing is simply electric in its rapidity.'[4] Although such material was universally appreciated Dan was probably
regarded as a London comedian when he appeared in Birmingham and
Liverpool some weeks later. As with Harry Liston revisiting the North in
1868, audiences would have detected a shift in the emphasis of his songs
and patter. As late as the 1890s one northern galleryite was uneasy with
the abridgement of his clog-dancing routine. After performing seven
songs at a Newcastle music hall he was interrupted by the rude call "Eh
– cut your cackle, and bring on your clogs.'[5]

After concluding the tour at the South Coast seaside resorts of Mar-
gate and Brighton, Dan returned to the family lodgings at 91 Kennington Road. It was to prove a sad homecoming for, on 2 April 1887, Dan
and Lydia's second child Lydia Daisy died of an attack of croup at the

age of eight months. In December husband and wife started rehearsals for the next Surrey pantomime *Sinbad and the Little Old Man of the Sea; or, The Tinker, the Tailor, the Soldier, the Sailor, Apothecary, Ploughboy, Gentleman Thief*. The pantomime was to prove the last in which George Conquest appeared. He had been the most athletic of performers, an expert at turning somersaults and pirouettes when ejected from a counterbalanced 'star trap', but time had finally taken its toll. His body had not only been subjected to startling aerial manoeuvres, but had been contorted into countless curious shapes as he portrayed creatures as varied as spiders, monkeys, parrots, crabs, toads and octopuses. In his final pantomime George contented himself with squeezing into a jar. *The Era* reported:

> The Little Old Man of the Sea is fished up by the hero, who lands a strange-looking jar instead of a fish. But there is a queer fish inside, for Mr Conquest emerges from the jar, and, in spite of his ungainly appearance, begins to make love to the fair Aminè. When this is resented, the Old Man disappears with a suddenness that astonishes all. Waving a cloak around him, he flies, and when they attempt to seize him, he is gone. This mysterious disappearance was managed with the utmost skill …

> In the representation of Sinbad we have already shown what a tower of strength Mr Conquest himself was. The very Emperor of Pantomime, he still retains his position by right of pre-eminence, skill and originality. Not only in weird and fanciful ideas, but in striking ability as a pantomime actor, he stands in the front rank, and his Old Man of the Sea is worthy of the many fantastic figures he has already created. He received admirable support from the company, beginning with Mr Dan Leno, who made a capital Tinker, full of drollery and grotesque business. Some of his scenes were particularly good, and he was most humorous throughout the pantomime.[6]

Playing in the formidable shadow of George Conquest, Dan was still impressive. *The Stage* noted:

> Full of dry genuine humour Mr Dan Leno does not fail to accentuate the funny lines of his part of the Tinker. Every movement is a signal for laughter and his dance on the rolling vessel is a sight to see.

Dan also had to battle for a share of the limelight with his own wife. Once again *The Stage* reported: 'Miss Lydia Reynolds was a pert and pretty

Amine, and sang very sweetly many tuneful numbers.'[7] Although his second pantomime at the Surrey Theatre was to be his last, Dan did not lose touch with the Conquest family – he was soon reunited with George Junior at the Theatre Royal, Drury Lane, in 1888, while the youngest of George Conquest's sons, Arthur, became a perennial performer at the Lane, appearing in almost 30 of its pantomimes.

During the run of the *Sinbad* Dan was approached with an offer to appear in a musical burlesque, a form of entertainment that was extremely popular with middle-class audiences. Bearing no similarity to its seedy American namesake, British burlesque united elements of pantomime and music hall to produce light-hearted productions that gently satirised current events, fashions and theatrical productions. Men sometimes played women and, more frequently, women appeared as men. Songs and dialogue were full of convoluted word-play and a general air of topsy-turviness prevailed.

Oscar Barrett, the organiser of entertainments at the Crystal Palace, the gigantic glass and steel entertainment complex in South London, considered that Dan would make an ideal Dame Hatley in his new version of an old favourite, *Black-Eyed Susan*. Written by Horace Lennard with music by Barrett, *Too Lovely Black-Eyed Susan* was a curious concoction even for the eclectic world of nineteenth-century theatre. Originally written by John Gay, the song 'Black-Eyed Susan' had already been performed in ballad operas for over 100 years when Douglas Jerrold took its two characters, William and Susan, and constructed a three-act melodrama around them. With a rollicking, sea-faring plot the play was an immediate success when performed at the Surrey Theatre in 1829. After nearly 40 years as a serious play *Black-Eyed Susan* became the subject of a burlesque by F.C. Burnand, the future editor of the humorous magazine *Punch*. The Victorian fixation with puns, parody and pastiche found full expression in *The Latest Edition of Black-Eyed Susan; or, the Little Bill that Was Taken Up*, first produced in 1866.

It seems that Horace Lennard had been inspired by Charles Coborn's current music-hall hit 'Two Lovely Black Eyes' to write a new burlesque, loosely based on Burnand's original. Therein lay a major problem that affected Dan's casting. The comedy-female part allotted to Dan was Burnand's own creation, and as such he refused to allow the character to be re-used. Undaunted, Lennard re-arranged his burlesque, offering Dan the title role of Susan and assigning the part of William to Fanny (or Fannie) Leslie, a talented singer and dancer who alternated between music hall and burlesque.

To allow Dan to honour his music-hall commitments *Too Lovely Black-Eyed Susan* was presented as a matinee performance at the Crystal Palace. The opening performance on 2 April 1888, Easter Monday, was not well received:

The dialogue of *Too Lovely Black-Eyed Susan* is no worse, as re-
gards to point and polish, than that of most of the old burlesques;
and there is a commendable absence of that out-worn expedient,
the pun elaborate. The piece, however, according to our present
day ideas, is sadly 'slow'. There is a comparative scarcity of popular music hall airs, of ingenious and striking dances, of quaint
'wheezes', and of individual exploits on the part of leading performers. Miss Fanny Leslie as William did all that she could to
keep things going; but her material was scant, and she did not
introduce much novelty on her own account … Miss Dot Mario is
an acceptable Dolly Mayflower, and Mr Dan Leno appeared with
decided success as Susan. He gave a clever reading of the role on
the lines laid down by the author, but we cannot say we care for
the course adopted of making Susan a hideous elderly woman of
immoral tendencies. There is little humour and less good taste
displayed in the idea. It must, however, be owned that Mr Dan
Leno managed to create much amusement by the introduction of
various droll and original touches …[8]

Despite the burlesque's poor reception a trial matinee was arranged nine
days later at the Strand Theatre. Any chance the production had of a
longer run was dashed by more bad reviews and by a sudden illness that
undermined Dan's performance. *The Entr'acte* reported:

The Susan of Mr Dan Leno suffered on Wednesday from the hoarse-
ness which clouded this actor's performance. This, however, could
not conceal his humorous conceits, which were fresh, and not the
stereotyped article. Some of Mr Leno's movements forcibly re-
mind one of Mr Arthur Roberts, and certain is it that Mr Leno
with his great resources should be a most valuable burlesque dancer. His dancing is quite phenomenal …[9]

A heavy cold had made it impossible for Dan to sing, and extremely
difficult for him to deliver his spoken lines. Although his stage 'business'
and dancing won repeated applause, he felt that he had let Barrett,
Lennard and himself down. He broke down, sobbing as he spoke to the
author: 'To have a chance like this and not be able to take it! But it's not
so much that. I'm so sorry for you and Barrett; I've spoilt your show.'[10]

The disappointment was quickly forgotten. By the summer of 1888
he had received two further offers to appear in burlesques – one from
Willie Edouin, proprietor of the Strand Theatre, and another from
George Edwardes of London's famous Gaiety Theatre. Dan eventually
rejected both to concentrate on his music-hall career, which had been
boosted by two major song successes: 'I'll Be Waiting for Him Tonight'

and 'Young Men Taken In and Done For'. The former number, written
by Dan himself, dealt with the familiar topic of marital strife, but was
unusual in that it was a parody of an existing ballad. Unlike his future
colleague, Herbert Campbell, Dan seldom performed parodies, although
they represented an immensely popular music-hall genre. As with burlesque, song parodies would take a dramatic or sentimental original and
subject it to ridicule by use of comic substitution and inversion. So when
a dewy-eyed Leo Dryden appeared in the romantic costume of a gold
prospector to sing 'The Miner's Dream of Home', he immediately became
a sitting duck for the master of parody Herbert Campbell. The chorus of
Dryden's ballad evoked a chocolate-box England:

> I saw the old homestead and faces I love
> I saw England's valleys and dells.
> I listen'd with joy, as I did when a boy,
> To the sound of the old village bells.
> The log was burning brightly,
> 'Twas a night that should banish all sin,
> For the bells were ringing the old year out
> And the new year in.

Campbell was cruelly dismissive of such a golden vision. His alternative
version offered a domestic nightmare:

> I saw the back kitchen in which I was born
> I saw the old slum in the 'Dials'
> Where I played as a boy with a brick for a toy
> And was known as a moocher for miles.
> My pa was boozing nightly
> And my mother was shifting the gin
> And the lodger was taking the old girl out
> And the old man in.

Dan's parody was just as savage, taking the original's theme of romantic, passionate love and replacing it with cruel, malignant anger. Like so
many of his songs it centred on a 'bit of meat'. 'Queen of My Heart' had
originally been sung by C. Hayden Coffin in one of the Victorian era's
longest-running comic operas, *Dorothy*. As Harry Sherwood, the tall,
dark and handsome singer stood in a darkened baronial hall, illuminated
only by the glimmering embers of a dying fire. He began a lovesick
serenade outside his beloved's bedroom door:

> I stand at your threshold sighing,
> As the cruel hours creep by;

And the time is slowly dying,
That once too quick did fly.
Your beauty o'er my being,
Has shed a subtle spell;
And alas! there is no fleeing
From the charms that you wield so well.
For my heart is wildly beating,
As it never beat before.
One word! One whispered greeting
In mercy I implore.

Chorus:
For from daylight a hint we might borrow,
And prudence might come with the light.
Then why should we wait till tomorrow?
You are queen of my heart tonight.

Dan upended this eighteenth-century idyll by presenting a shrewish wife waiting in a non-baronial hallway for the arrival of her abusive husband. Her intentions were made clear by the assortment of makeshift weapons that she carried with her. A gramophone recording made 15 years later preserves Dan's performance, a mock concert presentation, perhaps influenced by his few engagements as a 'serious' singer:

I scalded myself while a-frying
A nice piece of steak rather off,
And my sad headed baby was crying
He was bad with a nice whooping cough.
And the steak it got burnt to a cinder
Which made my old man rather wild,
Then he threw all the lot through the window
And struck me on the nose with the child.
And my nose began a-bleeding
As it never bled before
And while his mercy I was pleading
He rolled me up and down on the floor.

Chorus:
He punched me without any warning
And made my poor face such a fright,
He knocked corners off me this morning,
But I'll give him beans tonight.

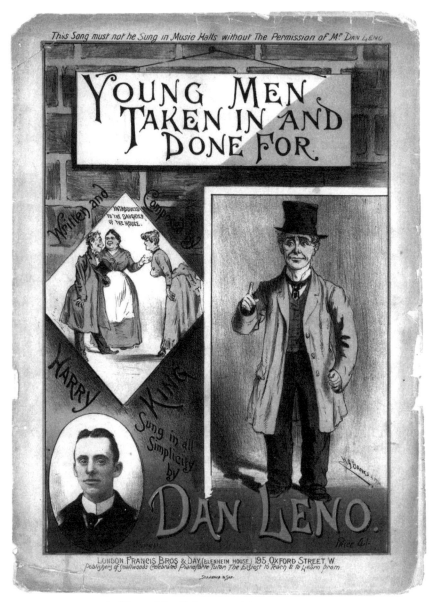

8 'Young Men Taken in and Done For', 1888

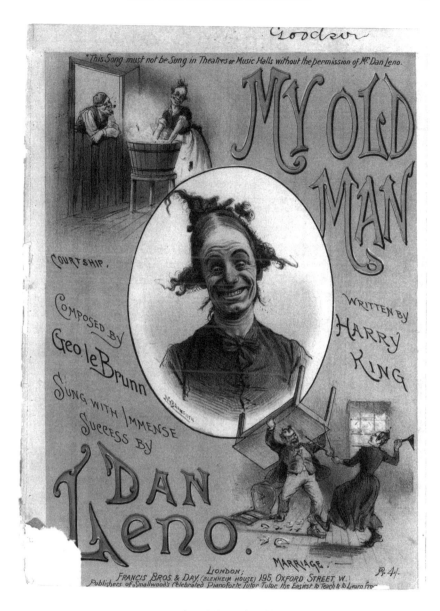

9 'My Old Man', 1888

A review of Dan's turn at the Royal Music Hall, Holborn, in June 1888 referred to the popularity of the song:

> The loudest laughter of the evening was provoked by Mr Dan Leno, who began singing about a nagging wife, who had robbed him of his boots, and exposed his poor feet to splinters – he produced one about twelve inches long and about a pound, at least, in weight; who drove away his Spanish cook employed to cook Spanish onions, and his Welsh cook specially engaged for the manufacture of Welsh rabbit; who used a gridiron to fry pancakes which ran through and put the fire out, and who generally made his life miserable. Another very laughable contribution by Mr Leno was descriptive of his courting days and of the problems caused by the arrival of twins that quickly leaned to 'talk shorthand'; while funniest of all was his parody of the well-known song 'Queen of my Heart', in which he represented an ill-used wife waiting with a big brick and a formidable chopper for the homecoming of her tyrant. The audience seemed unwilling to let Mr Leno depart, and he had to explain that if he did not move he would stand in the way of other artists, who, if they could not do their fair share of the evening's work, would be ashamed to take their salaries when Saturday came around.[11]

The war between the sexes also found expression in Dan's second hit of 1888, although the character he portrayed appears to have been taken captive soon after the commencement of hostilities. In his later songs Dan described an inconclusive guerrilla conflict, with both parties ambushing and sniping at their partners, but in 'Young Men Taken In and Done For' the action was swift and decisive:

> As smart a man as ever lived was I when in my prime,
> Until I met Miss Lucy Jaggs, she knocked me out of time.
> I called there for apartments, for I'd noticed one or twice,
> A card stuck in the window, and on it this device:
>
> Chorus:
> 'Young men taken in and done for.'
> Oh! I never thought that she,
> The girl I left my happy home for,
> Would have taken in and done for me.
>
> Being a lonely single man, I wanted lodgings bad,
> So Lucy Jaggs's mother then soon showed me what she had,
> I'd not stayed there about a week when Lucy came to me

And fondly kissed me on the cheek, then sat upon my knee.
Of course, just like a stupid, I must go and tie the knot
That brings us bliss and happiness – but that's all tommy rot.
I don't believe my wife loves me, it's the truth I'm telling you.
A wife can't love her husband if she beats him black and blue.

Miss Lucy Jaggs might well have dangled Dan upon her knee. He was short in height and weighed little, whereas the illustration on the sheet-music cover shows her to have been a well-proportioned young lady. Dan's slight physique, which contributed so much amusement to his portrayal of vituperative wives and downtrodden husbands, was already showing worrying signs of strain. In August 1888 he embarked on what for him was a remarkable course of action – he took a holiday. His *Era* card announced that he had gone to the seaside to 'refatten', a process that was apparently successful for, on his return, he jokingly claimed to have gained four stone in two weeks.[12] It was becoming difficult to retain the exhausting clog dance as part of his act. Some friends and critics exhorted him to drop it altogether:

> The other champion is a clog dancer, Mr Dan Leno; but those of our metropolitan music hall frequenters who know this gentleman – and who does not should immediately become familiar with his features as 'The Detective' – prefer his humorous talk to his clog 'patter'. Mr Leno's custom to conclude with a serious dance is now better honoured in the breach than in the observance. A shade of gloom used to come over him as he began it, which increased as he 'triples', and as fairly over-whelmed him as he concluded, breathless and exhausted. Not exhausting, but far more humorous is his parody of 'Queen of my heart'; and there is plenty of laughter to be squeezed from 'Taken in and done for' and from the song we have mentioned above, in which satire is levelled at the Criminal Investigations Department and Sir Charles Warren. In the interest of mirth we would ask Mr Leno, after our Monday night's expedition, to always omit his clog dance, which, whatever its qualities – we know them to be great – is, after all, a merely mechanical exercise, but instead of the melancholy beat of the clog step, give us humour, which, with him, is not mechanical, but unforced and fresh.[13]

Success as a comedian had rendered the challenges and counter-challenges of the clog-dancing world irreverent. Dan could now regard the stern-faced ritual with a degree of equanimity, even amusement. A 'friendly' clog-dancing contest was the highlight of J.L. Graydon's benefit evening at the Middlesex on 8 November 1888. Dan was pitted against J.H. Haslam, the prize offered to the winner being 'a handsome

pair of dark grey cobs'. When the votes were counted Haslam was ad-
judged better in 'tap' and 'time', while Dan proved superior in 'beauty
and grace' and 'elegance and deportment'. There was no option but to
separate the two magnificent steeds, which were only then revealed to be
children's rocking horses. Amid scenes of great amusement Dan declared
that he would keep his horse forever – attached to his watch chain.[14]

A more substantial prize had been presented to Dan earlier in the
year. He had come to the notice of Augustus Harris, who was combining
the role of lessee of the Theatre Royal, Drury Lane, with that of entertainment manager at the Empire Theatre of Varieties, Leicester Square.
After booking him for the Empire, Harris became convinced that Dan's
female impersonations would be ideally suited for pantomime at the
Theatre Royal. Dan and Lydia were engaged for the forthcoming production at a joint weekly salary of £28.

Before embarking on this formidable new venture, Dan was called
upon to help revive the flagging fortunes of a faltering burlesque –
Atalanta, a comedy set in Ancient Greece. After two weeks of falling box-
office receipts the writers George P. Hawtrey and A.E. Dyer persuaded
Dan to play Leontes in the show. He went on stage at the Strand Theatre
at very short notice, in his own words 'without knowing a bit of the
business or a line of the dialogue.'[15] But his improvised comedy was so
well received that he temporarily saved the show. Some of the most
successful scenes in the rejuvenated production were those in which Dan
played opposite Alma Stanley. Alma was a clever burlesque actress, but
her greatest asset was what a contemporary publication described as her
'magnificent physical development'.[16] Dan and Alma's disproportionate
pairing, emphasised in a spoof race-scene, was not to last long, for both
had pantomime commitments to fulfil. Their joint departure sealed the
fate of *Atalanta*. An epitaph for the burlesque was provided by J.M.
Glover, later to enjoy a close working relationship with Dan at the Theatre Royal. In *The Hawk* 'Jimmy' parodied a popular music hall song:

> The bookings went up, up, up,
> They came from all over the town!
> But when Stanley, or Leno
> Were not to be seen, oh!
> The bookings went down, down, down.[17]

For his first Drury Lane appearance Dan was cast as the Naughty Baroness, the reluctant and cantankerous wife of the Wicked Baron. Lydia also
swapped gender to appear as the outlaw Large William, although, unlike
Dan, her stay at the 'National Theatre' was to be of brief duration.

10

THE REIGN OF AUGUSTUS

Augustus Henry Glossop Harris, nicknamed 'Augustus Druriolanus', had a Roman emperor's love of spectacle. Since taking over the management of the Theatre Royal, Drury Lane, in 1879, he had consistently aimed for bigger, if not always better, productions. Under Harris the theatre presented spring and summer seasons of grand opera alternating with classic plays, followed in the autumn by melodramas that were packed with special set pieces such as earthquakes, train crashes and battle scenes. At Christmas he indulged his passion for the grandiose by mounting magnificent pantomimes whose tableaux and ballets occupied every inch of Drury Lane's immense stage. As a counterbalance to such breathtaking visual effects Harris chose to introduce well known music-hall performers and their broad comedy material, a move that dismayed his veteran writer, E. L. Blanchard.

'Druriolanus' relied on his comedians to cover the inevitable technical hitches and organisational breakdowns that occurred during the run of his pantomimes. On the first night of *Sinbad the Sailor* in 1882 Arthur Roberts and James Fawn were called upon to improvise in front of the curtain while stage carpenters battled to dismantle an enormous whale that had become stuck on stage. It was a disastrous evening, with the already long performance over-running by an hour and the actors subjected to abuse from the pit and gallery. Harris favoured music-hall humour to such an extent that he considered the Harlequinade out of date and unnecessary, severely curtailing the antics of Clown, Pantaloon and Harlequin and sometimes, when time was at a premium, omitting them entirely.

Audiences changed considerably during Harris' regime. As the arranger of music at the theatre for many years, 'Jimmy' Glover had studied its patrons closely. Writing in 1911 he observed:

The Drury Lane pantomime has wonderfully metamorphosed in the last three decades. From E.T. Smith, 1862, to Chatterton, 1879, and on to the present day, the three periods have been instructive. It is ridiculous to state that pantomime has declined.

It has not declined; it has, however, changed and increased its public. In Chatterton's time, the 'Opening' was quite a modest affair, and was once produced in September, and the Harlequinade which was added on Boxing Night became somewhat more elaborate; but Chatterton's public was a few rows of five-shilling or seven-shilling stalls, a huge eightpenny pit, and a seething mass of sixpenny and fourpenny galleryites, who cat-called the 'Opening' on Boxing Night till not a word on the stage was heard. The shilling pit and the sixpenny gallery boy shouted the latest music-hall songs. The better-educated audience of today is not the chorus-singing urchin or patron of the 'seventies'. The top gallery disappeared under the London County Council during the end of Harris' management, and the stalls on Boxing Night have developed into a kid-gloved army of *dilettante* patrons, across whose apathetic well-dined and gloriously gloved personalities it is a far run to get to the pit for a good honest round of applause.[1]

The 1888/89 Drury Lane production, *Babes in the Wood, and Robin Hood and his Merry Merry Men and Harlequin Who Killed Cock Robin*, was the last to be written by Blanchard. He had supplied the theatre's pantomimes since 1852, but as a traditionalist had become increasingly disillusioned with Harris' interference and rewriting. The cast was strewn with stars, most of whom were regulars at the theatre. The Babes were played by Herbert Campbell and Harry Nicholls, already performers in five Drury Lane pantomimes, and previously in six at the Grecian Theatre under George Conquest. It was also the fifth appearance for Charles Lauri (himself the son of a once popular clown at the theatre) who portrayed a poodle that delighted audiences by scampering around every part of the theatre. Among newcomers were two buxom female music-hall artists, Harriett Vernon as Robin Hood and Maggie Duggan as Will Scarlet. Lydia played another merry man, but soon left the cast, probably due to the forthcoming birth of her fourth child.

Now, without Lydia, Will or Johnny for support, Dan must have felt particularly isolated. To achieve success he had to stand out from an eye-catching cast, to score points off a well-established comedy team and to offer himself for judgment by the intimidating patrons of the stalls and dress circle. He had been tried and tested throughout his already long career, but such experiences had exacerbated rather than eradicated his professional sensitivity. He was his own harshest critic, with a nagging concern over his own level of skill and the loyalty of his audience. The public, however, had no reservations about his first Drury Lane performance, and their verdict was resoundingly favourable.

10 Augustus Harris

Campbell and Nicholls created much laughter with a spoof ballet in which Harry played the premiere danseuse and eighteen-stone Herbert appeared as an extremely chubby cupid. Dan had no such major scenes to exploit, but he made the most of any opportunities that came his way. His talent was immediately obvious to public and press alike:

> I am inclined to think 'the cake' for frolicsome humour is taken by the dapper new-comer, Mr Dan Leno, who is sketched as the galvanic baroness in a wonderfully amusing dance which sets the house in a roar. The substantial 'Babes', Mr Herbert Campbell and Mr Harry Nicholls, would have no excuse if they did not vie in drollery with light-footed Dan Leno and jolly Victor Stevens ...[2]

The pantomime was a personal triumph for 'Druriolanus', breaking all box-office records by running through to the Easter holiday. Dan's music-hall engagements were consequently less numerous in 1889. Between April and October he appeared at the Empire (for six months), the Oxford (five months), the Canterbury, the Middlesex and the Paragon. His turn at the Canterbury was described by *The Era* at the beginning of June:

> ... we meet with the name of Mr Dan Leno, who as an old lady dilates on domestic affairs, and praises a husband who is a model of contentment all the week on bread and cheese, but 'he must have a bit of meat on Sunday'. Mr Leno, also comically deplores the lot of a travelling muffin man whose wife is a roamer that returns not, and likewise moved the house to laughter in his descriptive sketch of moving, increasing his comic impressiveness by carrying a baby's chair, a clock, and a frying pan tied to his coat tails. His quaint dancing, his burlesque hornpipe, and his whimsically delivered patter were, of course, loudly laughed at, and the audience were loath to let him depart from the Canterbury.[3]

By now he had engagements booked for three years in advance, a situation that forced him to reject an offer from the actor-manager Charles H. Hawtrey to appear in *Uncles and Aunts* at the Comedy Theatre. His packed schedule allowed one brief appearance in George P. Hawtrey's *Penelope*, a musical version of a famous farce, *The Area Belle*. Dan played Pitcher to the Tosser of the celebrated Gilbert and Sullivan comedian Rutland Barrington in a matinee presented, on behalf of the Holborn Lodge for Shop Girls, at the Comedy Theatre on 9 May 1889. A scene in which Dan was taken for a ghost after wrapping himself in a sheet created much amusement, but overall the *Times* critic considered that his performance treated the piece 'too much in the manner of pantomime'.[4]

In October Dan embarked on another provincial tour before returning to London to start rehearsals for the next Drury Lane pantomime.

'Druriolanus' surpassed himself, as he always did, with the 1889/90 pantomime *Jack and the Beanstalk; or, Harlequin and the Midwinter Night's Dream*. Having finally freed himself from the restraining influence of Blanchard, Harris, in collaboration with Harry Nicholls, produced a script that was widely criticised for its vulgarity. References to drunkenness abounded, while the main element of the comedy consisted of poking fun at the hypocrisies of bourgeois respectability. As King Henry the Bounder, Harry arrived home after a night on the town that would have put any *Lion Comique* to shame. Any excuses that he might concoct – 'Club? Smoking Concert? Lodge?' – were less than useless, for Queen Fanny the Flirt, played by Herbert Campbell, had heard them all from previous husbands. She had entrapped King Henry with a misleading newspaper advertisement, but the regal roué found consolation with a number of pretty maidens whom he kissed and cuddled in the town market-place.

England's greatest playwright was commandeered to provide a thin cultural veneer. A long procession, one of Harris' favourite and most time-consuming devices, represented heroines from the works of Shakespeare, while the opening scene, 'Oberon's Bower', was populated by chorus girls underdressed as fairies. Despite widespread criticism of his taste Harris knew the Drury Lane audience very well. Middle-class families were excited by a glimpse of the racy world of music hall; the working-class element could see their comedy favourites in unfamiliar and more extended roles; and everyone, including those often-neglected patrons of the pantomime, children, was excited by the gorgeously-fashioned and beautifully-lit scenic effects.

Following the success of his first Drury Lane appearance, Dan was allowed more time on stage. Back in 'widow's weeds', he played the dairy owner Mrs Simpson, struggling to control a rampant cow, played by the Brothers Griffiths, and bandying words with her errant son Jack, portrayed by stately Harriett Vernon. As tradition dictated the dialogue was in convoluted rhyming couplets, published in a shilling 'book of words':

JACK: (*Outside*) Mother! Mother!
Mrs S: Ah! Here he is.
(*Enter* JACK *enthusiastically*)
JACK: See, Ma, what I have got!
Mrs S: Something to eat, my dear?
JACK: No!
Mrs S: I thought not!
JACK: (*Aside*) I wonder if there's going to be a row?

Mrs S: (*Crying*) I can't go on much longer – (*Suddenly*) Where's the cow?
JACK: (*Aside*) Now for it! (*Aloud*) Ma dear, it is gone!
Mrs S: (*Shrieking*) What dead!
JACK: No!
Mrs S: (*Seizing him*) Give it me! Or else I'll punch your head!

Dan also had an effective novelty song – a ballad dedicated to Mother Nature. The setting, 'Mrs Simpson's Back Garden', was not an idyllic floral retreat, but a small patch of ground hemmed in by squalid housing. Tom cats faced off on a rickety fence, a silhouette was seen in a window swigging from a bottle, and a receding line of crazily-orientated chimney pots indicated a poor, urban street such as Eve Place or the back-to-back terraces of Manchester and Sheffield. *Jack and the Beanstalk* presented a make-believe world in which reality, like Giant Gorgibuster, often raised its ugly head. Like many Victorian families, the King and Queen struggled to meet their financial commitments. A running joke involved their attempts to avoid paying a long-overdue milk bill, while King Henry's first appearance saw him involved in an undignified squabble with a hansom-cab driver over a fare.

In Mrs Simpson's song the ideal and the actuality of the natural world clashed violently:

Our mother Nature seems to seek
A well-earned rest at close of day!
Her task is done; and (so to speak)
She's 'washed up' and she's 'cleared away!'
And like a good dame, always will
At eventide with cosy chat
With her sweet voice the silence fill
With sounds of peace (*CAT outside* 'Miow!')
There's a cat.

Ah me! What lessons can we learn!
If we but hearken to her – (Miow!)
On all sides – ev'ry way we turn
She'll teach us (Miow!) Oh! Stop that.
By rippling stream – through wood and dell
In peaceful vale – on mountain's brow;
You'll hear her (Miow?) I mean – (Miow!) well
I think I'll give it up! (Miow! Miow!)
Whatever trials we're doomed to know –
Whatever greatness we achieve –
We turn to her at last – (*DOG outside* 'Bow-wow!')

And if we've sought the – (Miow) Oh law!
The good, the beautiful, and true,
We need not fear the last (*DONKEY* 'Hee-haw!')
But smile, and – (*COCK* 'Cock-a-doodle-doo!')
(*In a frightful rage*)

Ah me, what lessons, etc.
Ending with everything joining in.

With his salary at Drury Lane doubled and a diary filled with lucrative engagements, Dan's bread was becoming fairly well buttered. His increasing earnings not only allowed Lydia to retire from the stage, but provided Louisa and Will with a comfortable home in Salford. It seems improbable that the elder Lenos had given up performing altogether – indeed the 1891 census still recorded Louisa as a vocalist and Will as a comedian. Louisa's health was failing, however, and in May 1890 Dan was reported to be hurrying back to visit his mother on her deathbed. It was a false alarm for Louisa's demise did not take place until 12 December 1891. The cause of her death, cirrhosis of the liver and dropsy, suggest that she might have joined her husband in the odd tipple. Whenever Dan visited Salford, Will insisted on taking him round his various drinking haunts. Very much as he used to announce his step-son's dancing feats from the stage, Will lectured his cronies: 'There he stands! There he stands! Dan Leno! *My* boy! The most famous man on earth – and *I* trained him!' As a rousing conclusion to his essay in self-congratulation Will grasped Dan's hand, drawing attention to an impressive diamond ring: 'See that? Things like that don't grow on gooseberry bushes, do they? Who is responsible for putting that ring on that finger? Ask the boy! *He'll* tell you! I am!'[5] As he had celebrated the championship belt Will continued to celebrate the ring for some years, finally succumbing, like Louisa, to cirrhosis in June 1896.

Perhaps Dan introduced some of Will's personal characteristics into his portrayal of Mr Lombarde Streete, father of Beauty in the 1890/91 Drury Lane production *Beauty and the Beast*. In answer to Harris's pre-pantomime enquiry, 'Dan, how do you think you'd be as a man?' he had responded positively: 'Well I don't know, but I think I *ought* to be all right; because, you see, I was born that way.'[6] There had been a sudden change in the choice of pantomimes. The scheduled *Dick Whittington* was abandoned when Harris was provided with a lucrative opportunity to exploit a sensational divorce case involving the daughter of an Aldershot canteen sergeant and the son of an Irish earl.

11   Belle Bilton

Belle Bilton, with her sister Flo, had been a highly popular music-hall performer before secretly marrying young Lord Dunlo in 1889. Not surprisingly, the Fourth Earl of Clancarty objected to having the short-skirted singer of 'Fresh, Fresh, Fresh as the Morning' as a daughter-in-law. The suitably chastened Dunlo was packed off to Australia and ordered to petition for divorce on doubtful charges of adultery. In the summer of 1890 proceedings ended in public jubilation when Dunlo, having developed a backbone during his Antipodean exile, returned home to assert his wife's innocence. The charming French fairy tale did not really parallel the real-life drama, but the presence of Belle playing her namesake Beauty, and a Beast who eventually became Prince Courage was sufficient to generate massive publicity for the production.

Belle and Dan were joined in the cast by the male impersonator Vesta Tilley, who played the Prince, John D'Auban as the Prince's beastly alter ego, and Campbell and Nicholls as Belle's sisters, Sarah Jane and Mary Ann. On the first night of the pantomime Belle's sister and husband were prominently seated in the grand tier prompt-side box. A reviewer for the *Penny Illustrated Paper* commented: 'I didn't observe Lord Clancarty among the crowded audience; but it was easy to note that his lordship's son was quite proud of his dainty little wife's lace-petticoat dancing, and donkey cart driving in a smart Newmarket coat.'[7] Beauty's cart, drawn by donkeys played by the Brothers Griffiths, was accompanied on its way to the docks by two other vehicles – a four-wheeled cycle pedalled by Sarah Jane and Mary Ann, and a three-wheeled 'boneshaker' driven at breakneck speed by Lombarde Streete. Drunkenness again provided the subject for a comic scene when a wavering Mr Streete was escorted from the palace 'after a too liberal allowance of the wine-cup'.[8]

In one of their scenes Herbert and Harry burlesqued sister acts such as the Biltons:

The far-famed Sisters Frillings we, of very great renown,
The pets of all frequenters of the music-halls in town.
Distinct originality's the specialty we claim,
And so we always sing, and dance, and act, and dress the same.

Wherever we may go
We're seen together – so,
Arms around each other's waists lovingly entwined.
And every move we make
In unison we take,
Two artists more original than us you'll never find.

It was to be their last duet, for Nicholls left Drury Lane after the pantomime to pursue his career at the Adelphi Theatre. Dan and Herbert had
already become firm friends, and their rapport on stage was clear to all.
Unlike Nicholls, with a background in the theatre, they shared many
years of music-hall experience both having fought their way out of poverty to achieve popular acclaim. Without Will, Henry or Johnny, Herbert became Dan's mainstay in pantomime for many years to come.

Beauty and the Beast proved to be Belle Bilton's last appearance. With
the sudden death of her father-in-law she became Lady Clancarty, a title
she held with dignity and good grace. Though never received at court,
she was extremely popular with her tenants and neighbours at the family
seat in Galway, Ireland. Having given birth to five children, Isabel
Maude Penrice died of cancer at the age of 36. Lydia, too, never resumed
her professional career, although she sometimes performed at charity
events. Following the death of her younger sister Lydia Daisy (19 September 1886–2 April 1887), Georgina was joined by John William born on
16 April 1888; Ernest George, 26 May 1889; Sidney Paul, 11 July 1891;
Herbert Dan, 3 May 1893; and, finally, May Lillian, 10 March 1896.

11

CRUFFINS AND MUMPETS FOR TEA

The fragile roots of comedy are not easily transplanted from one culture to another. Like flowers pressed in heavy albums the jokes that amused our ancestors linger on in their outward form, but, removed from their original context, provide only a suggestion of the laughter which they once provoked. An archive dedicated to preserving nineteenth-century humour would be a gloomy place, packed with frivolous magazines bound into heavy volumes; flimsy chap books locked away in filing cabinets; colourful pictorial song-sheets bundled together and placed in drab boxes. At such a distance in time and in such a different society it is almost impossible to recreate, or even imagine, the motivation for much Victorian humour. Yet, in their unselfconsciousness and lack of formality the desiccated remains of comedy represent a major insight into the everyday life of the past.

By the early 1890s Dan's increased earnings made it possible for him to purchase songs from the foremost music-hall writers and composers. He was considered by many to be Britain's leading comic singer, his only significant rival being a newcomer to the variety stage, Albert Chevalier. Despite regularly portraying aspects of working-class life, the two comedians differed radically in their personal background and stage technique. Chevalier was a supremely skilful character actor, but a romantic who stuck closely to existing music-hall forms. Dan, on the other hand, was a realist, abandoning many of the conventions of the comic song. Together they represented the opposite poles of cockney comedy, with Chevalier's idealised barrow-boys and Dan's downtrodden drabs providing the outer limits within which most other comic singers performed.

Born in 1861, just a few months after Dan, Hereen Albert Onezime Algarth Britannicus Garfleur Alphonse Chevalier was brought up in a comfortable middle-class home in North Kensington, London. He had been an established actor for some years before his talent for performing humorous songs led him, in 1891, to transfer to the music-hall stage. Friends warned that the move was professional 'suicide', but Chevalier's success was such that he had many offers to return to the legitimate theatre. His carefully studied performances in cockney songs such as 'My

Old Dutch', 'The Coster's Serenade' and 'Knocked 'Em in the Old Kent Road' relied more on literary tradition and theatrical custom than on empathy and audience involvement. At a time when music halls were attempting to attract a more respectable audience, Chevalier appealed to a middle-class conception of what working-class life *should* be like. Several critics detected a refining influence in his songs, their artistic treatment likely to lift music-hall entertainment from its slough of vulgarity.

Although Chevalier and Dan were the top music-hall comedians of the day their styles were so dissimilar that they were seldom compared. The extreme sentimentality expressed in many of Chevalier's songs was not an area that Dan chose to explore, while Chevalier's training and long experience as an actor made him wary of spontaneity and of communicating with his audience. Paradoxically, Dan, who had spent most of his career as a singer and dancer, developed a routine that depended for its effect on the spoken word, whereas the actor Chevalier achieved his greatest music-hall hits with melodic chorus songs. In the songs 'The Future Mrs 'Awkins' (1892) and 'Her Mother's at the Bottom of it All' (1890) Albert and Dan provided their own individualistic interpretations of love and marriage. Chevalier's 'coster' sauntered on stage, dressed in his Sunday best costume, decorated with pearl buttons and velvet trimmings. Softly he crooned a tale of growing affection:

> I shan't forgit our meetin', 'G'arn', was 'er greetin'
> 'Just yer mind wot you're about;'
> 'Er pretty 'ead she throws up, then she turns 'er nose up
> Saying 'Let me go. I'll shout!'
> Cops 'er round the waist like this!
> Sez she 'I must be dreamin', chuck it I'll start screaming'
> 'If yer do' sez I 'I'll kiss.'
>
> Chorus:
> Oh! Lizer Sweet Lizer!
> If yer die an old maid you'll 'ave only yerself to blame
> D'y'ear Lizer? *Dear* Lizer!
> 'Ow d'yer fancy 'Awkins for your other name?
>
> She wears an artful bonnit, feathers stuck upon it
> Coverin' a fringe all curled;
> She's just about the sweetest, prettiest and neatest
> Doner in the wide, wide world!
> And she'll be Mrs 'Awkins, Mrs 'Enery 'Awkins
> Got 'er for to name the day;
> Settled it last Monday so to the church on Sunday
> Off we trots the donkey shay!

Dan's hero was less eloquent, but equally lovesick. Mr Pipkins' account
of a convoluted courtship was gushing and garbled:

> It was very strange that I should first meet my wife in the Maze.
> I'd never been in the Maze before (well, I've never been out of it
> since). I think every married man's a bit mazy, more or less. Well,
> to make a long story thick, I was walking up and down, and after
> walking for about two hours I found I hadn't moved; somehow or
> other I'd mislaid myself. I tried to find a side door at the back, but
> no. Then it struck me all of a lump that I was lost. Well it's dan-
> gerous to lose a person like me. So I began to cry, when someone
> over the other side of the hedge said, 'Don't cry, little boy, here's
> some nuts.' Oh, I was so pleased that I was found; and I found it
> was a lady that was speaking, I shall never forget how I felt. I
> went all of a cold perspiration, and I said, 'I ain't a little boy.' She
> said, 'I beg your pardon.' I said, 'You're welcome.' So one word
> got to another; then she told me my name, and I told her hers. I
> asked her to go for a stroll when we got outside, she said she'd be
> delighted a lot, but how was she to know me? I said, 'When we get
> out I'll cough twice.' So when I got out I coughed a lovely cough,
> and the man at the gate said, 'You've got hydrophobia.' I said, 'I
> beg to differ', and then up came the girl. Oh, I was so bashful. I
> asked her to have some wine, so she ordered a pint of shandy-gaff.
> I said, 'No, let's have two.' So I ordered two pints of shandy-gaff. I
> gave the waiter half-a-sovereign – no, let me see – fourpence; I get
> mixed a little. Then I ordered tea. I said, 'What will you have for
> tea?' She said, 'Anything you like.' So I ordered two plates of any-
> thing you like, and cruffins and mumpets. Oh, and we did have a
> game! I burnt her hand with a teaspoon, and she filled my cup
> with salt and I was sick. Oh, we did enjoy ourselves! Then we went
> home. But after leaving her I couldn't rest, nor eat my supper. I
> had to call my landlady up to sit with me a couple of hours. She
> said, 'Lor! Mr Pipkins, what's the matter with you?' I told her I'd
> met my divinity. She said, 'Lor, have a mustard-plaster on at
> once.' I said, 'No, it's my sweetheart.' And I believe if her mother
> hadn't interfered we should have been happy. But! Lor, married
> life makes a man of you. Before I was married I didn't say a word;
> now look at the difference. I daren't open my mouth at all.

A major difference between the two comedians lay in their approach to
original material. Chevalier wrote most of his own songs, carefully planning and choreographing their effect. Dan purchased the majority of his
songs from professional writers, later developing their content to suit his
own style. Writing to Horace Lennard he explained:

The characters of my songs are all 'founded on fact'. To get the effect out of songs is not as easy as it looks. In the first place you've got to catch your song, and you'll understand the difficulty when I tell you I've over 150 songs at home for which I've paid one to five guineas each, and which are utterly useless. Sometimes I sit up all night studying the song, trying to see the chances of effect in it, till I get out of temper, and chuck it in the fire. I study hard for all my songs, my favourite way is to walk a few miles in the rain, keeping the tune with my feet.[1]

Many of Dan's early successes were written and composed by Harry King, but other, better-known songwriters were soon engaged. Among those to supply Dan with numbers were Fred Bowyer, author of many songs for Herbert Campbell; Harry Dacre, who wrote the bicycling anthem 'Daisy Bell'; Joseph Tabrar, creator of 'Daddy Wouldn't Buy Me a Bow-Wow'; and Fred Gilbert, who was responsible for music hall's most rousing chorus song, 'The Man That Broke the Bank at Monte Carlo'. From the mid-1890s Dan's principal songwriter was Herbert Darnley, a well-known music-hall comedian and one of the early recording industry's most popular performers.

Although usually set within a narrow social compass Dan's songs stood out from those of many of his contemporaries by introducing widely differing characters. Such variety did not dilute Dan's own distinctive style, for the songs were carefully adapted to suite his performance. Another unifying factor was the musical accompaniment, often provided by one of music hall's greatest composers, George Le Brunn. Music played a diminishing role in Dan's 'songs', but Le Brunn's stylish introductions and catchy choruses not only helped define individual numbers but also supplied a degree of homogeneity to the comedian's repertoire.

The composer was introduced to Dan by Johnny Danvers in about 1888. According to his frequent collaborator John P. Harrington:

... any old place and any old time, George could compose songs as easily as another man might write a letter. A rapid glance at the lyrics, a grunted 'This is six-eight time?' and after my nod of acquiescence, pronto! His fluent pen would positively fly over the sheet of music-paper, and the melody was written ere you had time to gasp 'Geewhiz!'

Seldom, if ever, was so much as a note uttered afterwards, and never once was the piano touched until the melody was complete. I have known him to reel off half-a-dozen melodies in this fashion, and some of our most popular songs were composed in five or ten minutes ...[2]

Le Brunn composed over 1,000 songs, including such music-hall classics as 'If it Wasn't For the 'Ouses in Between' and 'It's a Great Big Shame' for Gus Elen; 'The City Waif' for Jenny Hill; and 'Wink the Other Eye', 'Oh, Mr Porter' and 'Everything in the Garden's Lovely' for Marie Lloyd. He was particularly associated with Charles Godfrey, regularly embarking on pub crawls with the comedian, which sometimes resulted in the temporary loss of important 'band parts'. For Dan his compositions included 'The Detective', 'My Old Man', 'Chimney on Fire', 'The Fasting Man', 'The Detective Camera', 'All Through a Little Piece of Bacon' and 'The Jap'. During the early 1890s Le Brunn provided the accompaniment for three of Dan's most celebrated numbers, comic studies of characters pursuing specific occupations – 'The Railway Guard' (1890), 'The Shop-walker' and 'The Waiter' (both 1891).

Trade songs had always been popular on the stage, supplying ready made-characters in both appearance and anticipated behaviour. Before the advent of music hall Joseph Grimaldi had looked to the streets of his native London for inspiration. His most famous song, 'Hot Codlings', told the story of a drunken toffee-apple seller, while in 'Pretty Betty Brill' he sang of a sweetheart who sold sprats on Fish Street Hill. In 1807 he performed 'The Odd-Dealer', a song whose enumerative theme was to be revisited by other comedians many times over the next century:

> I keep a little shop
> None beat me at buying or selling can,
> In merry customers hop,
> 'Tis the sign of the frog and the frying-pan,
> You buy threads, pins and needles of me,
> For my catalogue never goes awry.
> Beside the best sugar and tea,
> Mugs, mouse traps, and all other grocery.

Like 'The Odd-Dealer' many subsequent songs were confined to descriptions of tradespeople and their services or wares, often employing a familiar street cry. As a vendor of cheap plaster ornaments Jacky Sharp sung 'Who'll Buy My Image?' during the 1850s. A decade later George Leybourne appeared as the raggedly-dressed 'Mousetrap Man' (1867):

> 'Mousetraps! Mousetraps,' I cry!
> 'Mousetraps! a penny who'll buy?
> Strong as a house, just have one and try!
> Mousetraps a penny! A penny who'll buy?'

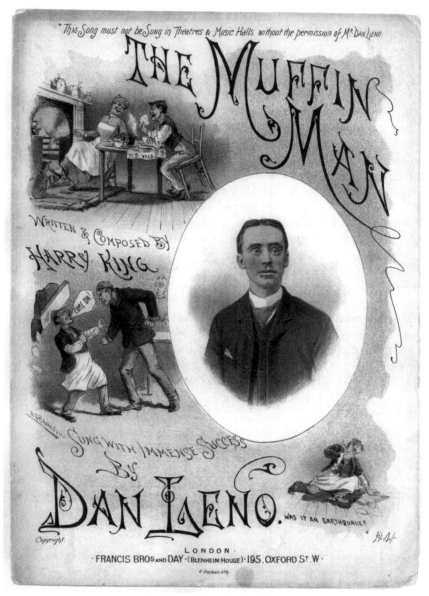

12 'The Muffin Man', 1889

In 1868 Leybourne's rival the Great Vance countered with his impersonation of Martha Gunn, a bathing-machine attendant who cried:

Come to your Martha, come, come, come,
The water is warm in the sun, sun, sun.

Sometimes a romantic narrative was introduced into the song. Harry Clifton's 'Polly Perkins of Paddington Green' (1863) placed three workers in an unhappy love triangle. A 'broken hearted milkman' sang of his love for a 'young servant maid', and of his rejection in favour of a 'bow legged conductor of a Tuppenny Bus'.

In one of his earliest trade songs, 'The Muffin Man' (1888), Dan told a similar tale of feminine fecklessness:

> I've been deceived, I've been betrayed, and treated most unkindly,
> By a cruel wicked jade I loved her madly, blindly,
> She kept a little sweet stuff shop, did false Miss Quisby Splinter,
> She sold ice cream, and ginger pop, and crumpet in the winter.

> Chorus:
> Oh! Muffins and crumpets for tea,
> I never thought she'd have sold me,
> She said 'She was fair gone on me',
> And I took it all in as she told me;
> While I was trying to earn a bob,
> She would be having a spree,
> And this other fellow would be on the job,
> Having muffins and crumpets for tea.

The worst aspect of Quisby's treachery appears to have been that she was undermining the muffin-man's trade: 'And she was actually learning him to punch muffins, taking my business out of my hands.' There were a number of moments during the song when Dan and, through him, his audience were compelled to pause and re-evaluate the situation unfolding before them: 'Those were happy days, one by one I used to put up those shutters (well there was only one to put up)' And again : 'He used to be in the shop every day, and I never noticed it, but he was so artful; he used to walk in backwards to make me think he was always coming out.'

Dan's next trade characterisation 'The Railway Guard' was a manic character with a spiky beard, ill-fitting uniform and gigantic whistle. His behaviour was based on an actual railway official that Dan had observed – 'a fussy little man I used to see at Brixton Station, always rushing up and down, shouting at everybody, and himself doing nothing whatever'. In Dan's hands the character was transformed into a frenetic harbinger of doom:

> I've seen our engine so hot it's scorched all the whiskers of the passengers' faces! Yesterday we started at such a rate, we flew past the terminus right up a back street. If some person hadn't got hold of the bridle we should have been dashed to pieces ... But, lor!

What an accident that was. I'll never forget it, it's a wonder all the passengers weren't killed, they would have been, only it happened there was nobody on the train.

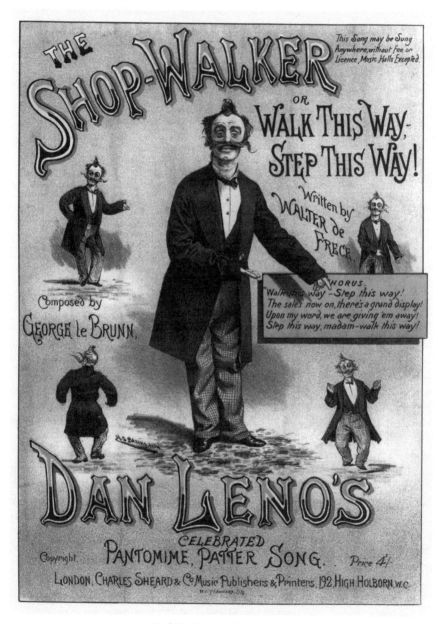

13 'The Shop-walker', 1891

'The Shop-walker' mixed verbal comedy with a far greater degree of pantomime than Dan had previously employed. His excruciatingly solicitous draper's-shop assistant strutted around the stage, beckoning to imaginary customers and requesting them to 'walk this way, step this way'. The offer of a temporary respite ('take a chair – thank you!') was merely the prelude to a prolonged selling campaign:

> Something about half-a-sovereign? No? One–and-six? I'm afraid we haven't got any at that price. Oh, yes! There's some in the window, but they're only glued to the glass. Try these, I'm sure they will give you terrible satisfaction. Two pairs? – sure you won't have half-dozen? No? – thank you! Now the next article? Black tie? – thank you! For yourself? – thank you! Sure you want a black tie? – thank you! Would you like a nice white with a blue stripe? Black? – thank you! Perhaps you would like to see one of our new shades – 'pink puce' – very becoming! No? Black – thank you! Are you quite sure no other colour would do? – quite sure? Well, I'm very sorry we are out of black, we shall have some more in, in about a fortnight. Nothing else? Good morning! Mind the step! Nice shower after the rain! What for you, madam? Stay-laces?

Unlike 'The Shop-walker' who was inordinately proud of his position 'The Waiter' radiated self-pity and indignation. As he raced around a cheap restaurant he dished out excuses faster than hot dinners:

> No we don't keep toothpicks, we lose so many of them; people used to use them and take 'em away, sir … what's the matter with the tripe? Green! Oh, yes, that's the only colour we keep now, we don't keep the common unbleached tripe … what, the chop smells? Didn't know you wanted to smell it, thought you wanted to eat it.

He was overworked, overwrought and very nearly overwhelmed as he attempted to meet the demands of a roomful of customers, subtly suggested by a series of one-sided conversations and indicative movements. His costume appeared to have been designed to emphasise frantic haste; flowing mutton-chop whiskers, a flapping coat and a billowing white napkin that at any moment seemed likely to be raised as a token of surrender. Both waiter and waited on were locked in a battle for survival:

> Journey! 'pon my word, some people think a waiter's on wheels. When I came here first, I was six inches taller than I am now. That

will give you an idea how I have to run about. I've worn myself down to a point. I've got no feet, I've worn 'em off. I've had to have the bottoms of my legs turned up to make feet. Well! You can believe me, these trousers were knickerbockers when I came here first. And what you have to put up with! Yesterday, a gentleman came in and wanted a steak. I brought it, with bits of parsley all round it to hide the rough edges. Then he said he couldn't get his teeth in it. No wonder! He'd only got false ones, and those he'd put in his coat-tail pocket. I told him he'd have to sit on the steak to eat it, if he kept his teeth in his pocket. Then he grumbled about it being tough. Then I lost my temper, and told him I wasn't going to chew it for him. Then another gentleman orders a spring chicken and a bottle of '64 port, and when I bring them he won't pay for them, because he says they are a spring port and '64 chicken ... My word, instead of giving a man seven years for life, they should make a waiter of him. You've more wear and tear to the soles of your feet than you have to the seat of the chairs; for all day long someone's calling –

'Now then, Waiter! Waiter! Waiter!
This mutton's raw, bring some more, the cabbage isn't done.
I say waiter! Waiter! Waiter!'
'I'm coming sir! I'm coming!' 'Why the dickens don't you come?'

As single songs in a stage turn 'The Railway Guard', 'The Shop-walker' and 'The Waiter' were remarkable for their distinctiveness. In his act Dan provided the audience with an ever-changing display of characters, each individual sharply defined, both in rapidly assumed costume and in psychological interpretation. Such a closely observed and varied cross-section of society had not previously been represented on the music-hall stage. Several performers possessed comparable acting ability, but no one had yet had the confidence or the audacity to present so many differing personalities within such a compressed period of time.

14 'The Swimming Instructor', 1898

DAN LENO. "THE DIVER"

15 Dan Leno at the sea-side

12

A LARGE, GENIAL GENTLEMAN

On stage Dan and Herbert were opposites that created the greatest possible attraction. With temperaments and physiques differing so dramatically their association exuded a humour that extended far beyond the auditorium of the Theatre Royal. Reports of their off-stage exploits and practical jokes were a source of continual amusement to the general public, as were the stream of cartoons and photographs that appeared in newspapers and magazines. Their partnership rapidly became celebrated as a national institution, remaining a stable feature throughout an unsettled and eventually disastrous decade.

An interviewer for *The London Magazine* described the last pantomime in which they appeared:

> Regarded solely from the point of pantomime, the effectiveness of physical contrast has, in some measure, increased the value of Mr Campbell's service. The possession of a singularly placid temperament and a rigidly methodical mode of living have, it is probable, been contributory causes of the comedian's present ample proportions. In short, Herbert Campbell, being a large, genial gentleman of physical as well as artistic breadth, makes an admirable foil to one of comparatively diminutive stature and widely different methods. Hence the long and brilliantly successful association with Dan Leno. Surely no broader contrast either in the physical or artistic sense was ever furnished by any other pair of jesters – the one plump, unctuous and deliberate, the other lean, perky and spasmodic.[1]

Dan and Herbert's partnership conformed to the popular stereotypes that have applied to successful double acts from time immemorial. Footit and Chocolat, Laurel and Hardy, Abbott and Costello, Morecambe and Wise all achieved their humour by a series of contradictions; inequalities of size, strength and intelligence combined with the subversion of each other's position and the adoption of attitudes and qualities that were more suited to their partner. Although both comedians

were products of the British music hall they approached their stage business very differently. Herbert was a creature of the past, a highly divert-
ing dinosaur whose style changed little in 40 years. Dan provided a
glimpse of the future, anticipating both the surreal and observational
style of later comedians. Unlike Dan who in his treatment of 'drunkenness, quarrelsomeness, petty poverty; still hunger, even crime ... trans-
muted mud to gold',[2] Herbert's vulgarity appears to have been a con-
scious protest against propriety and middle-class morality.

While often expressing admiration for Dan's subtlety and finesse,
Max Beerbohm also respected Herbert's more uncomplicated approach:

> He was the last guardian and exemplar of the old indigenous
> music hall tradition. James Fawn, and the Great McDermott, and
> all those other guardians and exemplars, had gone, one by one,
> before him. He alone lingered, a terrific embodiment of things van-
> ished and forgotten. Much we marvelled at him; yet, marvelling,
> much loved him. 'Our Herbert'! No subtlist, he. Offspring, as it
> were, of some mystic union between beef and thunder, he imposed
> as little strain on our intellects as on our ears. Artist he was; but
> his art was sheerly physical. He made his 'points' well; but then,
> for him, in every song every word was a 'point' to be hammered
> home by the unparallel power of his lungs. Wide-eyed, wide-
> mouthed, he looked us straight in the face, and let us have it for all
> it was worth.[3]

When Dan and Herbert began their partnership in the 1891/92 pantomime *Humpty Dumpty*, the older comedian had already been a leading
London performer for more than 20 years. Herbert Edward Story was
born almost exactly 16 years before Dan, in December 1844, at 16 Hamilton Street, Vauxhall, within flooding distance of the noisome waters of
the River Thames. After a period as an office boy employed by the *Sun*
newspaper in the Strand, he became an apprentice engineer at the
Armstrong gun factory at Woolwich Arsenal, South-East London. In-
explicably at this time of imperial belligerence, the demand for ordnance
appears to have slackened, causing Herbert and many of fellow workers
to be thrown out of work. Swapping quick-firing guns for quick-fire
jokes, he joined a travelling black-face minstrel show. He had already
appeared in many amateur concerts, but as 'Bones Corner' he was to find
that the life of a professional entertainer was not always an easy one. On
one occasion business was so bad that the troupe were forced to walk
back to London from Oxford, a distance of some 50 miles. Herbert
recalled trudging through Henley-on-Thames on Christmas Day, his hunger and thirst seemingly mocked by 'the sounds of feasting and merriment that came from the revellers'.[4]

16   Herbert Campbell

In 1865 Herbert's career took a major step forward when he joined two other performers to form Harman, Elston and Campbell, a black-face music-hall act. Elston sang 'drawing room' ballads, Harman told jokes and Herbert acted as the 'straight' man or 'feed'. Having spent three years establishing themselves as a popular turn, a dispute led to Herbert parting company with his partners in Edinburgh in October 1868. Once more he headed home, arriving in London almost penniless. It was make-or-break time. In dire need of funds Herbert decided to change his act, abandoning black-face to become a conventional solo comedian. A highly successful engagement at Collins', Islington Green, in the autumn of 1868 was followed by bookings at all the major London music-halls. By the end of April 1871 he had been engaged in the capital for 134 consecutive weeks.

The coloured cover of a song sheet published in 1870 shows Herbert at the commencement of his solo career. He is depicted as tall and narrow-waisted, a confident *Lion Comique* in tight dark trousers, wide-lapelled jacket, heavy gold watch-chain and jaunty top hat. His fashionable costume is somewhat at variance with the subject of the song 'The Oil Shop'; a sad tale of a young man whose love for his sweetheart is tempered by the lingering aroma of her father's business premises:

Soup, Starch and Candles, Flanders Brick and Turpentine.
Pepper, Glue and Mustard, Colza oil and Scent,
Black lead and Clothes lines, Peas and British Wine.
Colours mixed for Painting and Brushes lent.

Throughout the 1870s he established himself as one of the country's premier pantomime performers. Appearances at the Theatre Royal, Liverpool, in 1871/72 and 1872/73 were followed by five successive pantomimes for George Conquest at the Grecian Theatre. When Conquest announced his intention of moving to the Theatre Royal, Convent Garden, Herbert naturally went with him, scoring a personal triumph as Mrs Simpson in *Jack and the Beanstalk*. With Fanny Leslie, the Great MacDermott, Charles Lauri and the clown Harry Payne also contributing outstanding performances, the production was so successful that audiences were attracted away from the nearby Theatre Royal, Drury Lane, causing a financial crisis that led to the temporary closure of the theatre in February 1879. When Augustus Harris became the lessee of Drury Lane later in the year, one of his first acts was to strengthen the comedy content of its pantomimes. From 1882/83, when he appeared with Vesta Tilley, Arthur Roberts and James Fawn in *Sinbad*, Herbert became a regular performer at the theatre. In the following year's *Cinderella*, Herbert was joined by an old Grecian colleague Harry Nicholls, their partnership lasting until Dan's arrival.

From the 1870s onward Herbert's mighty voice boomed out songs chronicling the ups and downs of cockney life. Such numbers as 'In My Fust 'Usband's Time', 'Patching the Seats of the Mighty', 'They're All Very Fine and Large' and 'Up I Came With My Little Lot' were inherently coarse and ribald, but full of humour. His outlook was as rigidly set as that of the old woman he impersonated in 'At My Time of Life':

Now fancy me – Old Mother Scrubbs
A jineing these 'ere Totties' clubs,
Fancy me deserting the pubs
At my time of life.

His debunking of songs that expressed 'high flown' sentiments seems to have been from deep personal conviction. When the Great MacDermott's famous chorus song, performed in 1878 at the height of concern about Russian expansionism, inspired 'Jingoists' to demonstrate to its rousing refrain: 'We don't want to fight, but by Jingo, if we do, We've got the ships, we've got the men, we've got the money too', Herbert's parody expressed the less patriotic point of view of an ordinary rank and file soldier: 'I don't want to fight, I'll be slaughtered if I do; I'll change my togs, I'll sell my kit, and pop [pawn] my rifle too.' He was blunt and outspoken, with an aversion to hypocrisy that either met with unqualified approval or strong criticism. When John McDougall, a crusading member of the National Vigilance Association, attacked the morals of the London music halls, Herbert received much applause during the 1889/90 pantomime with his satirical song 'The Great McNoodle Went to Town'. But a year earlier he had caused offence with a number entitled 'Old Clo!' in which he sneered at former Prime Minister Gladstone, and made allusions 'in the worst possible taste'[5] to Sir Charles Dilke, a prominent Liberal politician who had been disgraced following an infamous 'three in a bed' scandal.

Herbert's 'rigidly methodical mode of living' included the regular consumption of fat cigars and large glasses of whisky, which he referred to as 'cups of tea'. On returning home to North London after his Saturday evening shows he would invariably call in at the Constitutional Club, Canonbury Tower, where he met with theatrical colleagues such as the pantomime author Geoffrey Thorn, his favourite song writer Fred Bowyer and comedians Harry Randall and Fred and Arthur Williams. Late nights imbibing numerous 'cups of tea' did not prevent him from heading off to the Green Man Tavern, Enfield, on Sunday mornings, conveyed along country lanes in his own stylish hansom cab. Sunday evenings would find him ensconced in the saloon bar of the White Swan, Highbury Corner, after which he would adjourn for further refreshment to his own home or that of numerous local friends. There was usually

someone waiting for Herbert at his pleasant stucco-fronted villa in
Quadrant Road. He had lost his wife Lizzie in 1884, after 17 years of
marriage, but soon met an actress, Rose Wiltshire, with whom he lived
until her death in 1891. Finally, Ellen Maud Bartram took up residence,
inheriting his estate of £4,500 after a bitter legal wrangle.

17   *Humpty Dumpty*, 1891

Although Nicholls did not appear in the 1891/92 Drury Lane production, Herbert would have been well acquainted with all the new members
of the cast. For *Humpty Dumpty; or, Harlequin the Yellow Dwarf and the
Fair One with the Golden Locks* Harris engaged even more music-hall
stars. Herbert and Dan were joined by Fanny Leslie as King Dulcimar,
the diminutive Little Tich in the title role and Marie Lloyd playing Princess Allfair. Only 20 years old, Marie had already established a reputation as an uninhibited singer of 'saucy' songs, delivering her *risqué* lyrics
with wide-eyed, but provocative innocence. Her brand of pouting pu-
dency was particularly popular on the halls with the archetypal 'Boy in
the Gallery', an individual she had notably celebrated in an early song
borrowed from Nelly Power. The 'gods' at Drury Lane were no different,
providing her with a great ovation when she performed a high-kicking
song and dance about corporal punishment entitled 'Whacky, Whack,
Whack'.

Herbert and Dan were cast as the quarrelsome King and Queen of Hearts, a married couple who threatened to inflict severe injuries on each other throughout the production's 11 scenes. A real episode of marital disharmony, however, tainted the latter stages of the pantomime. In the early hours of 12 January 1892 Marie and her husband Percy Courtenay were involved in a drunken brawl in her Drury Lane dressing room. In keeping with his theatrical surroundings Courtenay removed a sword from the wall and threatened to cut his wife's throat. Marie escaped, bruised but otherwise unharmed, and reported the assault at the nearby Bow Street police station. A few weeks later Herbert also made an appearance at Bow Street, having been arrested at the Albion Tavern, adjacent to the Theatre Royal, where he had been drinking after hours with the clown Harry Payne and several other members of the *Humpty Dumpty* cast.[6]

'Druriolanus' continued to ignore criticism of his pantomimes. As long as some members of royalty were present on the opening night, and while the gallery roared its vocal accompaniment to the tunes of popular songs, he felt vindicated in following the same policy. For the 1892/93 production, *Little Bo-Peep, Little Red Riding Hood and Hop O' My Thumb*, most of the previous year's performers were re-engaged, with additional music-hall talent drafted in. Once again there were complaints about the quality of the script:

> Someone should tell Sir Augustus Harris how very far his 'book of words' falls short of what the occasion requires. Life (at Drury Lane) would be tolerable if it were not for its humour. The humour of this Pantomime is of the roughest Cockney texture. In our over-plus of literature there must surely be someone who can write a really brilliant pantomime book; but it is clearly not Sir Augustus Harris, nor his colleague, Mr Wilton Jones.[7]

The narrative of the pantomime was rendered almost incomprehensible by lengthy and spectacular scenes, such as a procession illustrating 39 nursery rhymes and a gigantic hall of mirrors which reflected a Watteau-inspired ballet. Once again Marie was given free reign to introduce her music-hall hits, including a rewritten version of her celebrated song 'Oh, Mr Porter'. As Goody Thumb, Herbert towered over Little Tich, who played his son Tom. Dan, as Daddy Thumb, was also in the shadow of his wife's formidable form, but he found a means of escape when he briefly became a socialist orator in his song 'The Midnight March':

> Plain to see I am tir'd
> Nearly worn away to skin and bone,
> Not the sort of man to be admir'd,

Even by the misses all alone.
Here I have been spoutin' to the workin' classes.
Tellin' them as 'ow they are downright asses;
Tryin' to improve 'em such a bootless farce is,
I haven't got a blucher [boot] fit to own.

At Christmas 1893 there was an attempt to produce a fresher, more inno-
cent pantomime – not at Drury Lane, however, but at the nearby Lyceum Theatre. While Harris' processions lengthened and his comedians
queued up to outgag each other, Oscar Barrett received the best possible
reviews for his fairy-tale pantomime *Cinderella*:

> It is open to doubt if the London stage has ever seen any Christ-
> mas play of the kind conceived and executed in such faultless
> taste. It is hardly fair to call this dainty and charming Cinderella a
> Pantomime, for the modern Pantomime is associated with dances
> and music hall songs. Nothing of the kind is found at the Lyceum
> … Mr Oscar Barrett has out of the legend of Cinderella con-
> structed a fairy opera beautiful to behold and delightful to listen.[8]

18   A dress rehearsal at Drury Lane

Written by Dan's friend Horace Lennard, *Cinderella* was performed by actors, the only music-hall artist being Charles Lauri, who played the cat. The pantomime remained faithful to its fairy-tale original, with comedy not gratuitously added, but strictly subordinate to the plot. Playing to packed houses for 12 weeks *Cinderella* provided stiff opposition to Drury Lane's *Robinson Crusoe*. Harris had not allowed for a change in the public's taste, and had produced a bigger and blowsier pantomime, which many critics felt was excessive, even by his unrestrained standards. There were more lapses into juvenile vulgarity which amused the pit and gallery, but offended other members of the audience. Marie, as Polly Perkins, wore a low-cut dress and sang 'The Bar Maid', 'The Naughty Continong' and 'A Tasty Bit of Crackling'. In the scene where she prepared for bed an impromptu search for a chamber pot caused widespread disapproval. Even without the hunt for the illusive 'jerry', one critic found the scene hard to stomach:

> Nothing, apparently, can subdue Mr Dan Leno, who appeared as Crusoe's mother. The most successful incident of the evening was the bedroom scene, in which Miss Marie Lloyd modestly disrobed and retired to rest. At every string she untied, the gallery gave a gasp of satisfaction; and when Mr Dan Leno exhibited himself in a red flannel petticoat and a pair of stays, the whole house literally roared with delight. You may think it odd, and even ungallant, but somehow I don't seem to yearn for the privilege of assisting at Miss Marie Lloyd's toilet, or admiring Mr Dan Leno in dishabille; but amid all that vast audience, I was evidently in a minority of one.[9]

With a colossal budget the success or failure of Harris's productions was finely balanced. The overall coarseness of the writing and the indecorous songs and antics associated with Marie and Herbert proved such a deterrent to Drury Lane's regular audiences that the 1893/94 pantomime made a reputed loss of £30,000. *Robinson Crusoe's* faltering fortunes were mirrored by Harris's own precarious state of health – in February 1894 he was confined to bed with a serious illness, compelled to listen to Marie, Dan and Herbert via a telephone link to his Regent's Park home.

13

POPULARITY

A 13-foot long oil painting that hangs in the Museum of London depicts a group of over 200 variety artists. 'Popularity', painted by female impersonator Walter H. Lambert under his stage name Lydia Dreams, is a striking visual record of the elite of the music-hall world during the early 1900s. But in its portrayal of ranks of chattering, gesticulating performers the painting also suggests the homogeneous nature of the profession and its love of both informal and organised social gatherings. The happy crowd are placed in the middle of Waterloo Road, at the corner of Lower Marsh near the Canterbury Music Hall and the Old Vic theatre. Dan is at the centre of the throng, waving towards the artist, while behind him can be seen the spire of St John's Church, where his parents were married 50 years previously.

19 Dan Leno on stage, 1895, by Charles Dana Gibson

With the exception of Herbert's Canonbury colony, most music-hall performers lived close to the area of South-East London depicted in the background of the painting. Many inhabited the Kennington Road, which ran from Waterloo to Kennington Park, while others were based slightly further south in Brixton Road. Depending on their current levels of success variety artists might reside in comfortable detached villas, apartments in elegant Georgian terraces, or squalid attics such as that occupied by the young Charles Chaplin and his performer mother. Charlie's grim struggle for existence was lightened on Sunday mornings when 'The Profession' took to their carriages to embark on a Bacchanalian odyssey along the local thoroughfares:

> On Sunday mornings along the Kennington Road one could see a smart pony and trap outside a house, ready to take a vaudevillian for a ten mile drive as far as Norwood or Merton, stopping on the way back at the various pubs, the White Horse, the Horns and the Tankard in the Kennington Road.[1]

The author Thomas Burke described the interior of one of these popular wayside stops:

> When I was a boy, Camberwell, Kennington, Brixton and Stockwell were thick with music-hall artists, and on Sunday mornings they rallied upon a central point – the *White Horse* in Brixton Road – then the most completely Cockney public-house in London. In the lounge of that house you might see, at midday on a Sunday, most of those stars of the halls who were not on tour; a good quarter of the crowd to be seen in that well-known conglomerate picture of the music-hall profession, 'Popularity'. I myself, as a boy, sitting in a corner, arrayed with heartcake and lemonade saw most of the gods, and it was more than likely that Charles [Chaplin] and I, unknown to each other, sat there together. Some of them recur to me in image – George Lashwood, marvellously tailored. Dan Leno in his old gardening suit. George Chirgwin, Witty Watty Walton, one of the Poluskis, Phil Ray, Harry Ford, Tom Costello, Joe Elvin.[2]

Such harmony was always likely to be disturbed in an intensely competitive and Bohemian profession. Drink, as ever, took a heavy toll. Chaplin's own father, a highly popular 'comic and descriptive' singer, died of an alcohol-related illness at the age of 37. Fights, feuds and infidelities were commonplace, with an occasional suicide or murder providing a temporary talking point in the lounge bar of the White Horse. Probably, the most frequently discussed subject was unemployment, the

ever-present fear of being 'out of a shop'. Close to St John's Church stood
a gaudy pub and a row of dingy houses occupied by music-hall agents.
Here at the intersection of Waterloo Road and York Road, popularly or
unpopularly known as 'Poverty Corner', performers gathered to exchange information, to borrow money and to seek work. They represented a far less happy gathering than that depicted in 'Popularity', and
tempers were often at breaking point. In 1884 a Waterloo Road agent
named Wolf Goldstein was charged with assaulting his client Rose
Pritchard, known on the halls as 'Dashing' Eva Lester. Rose, a friend of
Chaplin's mother, was counter-summoned by her agent, but the case was
found in her favour.[3] Fifteen years later, Chaplin and his mother had a
chance meeting with the once exuberant star. She was ragged and desti-
tute, tormented by a gang of street urchins.[4]

A number of societies were set up within the profession to meet the
needs of the less well paid and those, like Rose, who had fallen on hard
times. Since 1867 the Music Hall Sick Fund Provident Society had provided an opportunity for performers to put money aside on a weekly
basis to provide benefits for periods of sickness. There was a poor take-
up, however, with the notoriously improvident nature of variety entertainers resulting in a membership that was never high. In 1888 the comedian Charles Coborn and the theatrical agent Richard Warner established the Music Hall Benevolent Fund, a charity that raised money by
an annual subscription and by public events such as the annual Music
Hall Sports. Two years later the Terriers Association was founded as a
friendly society, with the object of providing sickness benefits and funeral expenses to its members. Several less formal societies such as the 'J's',
the 'Stags' and the 'Water Rats' combined fund-raising with smoking
concerts, dinner dances, sporting occasions and, most popularly, outings.
It was a charitable alliance that demonstrated not only an insatiable
appetite for entertainment, but an impressive ability to protect its membership. In 1906 the Music Hall Artistes' Railway Association, an organisation co-founded by Dan, collaborated with the 'Water Rats' to form
the first music-hall trade union.

Such societies provided Dan with an outlet for his seemingly inex-
haustible energy and compulsively charitable inclinations. Perhaps the
insecurity of earlier times had created within him a need for reassurance
and approbation. An incessant quest for applause dominated public and
private life alike. Hickory Wood recalled:

> I can honestly say that I never saw him absolutely at rest. He was
> always doing something, and had something else to do afterwards;
> or he had just been somewhere, was going somewhere else, and had
> several other appointments to follow.[5]

In an attempt to elicit laughter Dan sometimes perpetrated cruel practical jokes, particularly on his long-suffering friend Herbert. Once, when
Herbert had purchased a new raincoat, Dan cut it into fragments which
he distributed to the cast at Drury Lane with the explanation that they
were 'a little souvenir, with Herbert Campbell's compliments'. On another occasion, knowing that it was Herbert's routine after a matinee to
return home for a rest prior to the evening performance, Dan attempted
to thwart his partner's plans by spinning out the duration of their scenes.
Despite such inconsiderate pranks the two comedians remained the
firmest of friends, with Dan naming his fifth child Herbert Dan.

Charity with Dan took two forms. There were many undisclosed acts
of kindness, performed when he was convinced that a genuine need existed. Then there were conspicuous displays of generosity in which he played
the part of a public benefactor, scattering coins to boys in the street and
handing out 'small considerations' to the scroungers who shadowed his
every movement. But there were times when even he felt the need to re-
strict his largesse. Hickory Wood remembered an unusual first meeting
when the comedian leapt from the front seat of his brougham and made a
frantic dive through the Drury Lane stage door. Well used to the impor-
tuning gauntlet that Dan ran every day, the stage-door keeper observed:
'He's that soft-hearted that three minutes among the crowd outside
there would cost him over a tenner.'[6]

The comedian Arthur Roberts recalled a Fagin-like character who organised a gang of 'touts, cadgers and beggars' to 'tap' well known performers. On one occasion Roberts, with fellow actors Teddy Payne and
Lionel Brough, was on his way to the Bun House, a popular resort of
theatrical folk in the Strand, when they were intercepted by a frantic
Dan who explained that a group of 'ear-biters' were awaiting them at the
pub. The quartet of comedians crossed the road and took refuge in the
bar of the Adelphi Hotel. Their change of plan proved too late, for within
a few minutes they were joined by a shabby, but expectant-looking
stranger. 'How are you, Mr Leno?' inquired the newcomer. 'I'm delighted to see you in such good health. I'm afraid you don't remember me,
but we were last together on the bill at Newcastle.' Over a drink, purchased, of course, by Dan, the stranger explained that the fate of his
starving wife and family lay in the comedian's hands. All he needed was
the price of a railway ticket to the North of England, where he had somehow managed to secure a well-paid engagement. It was a familiar and
unimaginative tale, but Dan handed over the requested amount. Minutes later he discovered his supposed ex-colleague splitting the 'loan'
with the cadger king who had supplied him with the necessary background information.[7]

Dan's generosity with time and money did not extend to his professional material, which he guarded zealously. To appreciate his loathing

of those who were suspected of appropriating aspects of his stage routine
it is necessary to understand his approach to his act. It was a complex
process, initially reliant on a framework represented by make-up, costume and an array of gestures, steps and facial expressions that he had
developed over many years. He was understandably anxious to protect
the building blocks of his performance, often accusing fellow artists of
plagiarism. Early in 1888 he publicly warned Tom Costello about stealing 'gags' and make-up for a Manchester pantomime appearance,[8] while
another famous comedian, George Robey, was rebuked from the stage of
the Tivoli Music Hall. Harry Randall witnessed Dan's rage:

> At the risk of fluttering dovecotes, I may say that the thick, black,
> arched eyebrows, usually associated with George Robey, were ori-
> ginally the stock-in-trade of Dan. So were the large, square-toed
> shoes and Dan's characteristic entrance on the music-halls: a
> quick run down to the footlights, a roll like a drum with his feet,
> his leg raised, and brought down with a loud clap from the foot.

> I well remember one Saturday afternoon at the Tivoli. I was
> standing at the back of the circle watching the show, and George
> Robey came on and did the Leno rattle and finish before com-
> mencing his song. A few turns later Dan Leno's number went up,
> and when he came on, I could see he was somewhat excited. He
> came down to the front as usual, gave his roll and flap, then
> stopped dead, and he did it once again. 'You see that?' he said to
> the audience, 'you saw something *like* that a little while ago – but
> it's *mine!*' I saw his eyes blaze. The audience unmistakably let him
> know that they had seen it, too.[9]

Having prepared the outward appearance of the character Dan gradually developed a credible personality on stage, adding and adjusting
words and actions until he was totally satisfied with the results. He explained:

> The continual thinking out of ideas is, as may be imagined, trying
> work. I could not do it if I did not love my profession, and unless a
> man loves his profession he cannot get on in it. Some people, too,
> work out their ideas in bed. I never do that. But what a nightmare
> I have sometimes when a new song has been a failure. I am think-
> ing of it all night, wondering what was wrong, and going over it
> again and again, until I have thought of something which will put
> it right. It is very trying sometimes, too, when I produce a new
> sketch with some good 'gags' in it, and the next morning some
> paper comes out with them all, and they are all at once stale.

It is curious how ideas sometimes suggest themselves. More often than not you will come across them while you are performing. The first night of a new turn is generally the time when the new ideas come. A situation presents itself, you will see an opportunity, take it, the audience is appreciative, and there you have a new 'gag' for future performances. I myself have almost come to count upon these first-night ideas now.[10]

20 'The Recruiting Sergeant', 1893

Although new characterisations were invariably well observed they remained only clever studies awaiting a vital infusion of life. At this stage many performers would have considered their work complete. Chevalier, for instance, gave an immaculately acted performance, but one that was sometimes criticised as being stilted and mechanical. Dan, however, needed to reach a point of consensus with his audience. 'A new performance by Dan Leno,' wrote Max Beerbohm, 'was almost always a dull thing in itself ... he was unable to do himself justice until he had, as it were, collaborated for many nights with the public.'[11] A combination of experience and empathy made him an adept judge of audience reaction, able to draw guidance from a ripple of applause, a burst of laughter or an ominous silence. His most successful numbers may have originated with several pages of text, but they were 'dished up', as he put it, on stage.

The traditional verses of the comic song were often replaced by long passages of patter, during which he could more easily monitor his public. It was no accident that his audiences were frequently provided with an honorary role within the song; becoming the proletarian rabble harangued by the orator in 'The Midnight March', the passengers waiting on the platform in 'The Railway Guard' or the band of tourists following an old Beefeater in 'The Tower of London'. In 'Clever Mr Green' the audience were cast as electors answering rhetorical questions posed to them by a self-important town councillor:

> Who was it suggested we have a mad house? Green! Who was it
> suggested we have a work house? Green! Who was it suggested
> we have a prison? Green! And who was the first man in it? Green,
> no, I mean Brown!'

His act was such a fusion of intuition and invention that it was not surprising that he took exception to unauthorised borrowing. Other performers adopting or adapting his stage business demonstrated a lack of respect for Dan and his audience and, even worse, appeared to have little understanding of the unity and balance required for his comedy.

When it came to seeing himself and his creations represented on stage Dan was less bothered by performers who imitated his act, although the repetition of his jokes was a continual source of irritation. The impersonator Bransby Williams was a personal friend, and when he first offered his version of 'Mr Dan Leno' at the London Pavilion, Dan and Herbert were present in the audience to heckle and pelt him with chocolates.[12] A less gifted mimic was treated with generosity when Dan encountered him at a seaside concert-hall. Spotting the great comedian the performer bravely announced 'I will now give my celebrated imitation of a gentleman who is at the moment among the audience – Mr Dan Leno!' After witnessing a drawn-out performance Dan eventually visited the entertainer in his dressing room, and presented his imitator with half a sovereign, explaining: 'This isn't for your talent; it's for your confounded cheek.'[13]

By the 1890s Dan was widely acknowledged to be one of the greatest 'low' comedians of the century. He had become the latest in a distinguished lineage of performers who had challenged their audience's emotional response by moving effortlessly between merriment and pathos. As such he was often compared to actors such as John Sleeper Clarke (1833–99), an American who had achieved long-term fame in England, Jimmy Rogers (1821–63), the original Widow Twankey, and the evergreen comedian and club-land hero J.L. Toole (1830–1906). It was a great compliment, but also an onerous responsibility when his efforts were likely to be ranked against performances deeply embedded in the collective theatrical memory. Of all past performers Dan had most in common with Frederick Robson (1821–64), a slightly-built, galvanic cockney comedian whose career as an actor and singer was cut short, like Dan's, at the age of 43. 'The Great Little Robson' was 'haunted by an idea that there was some delusion in his success and that his fall would be as sudden and marked as his rise'.[14] Sharing first-night nerves with Dan, he succumbed to overwork and a reliance on brandy and water.

In his 1899 introduction to *Dan Leno: Hys Booke*, the dramatic critic Clement Scott referred to the comedian's remarkable relationship with his audience:

> The comedian who laughs at his own jokes soon becomes wearisome, but it is Dan Leno's astonished face when he looks at the laughing audience that gives him his power. In brief, a most admirable, versatile, persuasive, volatile, and intense comedian and artist. Whenever he is on the stage, be it theatre or music-hall, he literally holds his audience tight in his power. They cannot get away from him. He is monarch of all he surveys.[15]

On one occasion Dan's grasp on a member of his audience was too intense. In November 1897 a woman in the gallery of the Empire Music Hall, Birmingham, laughed so much during his turn that she had an apoplectic fit, dying before a doctor from the audience could be of any assistance.[16]

Few critics had a negative comment to make about his performances, but those that did caused considerable annoyance. His vociferously expressed indignation at what he considered to be unfair remarks in the reviews forwarded to him by a cuttings agency provoked Herbert to comment 'Serves you right for buying a guinea's worth of trouble.'[17] Towards the end of his career Dan became weighed down by public

acclaim and expectation. His sense of oneness with the audience sometimes seemed on the verge of breaking. Hickory Wood remembered:

> He had peculiar views on the subject of his own popularity, and I
> well remember him, on the afternoon of a certain Boxing Day,
> some three hours before performance, turning to me, with a most
> doleful expression on his countenance, and gloomily remarking,
> 'Nobody cares for me – nobody!'

> In reply I ventured to point out to him (as actually happened
> afterwards) that his appearance on the stage that evening would
> be the signal for such a shout of welcome only one other actor
> could awake within the walls of Drury Lane theatre.

> He merely remarked, in the same pessimistic tone – 'Yes; but
> that's not for *me*! It's for what I've done!'[18]

Dan's widespread popularity within his own profession was recognised in
1891 when he was elected 'King Rat'. He might well have been titled
'King Magpie' had it not been for a sudden shower of rain that brought a
premature end to a music-hall jaunt. The comedian Joe Elvin had acquired a lively pony in the North of England, reportedly transporting it
back to London in a first-class railway carriage. Named Magpie, after a
riverside pub frequented by music-hall folk, the pony was stabled in
Kennington, from whence it sallied forth to participate in trotting races
along the streets of South-East London. Despite police objections to
horse-drawn traps racing on public roads, a small syndicate was set up to
maintain the pony and share any winnings that might accrue. Magpie
was baptised with a new name during a thunderstorm when the driver of
a passing omnibus suggested that it looked more like 'a bloody water
rat'. It was a chance comment that became commemorated in the foun-
dation of 'The Pals of the Water Rat' in 1889. A year later the society's
original membership of 12 was doubled, with the objective of promoting
the causes of 'Philanthropy and Conviviality'. Harry Freeman, a comedian, was chosen as first 'King Rat', followed by Dan the next year.
Dan was re-elected in 1892 and again in 1897.

Dan revelled in and at the outings organised by the 'Rats'. Harry
Randall remembered him standing at the side of a steam launch, enthusiastically relating 'one of his funny yarns'. To everybody's consterna-
tion he overbalanced and fell into the river. Fred Griffiths threw off his
coat and dived after him, and seeing the incident several small boats
were launched from the bank. At the moment of rescue Dan and Fred
shook hands, kissed each other and sang the Water Rat's anthem:

This is the emblem of our Society
Each member acts with the greatest propriety.
Jolly old sports, to us they raise their hats,
A jolly lot of fellows are the Water Rats.
Rats! Rats! Rats![19]

It was, of course, a pre-arranged stunt, the sort of prank that was repeated many times in the ensuing years. During its early existence 'The Grand Order of Water Rats' met every Sunday evening in a room above the White Horse, a short distance from Dan's Brixton home.

Although an active 'Rat' Dan also worked hard to raise funds for the Music Hall Benevolent Fund, taking over the presidency on the death of Sir Augustus Harris. His contributions were usually of an extremely physical nature, the Music Hall Sports providing him with a huge arena, a massive audience and a 'turn' that extended over the whole day. Of all his activities on behalf of the profession the most influential was the setting-up of the Music Hall Artistes' Railway Association in 1897. Co-founded by Dan, C. Douglas Stuart (editor of the music-hall journal *The Encore*) and by black-face performer Eugene Stratton, the association negotiated cheaper rates of travel on trains and steamboats for groups of performers, also providing insurance against accident and loss of luggage. The M.H.A.R.A. offered free medical assistance and legal advice, and, increasingly, concerned itself with improving performers' working conditions. By 1906 over 7,000 music-hall artists were registered as members.

Popularity was often attended by prejudice during the 1890s. Although the heir to the throne regularly attended music halls, variety performers were not usually considered to be members of 'respectable' society. Actors were a step or two higher on the social ladder, but it was not until 1895 that the most eminent member of the profession, Henry Irving, was considered for a knighthood. Much to Irving's chagrin, an occasional bit-part actor had been honoured four years earlier, 'Druriolanus' receiving his knighthood for organising a reception to greet the visiting emperor of Germany.

While looking for a club in which to relax when appearing at Drury Lane, Dan received a hurtful rebuff. He had been proposed by H. Chance Newton for membership of the Yorick Club, in Covent Garden. Although the club had been established for 'gentlemen connected with Literature, the Drama, Music and the Arts', Dan was considered ineligible on the grounds that he was a music-hall performer. After Chance Newton complained that the club's president, the actor-manager Edward Terry, had himself appeared on the halls, the committee reversed their decision, but by then Dan had already decided that he no longer wished to join a club which would only reluctantly accept him as a member.[20] Another organ-

isation that excluded variety performers was the Drury Lane Theatrical
Fund, a form of pension scheme that was available to any actor or actress who had appeared at the theatre over three consecutive years. It is
unclear whether the fund was available to the ladies of the chorus, who
frequently gave their occupation as actress when arrested on charges of
prostitution.

21 Dan Leno takes a bath

Whenever he appeared in the provinces Dan attempted to recreate
the convivial atmosphere of Brixton and Lambeth by organising entertainments and excursions. In 1897 the young Bransby Williams was engaged at the Palace Music Hall, Sunderland, where he encountered Dan's
father-in-law 'a pompous chap [who] chucked his aitches about and was
a sort of old Malaprop'. Dan, who was playing in nearby Newcastle, arranged a day trip that skilfully circumvented the local licensing restric-
tions on Sunday drinking. Williams recalled:

> It was then arranged we should go out to the coast and visit the
> Pirate's Caves at Roker on the Sunday and that we would have a
> large brake and three horses. The day arrived. It was very misty
> and looked like being a failure, but Dan said, 'No, we'll go.' Sev-
> eral members of the Palace company joined us; one I remember
> was jolly Peggy Pryde, the daughter of the famous Jenny Hill.
> Slowly we started in the mist. About two streets away Dan cried

'Stop here.' He said: 'Now, we are travellers, see? No one knows how far we've come,' so into the 'public' we trooped and Dan ordered warm port and lemon. Back to the brake, and a short distance and the travellers once more imbibed warm port. I took plain lemonade like the good youth that I was. After repeating the stop quite half a dozen times I was feeling like a gassy balloon.

Eventually we arrived and explored the caves. It was cold and dreary, but Dan kept us merry and found where we could all have tea. We were all tired and drowsy and did a non-stop back to Sunderland. Then I thought I might be able to do the grand and asked them all in to a meal and in they trooped. The manageress recognised Dan and said all she could offer was a fine gammon rasher each and two poached eggs. It was a jolly meal, and when cleared away we were shown to the coffee-room, where three old 'commercials' were spending the evening. Dan was indeed welcomed, and now he became the host and refreshments were ordered for all, and Dan started telling stories of the old days and made us all very merry. Those commercials joined in and each time enjoyed Dan's drinks and cigars. The greatest comic of the day was their generous host.

Even amid such convivial scenes Dan was to discover that national popularity provided little protection against personal slight:

When it got rather late and we thought of separating, one of the commercials, instead of thanking Dan, reminded him that we were all intruders in their 'commercial room'. Dan looked daggers at them. Then, taking a golden sovereign, he put it in the Commercial Traveller's Box for orphans and said: 'Well, the poor kiddies can't help it. Goodnight, gentlemen', and with that walked out and we followed, leaving the commercials to their own room.[21]

14

REGIME CHANGE IN DRURY LANE

Like the hero of his 1894 pantomime Augustus Harris performed a sudden about-turn. For *Dick Whittington and his Cat* he reduced the number of music-hall performers and curtailed the imposing but time-consuming processions. A stronger narrative was provided by playwrights Cecil Raleigh and Henry Hamilton, with Dan as Idle Jack and Herbert as Eliza the Cook given more coherent roles in the development of the plot. Although still not allowed to describe themselves as actors, the two comedians were increasingly expected to speak the lines allocated to them and to follow stage directions.

Despite this tighter control Dan and Herbert were still called upon to improvise, particularly when things were going wrong. On Boxing Night there were several delays in changing scenery, the worst causing one scene to be extended to such an extent that the audience became impatient even with their favourite comedians. A little later in the run an accident involving a genuine baked-potato barrow brought unexpected humour to one of Dan and Herbert's scenes. The authenticity of the street trader's cart was confirmed by a cloud of grey ash that enveloped the two partners, an effect that was so amusing to the audience that it was immediately written into the script. In the same way, casual ad-libs were carefully noted down for repeated use. It was obvious to many that Dan and Herbert were under greater constraints than before. *Punch* reported:

> On former occasions it has been said (by the dyspeptic and consequently disappointed) that 'the turns of the halls' have been too numerous. Those excellent comedians Messrs DAN LENO and HERBERT CAMPBELL have sometimes been a little too much in evidence to suit every taste. In 1894–95 they have plenty to do, but only enough to satisfy the most fastidious.[1]

A new approach was also detected by *The Sketch*:

The truth is that 'Dick Whittington' shows a change of policy. For some time Drury Lane pantomime has been on the wrong track, and 'Robinson Crusoe' showed the limit of the error. Doubtless, the uncharitable will suggest that Sir Augustus Harris is indebted to Mr Oscar Barrett and the Lyceum pantomime for showing him the true path. There may be some truth in this, but all the greater, then, the credit due to Sir Druriolanus for seeing the error of his ways and 'reforming it altogether'.[2]

Harris's reforms did not extend to the customary allusions to chronic drunkenness. On arriving at Highgate Church for his wedding Idle Jack gave a sozzled soliloquy, detailing the after effects of a wild stag night:

> At last this is my happy wedding morn,
> And I've had to put my hat on with a shoe-horn,
> And I'm to be Queen of the May, mother, I'm to be Queen of
> the May,
> The May, the might, the shall, the will love, honour and obey;
> That simile is rather mixed, I think,
> And so I rather think was last night's drink.
> Somehow this morning I can't think a thunk.
> Was pa-as-is-to-be also as drunk?

Meeting an old man Dan broke into an impersonation of R.G. Knowles, 'The Very Peculiar American' whose fast-talking, wise-cracking act had introduced a new kind of comedy to the British music hall. Dan's impression of his friend Knowles was a surprising and confusing break with the rhyming couplets so much associated with traditional pantomime:

> JACK: I say, are you the Sexton?
> OLD MAN: No, Sir, I'm the Verger.
> JACK: Where do you verge? I mean, look here – you know – I'm going to be married. [Drops into an imitation of R. G. Knowles] and my wife – that is, my wife that is to be – is rather late. I don't think she can have forgotten altogether, though it may have slipped her memory, till she took the cake – that is, the wedding-that-is-to-be-cake – with the milk. I don't mean the cake is going to marry the milk; but she took the cake and the milk for the wedding. I don't mean she mistook them – the cake and the milk, for a wedding – but being a Miss she took the cake and the milk in the morning. I don't mean the Miss took the cake and the milk mixed …

22 'My Sweet Face', 1894

When Dick's explanation had finally run its confusing course the Verger had his opportunity to make a simple request: 'I'm a little 'ard o' 'earing, Sir. Would you mind saying all that once over again?'

The Sexton's pay-off line was doubly amusing, for even with better hearing he, like the majority of the audience, would have struggled to make sense of Dan's impression of the American comedian. Off-stage Dan probably shared some interesting conversations with the veteran actor, for he was none other than Joe Cave, the banjo-playing proprietor of the Cosmotheca Music Hall.

The future was looking bright for Harris. He had taken a new lease on the Theatre Royal, which he had extensively refurbished. For the 1895/ 96 production, *Cinderella*, Harris found yet another way of amazing his ever-anticipatory audience. To the usual elaborate set pieces and beauti- fully designed scenery he added the wonders of electrical technology. The *Penny Illustrated Paper* eulogised the brilliantly lit production:

> The most notable novelty in the pantomime will be the very im- portant part electricity plays both as an illumination and as a motor in this most graceful and resplendent version of 'Cinderella' ... The gorgeous carriage in which Cinderella proceeds to the ball, though it makes the story very *fin de siècle* as a materialistic mat- ter of date, exemplifies in a conspicuous manner the wonders which Science, the veritable Fairy Godmother of today, showers upon us. Resplendent with hundreds of electric lamps, this auto- motor masterpiece wheels itself on to the stage without the aid of the tiny steeds of yore ... A specimen of the new colour-music is a welcome novelty. On a large wheel of electric lights will be thrown the colour harmonies which are the equivalents of the chords struck on a grand piano.[3]

Harris was well aware of a wide range of contemporary scientific de- velopments that had the potential to change the very nature of popular entertainment. The telephone link that enabled him to listen to perform- ances of *Robinson Crusoe* while sick at home, was almost certainly pro- vided by the Electrophone Company, an organisation that transmitted live shows and concerts to a network of subscribers. When the Prince of Wales installed an Electrophone in his rooms at Marlborough House in 1898, he was reported to have had the choice of listening to grand opera from Covent Garden or musical comedies from venues such as the Gaiety, the Shaftesbury, Daly's, the Prince of Wales and the Vaude- villle.[4] Dan himself had been included in a programme of entertainment relayed from Her Majesty's Theatre, Haymarket, to Windsor Castle to celebrate Queen Victoria's 80th birthday, although it is not known whether the elderly monarch listened to his contribution.[5]

Another marvel of technology, sound recording, had been introduced to England during the late 1880s. The American inventor Thomas Edison had refined his original primitive phonograph to produce a new 'improved' model which recorded onto cylinders made of durable wax rather than ephemeral tinfoil. Harris was invited to a private dinner party hosted by Edison's British agent, Colonel Gouraud, in October 1888, where recordings were made by distinguished guests, including the musician Sir Arthur Sullivan. No recording by Harris survives, but a cylinder held in the Edison Archive preserves the voice of Gouraud introducing 'Druriolanus' and explaining that his production of *The Armada* had 'eclipsed all of his previous brilliant efforts'. During the 1890s Edison struggled to enforce his patents and to protect the integrity of his invention, which he intended should be used as a means of preserving the voices of eminent personages. But entrepreneurs soon saw a different use for the phonograph, offering audiences a chance to listen to comic songs and band music at fairs and amusement arcades throughout Britain.

Edison's other great invention, motion pictures, followed a similar course of exploitation. Initially it was only possible to view the short films in the Kinetoscope peepshow machine. However, within a few months of its first exhibition in London, in October 1894, the Kinetoscope was copied by a number of British showmen, causing Edison to retaliate by cutting off the supply of American-made films. British inventors quickly produced their own movie cameras, filming several subjects, including variety acts, as early as the spring of 1895. Within a few months the Lumière brothers had developed the Cinématographe, a device that not only photographed motion pictures but also projected them onto a screen. After watching one of the first Cinématographe shows in Paris in January 1896, Harris became impressed by the entertainment possibilities of the new medium. A British inventor, R.W. Paul, was located and on 21 March 1896 Harris promoted one of the first commercial film exhibitions in Britain, charging the public sixpence to view 'Theatrograph' pictures at the Palmarium Hall, at Olympia in West London.[6]

It was to take a decade before film established itself as an independent form of entertainment. In the meantime motion pictures were shown as a 'turn' at music halls, as a dramatic device in plays and pantomimes and in 'penny gaff' shop theatres. In an attempt to integrate the new medium with pre-exiting entertainments, film makers often sought out stage celebrities to provide a celluloid endorsement. One of the first stars to appear on film was Johnny Danvers, photographed in Hastings, Sussex, on 1 July 1897. The Warwick Trading Company catalogue described the short film as: 'showing an audience leaving the Pier Pavilion, following Messrs. Danvers and Schofield, of the Mohawk Minstrels, who, in full costume, amuse the surrounding crowd by cutting many funny capers'.[7] Johnny's appearance was an isolated occurrence, but Dan was later to be seen in several films. He was also to embrace the new recording industry, making a considerable number of disc recordings for the Gramophone and Typewriter Company.

23   Dan Leno and Herbert Campbell in *Cinderella*, 1895

In the pantomime *Cinderella* Dan and Herbert were cast as the Baroness and Baron, with Isa Bowman, a one-time child friend of Lewis Carroll, playing the title role at a week's notice. Harris explained his initial approach to planning the pantomime:

> Having chosen the story (you've no idea of the importance of that task), I then set to work to invent a novel opening scene. Last year it was the 'cat camp'; this year it's 'Toyland'; next year it will be — well, if I tell you now it will be stale before next Christmas, won't it? Then, after the opening scene, I decide upon the following ones, always keeping the story in my mind, of course, but always on the look out for fresh ideas, new effects, striking novelties — anything, in fact, which will make the pantomime seem better than its predecessor.[8]

Writers Cecil Raleigh and Arthur Sturgess provided Herbert and Dan with pithy dialogue packed with jokes:

> BARON: (With fear again) Well, my love — you know, after all you were a barmaid.
> BARONESS: That's right. Throw the bar in my face. And what if I was a barmaid? I flatter myself there were few like me.
> BARON: None, my dear, none.
> BARONESS: People used to come from miles around to see me. Why, I made the name of the place.
> BARON: So you did — my dear — so you did. It got the name of the 'Old Curiosity Shop'.
> BARONESS: Oh, indeed! Then if I was a curiosity, why did you marry me?
> BARON: I was led to believe you had charge of the till.

Dan had one scene that ideally suited his visual humour. The Baron and Baroness were attempting to gate-crash the Prince's ball, and Herbert tried to slip past the doorman without being noticed, not easy for someone of his stature, while Dan attempted to reproduce the ingenious stratagem of the Muffin Man's rival, by walking in backward as if he was coming out. After Dandini, played by Alexandra Dagmar, had intervened on their behalf, Dan became less sure than he actually wanted to join the ball. With exclamations of 'Now I'm in, see?' and 'Now I'm out! Eh?' he tormented the flunkey, flouncing back and forth across the palace portal.[9]

On 22 June 1896 the theatrical world was stunned by the death of Sir Augustus Harris. His career could not have been fuller or more varied. He had rescued the 'National Theatre' at a time of crisis, resurrected

grand opera in Britain, stage-managed countless melodramas and pantomimes, and presided over the birth of the British film industry. He had
been an actor, a playwright, and a journalist with a weekly column in
The Sunday Times, a periodical that he also owned. All forms of popular
entertainment attracted him, and he was at times owner or co-owner of
the Palace Theatre of Varieties, the Empire Music Hall, Covent Garden
Theatre and the massive Olympia exhibition complex. As an enthusiastic freemason he had founded the Drury Lane Lodge, constructing a
temple within the Theatre Royal. He was a Sheriff of the City of London,
an elected London County Council member, President of the Variety
Artistes' Benevolent Fund and a tireless worker on behalf of several different charities. On taking over Drury Lane in 1879 he had a personal
fortune of £3.15s., which by the time of his death, at the age of 44, had
grown to £23,677.

Harris had put his life and soul into Drury Lane, involving himself
with every aspect of production. He was a hard taskmaster, but a generous employer. At five a.m. one Christmas Eve rehearsals had dragged on
for so long that Dan was discovered sprawled on the floor of the theatre,
trying to write a cheque for £3,000 to offer Harris to allow him to break
his engagement.[10] On another occasion Harris arrived at the theatre
flourishing a purse of coins:

> 'I have just come from the mint,' said Augustus one night, 'and
> here's some new money for luck, Dan: one for you. And one for the
> wife and – how many children have you?'
> 'Five.'
> 'One – two – three – four – five.'
> 'But,' said Dan, 'there's another on the road.'
> 'Oh,' said Harris, 'you're a terrible man!'
> 'Well, Sir Augustus,' quickly retorted Leno, 'I don't smoke.'[11]

If Druriolanus's ghost had joined the other wraiths that reputedly haunted the ancient fabric of Drury Lane, it would have been severely vexed
by the executor's choice of Oscar Barrett to produce the next year's
pantomime, *Aladdin*. His old rival collaborated with writers Arthur Sturgess and Horace Lennard to create a pantomime which was politely received, but generally considered to lack the Theatre Royal's usual gusto.
One aspect of the pantomime that would have pleased Harris was Dan's
portrayal of the washerwoman Widow Twankey. Ostensibly Chinese,
with silk jacket and tightly drawn top knot, Aladdin's mother was clearly a home-grown laundry lady, a close relative to his other dowdy, but
indomitable female creations. Dan had several scenes which were remembered long after the production. When confronted in her humble
kitchen by the Slave of the Lamp, played by music hall's greatest jug-

gler, Paul Cinquevalli, the widow looked on in amazement as the genii performed one incredible feat after another. On this occasion Cinquevalli, who was renowned for juggling cannon balls, limited himself to a Cockney delicacy, the humble saveloy. Netheretheless, the tricks he was able to perform with the spicy, red sausage were sufficiently spellbinding to reduce the usually garrulous widow to the repeated conclusion 'Yes, it is so! That's a saveloy right enough.'

When not amazed by the aerial gyrations of a sausage, the long-suffering widow was philosophical about her situation:

> Oh dear! What is it about washing that makes people so bad-tempered? I'm sorry I ever adopted it as a profession. But there when Mustapha left me to battle with an untrusting world what could I do? I tried lady barbering, but the customers were too attentive and I – poor simple child – was full of unsophisticated-ness and I believed their honeyed words. I remember young Lord Plumpler agitated me so much with his badinage that there was a slight accident. I believe he would have proposed to me, but in my confusion I cut the end of his nose off. Ah! It was a near shave … Then I had an idea. All society ladies were learning to be useful in dressmaking, millinery, painting and journalism. So I founded this select laundry for the daughters of decayed noblemen. It was alright at first, but I soon found that as my pupils left me, my trade decreased – every lady became her own laundress. Never mind; the weather forecast says it will rain in Brixton, so there may be a storm in Hackney. Then, if it rains, we shall have water and business will look up.

Just as it seemed that Barrett would gain control of Drury Lane, Harris's long-serving stage manager Arthur Collins managed to scrape together a £1,000 deposit to exercise his pre-existing option on the lease. More methodical and pragmatic than his old employer, Collins saw little reason to alter the theatre's overall policy. But there were a few adjustments to be made, the most fundamental of which was to alter the way in which Drury Lane utilised its most famous comedian. In future Dan's roles were to be even more closely scripted, carefully arranged to enhance what Collins considered to be his strongest qualities. For his part Dan was reluctant to change, uneasy to entrust even a portion of his future success to another's hands.

There is no doubt, however, that Dan's most memorable successes occurred under Collins's shrewd guidance. During a period of low inflation his original £28 weekly salary had grown to £80 when Collins took over the theatre. A few years later Dan was to be paid £240 a week by the grateful management. As Widow Twankey he had caused much amusement by shovelling gold sovereigns from a fireside scuttle. If Dan had adopted a similar approach to his own finances he would have had to extend his banking arrangements into the coal cellar or the outside bunker.

24 Dan Leno as 'Widow Twankey', 1896

15

THE FUNNIEST MAN ON EARTH

There is a story that during a period of mental confusion Dan was found queuing for one of his own shows. There is little doubt that he would have welcomed the opportunity of seeing himself from an audience's point of view, just as he liked to study fellow comedians from 'out front'. He was preoccupied with staying one step ahead of competitors, always concerned that the public would turn against him at the drop of a battered top hat:

> The penalty of such a position as mine is that I must be continual-ly thinking of and working out new ideas. In the old days folks did not specialise as they do now. At present [1901], when there are five or six good men each working the same kind of turn as myself, it is difficult work keeping the place the public has given me.'[1]

Dan's conservative estimation of his opposition must have been based on his own exacting standards, for the previous decade had seen a flowering of music hall talent.

Writing and composing had also reached new heights, although most songs belonged to a few, predictable stereotypes. There were dramatic songs about heroic acts and sentimental attachments; black-face songs evoking an idealised deep South; 'coster' songs about the life and loves of London's street traders; songs about 'Stage Door Johnnies' out on a spree; and songs about knowing young women well practised in the art of winking the other eye. Despite the familiarity of such themes the best songs were elevated from the commonplace by a rich use of vernacular language, by a pervasive sense of irony and by the interpretation of per-formers who were adept at adding meaning by phrasing and gesture.

Dan could easily have remained within the boundaries of the con-ventional music-hall song, but from an early stage of his career he had decided to emphasise the spoken word with long passages of patter that enabled him to create detailed descriptions and characterisations. Such characterisations, although rambling and absurd, were varied and essen-tially realistic. One of his main writers, J. Hickory Wood, wrote of him:

In each and every song he sang he played a separate and clearly defined part. He was never merely Dan Leno singing a song: but in make-up, gesture, and general demeanour, he was a consistent, if exaggerated type of character.[2]

Having depicted various ludicrous royal and aristocratic personages at Drury Lane, Dan began to introduce music-hall songs which ridiculed figures of authority. Two of the first, 'The Doctor' and 'The Recruiting Sergeant', appeared in 1893. It was hard to decide who was more life-threatening. Dr McFabback announced himself to be 'a most important member of the medical profession, with a practice that's esteem'd for many miles', but listening to his account of his activities it seemed that he was in danger of losing many of his patients:

> ... if my medicine's weak, my fees are strong, so that makes up for it. Bless your lives, there's no one so popular as the Doctor, and, though I say it myself, I may not have cured many, but I've killed thousands ... Oh! I never let a patient go once I get him. I've one old gentleman I've been attending for years. He'll never get any better (not so long as I attend him), and he has no idea what's the matter with him (and I'm certain I haven't). But he's very nervous so I generally walk behind him and drop my stick. See the idea? That jars his nerves (one pound eight, bottle of Nerve Mixture, three and three ...)

A visual counterpart to the Doctor's display of self-esteem was supplied by a long beard, a sign of gravitas on such eminent Victorians as Dickens or Tennyson, but on McFabback's chin, an undignified and animalistic tangle:

> Now, in the case of a lady, you must be careful in drawing a tooth, because you might dislocate the jaw – that's the lady's only weapon. I simply throw the whiskers over the lady's face; you see there's a kind of ozone on the whiskers that seems to soothe 'em, and before they know where they are, out comes the tooth.

Sergeant Smirks' principal stage prop was a cane with which he deftly demonstrated his skills as a swordsman. In an attempt to convey the thrills of soldiering he would thwack the stick against his thigh, repeating the stirring mantra 'And what a life! Oh, my word! Splendid life!' After somehow acquiring a chestful of medals Smirks had been let loose on the streets of London with orders to hang around pubs in search of lads ready to enlist in the army. He expounded on the ferocious battles in which he had participated: 'slashing, smashing, bashing, beer-eating'.

The greatest test of his sangfroid had occurred when the Colonel rushed into the canteen, declaring: 'Boys, there's no water'. Despite the severity of the situation Smirks remained calm. 'There,' he answered 'we shall have to drink it raw.'

When not poking fun at establishment figures, Dan often turned to that fertile source of gossip and aggravation, the family. The extended Galvin clan, and their convoluted relationship with the Danvers, was echoed in 'My Wife's Relations' (1901):

> And – er – during that time, our stepfather had married a third mother, and he'd pre-deceased also our second mother. So my brother met our third mother, fell in love with her and married her. Well now, that's where the trouble commenced. Because, you see, that made me my brother's son, and my sister-in-law was really my mother. Well now then, follow me closely, will you? There was an aunt by marriage – she had an adopted daughter. Left to her for rent, or something. And – er – the – this daughter fell in love with who built the house where my second mother lives. You see where we're getting to? Well now then, keep close to me, will you? This is rather intricate. You see the uncle – oh! oh, no, no, I'm wrong! I'm wrong!! I – no – yes – that's right! Oh, and, er – and there was a postman in it as well.

Much of Dan's material reflected his own early life. The search for cheap lodgings, so crucial when the family were touring, became central to several songs. Room had been at such a premium for the Lenos that they had put young George to bed in the 'second or third row of a chest of drawers'.[3] Later, when arriving at a new town, Will would request the boarding-house keeper to supply 'a room for myself and wife, and any old corner you may have where we can put the boy.' It appears that Mr Girking in 'Never More' (1890) was in need of several corners and a high-rise chest of drawers to accommodate his many offspring:

> You know a family like mine is no joke – eight children and two boys, and the wife she's very much larger than I am; not that I want to say anything about her. 'Cos whatever my wife *is*, she is my wife, oh yes, she's my wife! Then we looked for apartments, and got some. The landlady said, 'Is this all one family?' I said 'Yes.' 'What name?' she asked. '*Girking*' I replied; 'these are the little girkings, and I'm the cucumber.' They were very nice rooms – there was bed, bath, sitting and drawing room combined. It was very handy, 'cos if you wanted to go out of the sitting-room into the bed-room you stayed where you was. But I don't think it was

healthy, as I caught a nasty attack of whisky, and two of the children was laid up with the scarlet runner; so I said to myself:

Never more, never more
Will I be seen on the golden shore,
Dabbling my tootsies in the briny foam,
The next time I wash 'em
I'll wash 'em at home.

25 'The Grass Widower', 1891

Most of Dan's family songs concerned marriage. His relationship with Lydia appears to have been a happy one, unlike Johnny and Clara Jane who were divorced in 1894 because of her drunkenness and adultery with a public-house manager.[4] It is possible that Dan occasionally succumbed to temptation. He had a generous and engaging personality, and was a leading figure in a profession overpopulated with attractive woman seeking to further their careers. Details of this area of Dan's life are not available, but Harry Furniss recollected a backstage altercation between two of his 'lady friends':

> While I stood in the wings sketching the scene, Dan, or rather the Widow Twankey, had a few minutes off the stage. The time that should have been spent resting was devoted to a highly exciting altercation, of which Dan Leno was the subject, between two very overdressed ladies who had been permitted access to him. They were jointly, and severally, asserting their claims to the actor; attacking each other, and also poor Dan, in that determination to establish their ascendancy.

> Comic though the scene was – and I could not help being amused at the two over-dressed females, and between them the comedian in Widow Twankey's weeds, with pantomime cheek and red nose (a Widow Twankey as a Don Juan-cum-gay-Lothario!) – there was also the tragic side of the picture. For the unfortunate comedian's efforts were all concentrated in a frantic desire to prevent his wife, seated in a box close to the proscenium, from witnessing the incident. Surely it would be impossible to imagine a scene of more extravagant incongruity.[5]

In 'All Through a Little Piece of Bacon' (1892) marital harmony was destroyed, not by infidelity but by a wife's obsessesive tendencies:

> If you had seen the wife a month ago after we were married, sitting on the doorstep throwing bacon at herself and our little children – no, let me see, I've made a mistake; it would be more than a month after our marriage – but still, I took no notice of her strange ways. I thought perhaps it's a kind of pastime she's got. But, my word! – If you'd have seen the wife on our wedding morn! Oh, she did look pretty! – well, no, not pretty, far from it, but she's got such a – what shall I say, a face, a telling face. What the poets call a chisel face (no, that's not it); I have it, an open countenance. When she opens her mouth there's no countenance at all! And what a figure! Oh, dear, a kind of four-pound loaf sort of shape! And I looked a bit of a toff myself; oh, yes! Fancy these clothes were new! Well,

new to me; I don't know whether anyone else had worn them before! And what a wedding! Oh, dear, I should think there was thousands of people outside the church watching a dog fight; nothing to do with us, but still, it looked nice to see them there. And when the parson passed sentence, I mean when he said something and we both said no when we should have said yes, and the organ played the Lost Chord and a portion of the roof fell in and nearly smothered us. I thought this is happiness! And we would have had nought but bliss if this madness, this bacon fever hadn't come upon her. Fancy, she'd got bacon on the brain and I didn't know it.

Another long-suffering husband, 'The Grass Widower' (1891), was offered an unexpected holiday when his wife was advised to take a recuperative seaside break:

Well, when we got to the platform, I felt so overjoyed I could have cuddled the engine. I asked the guard what time the train went, he said, 'In five minutes.' I said, 'Send it off in three, and there's a pot of four-half for you.' He said 'Shall I lock the lady in?' I said, 'Nail her in! hammer her in!' And when the train left the station, I turned round and kissed all the porters; and I had two cabs home and ran between them, and I've invited the two dressmakers from next door to come and have a cup of tea and bring a bit of sewing; and I'm going to sit on the table, take my boots off, put my feet on the mantel-piece, spit on the ceiling, and throw all the cups and saucers out of the window.

Very occasionally Dan's character avoided the matrimonial trap. 'Mary Ann's Refused Me' (1895) told the story of a narrow escape:

Mary Ann's mother kept Mary and me courting for ten years. You'd say how? Why; ah, there you are – you didn't know Mary's mother. What a little vixen; oh! my word! She was only a little snipe of a woman, but what a temper. Well, I'm not a coward; I'd face a lion in a cage, but I'd no more contradict Mary Ann's mother than I'd think of cleaning my teeth with a whitewash brush. Oh, I've suffered, there's no mistake. That woman one day called me into the kitchen and said, 'Mr Beatrute, what are your intentions towards Mary Ann? Because the man that trifles with my daughter's heart, the longest knife in that drawer would not be long enough for him.' I said, 'Couldn't you get two knives and tie them together?' She flew into a temper, and it took three small drops of paraffin to soothe her:

Once I used to be so sad
Now I'm happy, now I'm glad;
With joy I think I shall go mad,
For Mary Ann's refus'd me.

The difficulties involved in describing working-class life to the middle-
and upper-class audiences who came increasingly to attend Dan's performances were encapsulated in an anecdote concerning either an aristocratic 'son of the house' or a royal equerry. Hickory Wood, Jimmy
Glover and Teddy Payne provide different versions of the story, all em-
phasising the gulf that lay between Dan and his new audience. The joke
at the centre of the story told how a wife tried to cook pancakes on a
grid-iron, only to find that the mixture ran through the bars: 'I like that
joke, Mr Leno, or whatever your blessed name may be – about the gwid-
iwon ['grid-iron' in everyday language] ... you see, I liked it so much
because I've seen a gwid-iwon.'[6] Fifty years after Benjamin Disraeli had
defined the rich and poor of England as 'two nations between whom
there is no intercourse and no sympathy; who are as ignorant of each
other's habits, thoughts and feelings, as if they were dwellers in different
zones, or inhabitants of different planets',[7] West End audiences would
have still struggled to understand many of the allusions in Dan's songs.
    It must have been with considerable trepidation that Dan approached
an entirely different public in the spring of 1897. He had accepted an
engagement at Hammerstein's Olympia Music Hall, a colossal 3,800-seat
variety theatre on Broadway in New York; it was not unusual for
variety performers to cross between Britain and the USA. When he set
sail in the SS *St Paul* Dan was following in the wake of such famous
artists as Charles Chaplin Senior, Lottie Collins, Marie Lloyd and, a year
previously, Albert Chevalier. To emulate their success Dan had to win
over a New York audience who were notoriously undemonstrative, both
in praise and condemnation. He was troubled that Americans would not
understand his humour, feeling that he would be appearing in 'a foreign
country, among foreigners who happened to have learned our speech'.[8]
There was also perhaps a degree of apprehension because the long run of
the Drury Lane pantomime had compelled him to postpone the engagement by several weeks. On arriving in New York his anxiety increased
when he was confronted by gigantic posters proclaiming him to be 'King
of Comedians' and 'The Funniest Man on Earth'. He explained to
Bransby Williams: 'You know, boy, when I walked on I felt there were a
lot who folded their arms and said "Well, show us!" and I felt I was up
for judgement and that spoilt my fun.'[9]
    Dan soon found himself among friends and fellow countrymen at the
Olympia. The stage manager was an old acquaintance from Lancashire;
the door-keeper was Irish, the *chef d'orchestre* a Yorkshireman and the

second fiddle a Tynesider. 'I am told that there are very few Americans in New York,' commented Dan 'and I can quite believe it.'[10] The British expatriate population turned up in force to support him when he made his debut, on Monday 12 April. At first the public back in England, connected to the USA only by the electric telegraph, received garbled reports that the appearance has been disastrous. Rumours abounded. It was said that the audience had hissed him; that he had fled from the stage in the face of a demonstration by anti-British Irish militiamen. In reality, one drunken heckler had been swiftly put in his place by a well-aimed put-down.

Shortly before he took the stage Dan joked with reporters that he was as cool as a cucumber, but the beads of sweat on his face and uneasy shifting from foot to foot suggested otherwise. Even for a performer of his experience it was a nerve-racking situation. The theatre was the largest that he had ever played, and his performance was not part of a variety bill, but isolated between the two acts of a drama, *In Great New York*. When he eventually bounded onto the stage the thunderous applause stopped him in his tracks. Blinking and apparently bewildered he thanked the audience for their reception 'I don't know when I had so many friends.' The tremble in his voice that reviewers detected during the first number 'The Horseshoe on the Door' soon wore off, and an early joke about the looseness of his trousers 'they were cut out for an overcoat' provoked roars of laughter. Song followed song: 'Courting the Widow' 'The North Pole', a polar exploration pastiche in which he was accompanied by a stuffed seal, 'The Grass Widower', and the ever-popular 'The Shop-walker'. After leaving the stage briefly he was called back. 'Give 'em "The Red Poppies", Dan!' demanded a lady from one of the 13 tiers of boxes. Dan obliged with the song, a mock black-face minstrel ballad of his own composition that 'had always been considered very good by those who have borrowed money from me'. After a strenuous dance Dan crawled on all fours from the stage, returning to accept a collection of oversized bouquets. 'In our country,' he responded 'flowers are given only to the beautiful and I suppose this is why they were handed up tonight ... I have only been in America for three days, but I feel as if I had been here a long time, I have received so many kindnesses.' He was not yet allowed to take his leave of the clamouring audience, giving a spoof ornithological lecture 'The Red Robin', after which he contrived finally to make his exit, as he had so often done in the past, with a breathtaking hornpipe. His turn had occupied almost an hour.[11]

The warmth of his reception had left him 'radiant with happiness', although immediately after the performance he told reporters: 'I was too nervous to do myself justice tonight and the orchestra played on too low a pitch for me; but I'll do better hereafter, now I know what they like. Of course, I'll change my songs to suit the audience.'[12] Within a few days some critical reviews appeared. Edward A. Dithman of *The New York Times* felt that genuinely American audiences were far from enthusiastic and that:

> He was well received at first because a large number of his own fellow countrymen, of the class and disposition to whom his art seems representative, were there to assist Mr Hammerstein's ushers with the applause. Thereafter the ushers were compelled to work almost alone.'[13]

Mr Hammerstein's ushers may well have been generous with their applause, but the length of Dan's appearances on the Olympia's giant stage suggests that some paying members of the audience were also appreciative. Throughout his four-week engagement his turn was never shorter than 35 minutes, and on one occasion extended to an hour and a quarter.

When Oscar Hammerstein, whose love of variety and grand opera equalled that of Augustus Harris, offered a return engagement Dan decided to decline. Despite repeated comments to the contrary, he had not been at ease in the USA. His first experience of the country was a confrontation with a pack of aggressive journalists who demanded to know about his methods, motivation and whether he felt he could make American audiences laugh. Hammerstein's fire-proof, well ventilated, brilliantly lit Olympia, with its seats stretching far into the distance, was an uncomfortable vision of the music hall of the future. In his hotel room he had fallen foul of an automated room-service device, a far cry from the traditional Liverpool landlady. Later, the American way of advertising, so shockingly exemplified on the hoardings announcing his arrival, was to trick him with a simple publicity device.

Dan had found what he considered to be a genuine $1,000 bill in the street. After allowing its owner three days to claim it back, he decided to use it to treat several of his American friends to a dinner party, a convivial event made merrier by the fact that it was generally recognised that the banknote was merely a cleverly printed advertisement for a local tradesman. Perhaps the discovery of the note was itself a piece of advertising, a publicity stunt conceived to flatter the New Yorker's sense of worldliness. Hickory Wood reported the restaurant manager's reaction when presented with the fake bill: 'See here, Mr Leno, they tell me you're a comedian, and I'm not going to deny it; but all I can say is, if a stale old joke like that goes down where you come from, they're a good deal easier to please than they are here.'[14] Dan's brief visit also left Oscar Hammerstein out of pocket. Following the latter's bankruptcy in 1899 he informed a meeting of creditors that the delayed appearance of the 'Funniest Man on Earth' had involved him in a loss of $30,000.

16

ORLANDO DANDO

Dan returned to a London busily preparing to celebrate the Queen's Diamond Jubilee. Colonial dignitaries and exotically uniformed troops from all parts of the British Empire were arriving to take part in a series of patriotic events, which were to culminate in a massive procession from Buckingham Palace to St Paul's cathedral. Streets and buildings were decorated with imperial symbols, souvenirs of all kinds were on sale and every newspaper and magazine carried surveys of the 60 'glorious' years of Victoria's reign On reflection, the speed and variety of changes that had occurred during the last decade led many commentators to describe it as a 'nervous age', a *fin-de-siècle* period after which nothing would be the same.

There had been major changes in the world of entertainment. Actor managers such as Sir Henry Irving and Herbert Beerbohm Tree had elevated the art of the theatre, overshadowing the efforts of their predecessors with spectacular and magnificently mounted productions. The simple farces of Andrew Halliday, Henry J. Byron and William Brough had given way to the complex plots and sophisticated wordplay of Henry Wing Pinero, Oscar Wilde and George Bernard Shaw. Burlesque and the minstrel show had become outdated, their audiences migrating to an elegant new form of entertainment, the musical comedy.

Music hall had entered a transitional stage. In the face of stricter regulation from local authorities many small halls had closed or were taken over by syndicates, such as those controlled by the Livermore Brothers, the Broadhead family and Edward Moss and Richard Thornton. When the latter two entrepreneurs joined with Oswald Stoll to form Moss Empires in 1899, the company had an authorised capital of £1 million. Funded by such massive investment scores of new Palaces, Hippodromes and Empires were built throughout the kingdom, their chief characteristics being elaborate decoration and increased capacity. Larger auditoriums reduced the effectiveness of solo comedians, their scale being more suited to sketches, acrobats, dancers and, increasingly, film exhibitions. Many proprietors were pleased to be phasing out the often unpredictable comedian in favour of acts whose content was less likely to cause offence – but in opting for such a course of action, spontaneity and vitality were lost. In 1904 the music hall reached a new level of grandeur when Stoll opened the London Coliseum, a giant music-hall similar in design and size to Hammerstein's New York Olympia.

Dan and Herbert's initial excursion into music-hall management was a more modest venture. Late in 1894, assisted by Harry Randall and Arthur Williams, they had put on a variety show for an audience of about 700 people in a small hall close to the smoky platforms of Clapham Junction railway station. They were launching a company to exploit the Grand Music Hall, formerly knows as Munt's Hall, on St John's Hill. In reality the area was Battersea, but Clapham, applied to both the station and the music-hall, sounded a social cut higher. The opening show at the Grand was not only star studded, but star studied, as many members of the variety profession had been persuaded to purchase shares in the new venture. Their faith in Dan, Herbert and co. was well founded, for the hall paid a healthy dividend after its first year. In December 1896 the directors mounted an unusual Christmas attraction, casting their own children in a specially written pantomime. *Little Cinderella* was a great success with Georgina Leno as Cinderella, being joined by Lulu Randall as the Fairy Godmother and by the talented offspring of several other well-known performers.

Dan's embryonic syndicate looked further afield for its next venture. An old Drury Lane acquaintance, Thomas Gardiner 'Spangles' Hales, leased them an ex-circus building in North End, Croydon, a rapidly expanding Surrey town. Spangles was a well-known London character, earning his nickname from the glittering decorations that he sold in his theatrical-costume shop in Bow Street. A second nickname had been conferred on him by the staff of Drury Lane, where he organised the supernumeraries. During a back stage poker game he had once triumphantly declared his hand to be 'Haces and Heights', thereafter becoming known at the theatre as 'Haces and Heights' Hales. The day-to-day management of the newly opened National Palace of Varieties was placed in the hands of Jessie Sparrow, a friend who had discovered Munt's Hall for the syndicate.

The Oriental Palace of Varieties on Denmark Hill, in the South-East London suburb of Camberwell was the syndicate's next acquisition. After a year the Oriental was rebuilt as a 2,000-seat music hall, opening its doors in December 1899 with a new name, the Camberwell Palace. Having taken over three pre-existing establishments the syndicate decided to build their very own music hall. A site was purchased at Walham Green, now known as Fulham Broadway, a busy working-class area on the borders of Chelsea. The design of the Granville was entrusted to Frank Matcham, who produced a beautiful and distinctive building décorated throughout with glistening Doulton tiles. Although accommodating an audience of only 1,000, from its opening on 19 September 1898 the theatre was immediately successful. At a private view held a few days earlier Dan declared that he and his fellow directors 'wanted to help the smaller fry of the profession'.[1]

Dan also thanked the variety profession for subscribing so heartily to the new venture. Analysis of shareholders in the Granville Theatre of Varieties Limited shows that, of 20,000 £1 shares, more than a quarter were held by investors with theatrical connections. Comedians, acrobats, ventriloquists, dancers, jugglers, pantomimists, song-writers, architects (including Matcham), theatrical agents and music-hall managers had joined forces with licensed victuallers, clerks, solicitors, book-makers, engineers, sign-writers, police officers and a diamond dealer to support the new venture. Some shareholders, such as a cigar importer and a glass-bottle manufacturer, had a vested interest in the entertainment industry, but the various gentlemen, married ladies, spinsters, teachers and medical practitioners who had invested in the Granville were probably attracted by Dan and Herbert's reputation. Of the directors Harry Randall had 367 shares, Fred Williams 466, Dan 566 and Herbert 567. Other well known music-hall artists to be represented were Ada Blanche (ten shares), Charles Lauri (25), Gus Elen (50), Fanny Lesley and Arthur Williams (100 each), Harry Champion (25) and Paul Martinetti (150).[2]

To complete their chain of music halls the syndicate replaced the small 'Grand' with a 'Grand' far more deserving of the name, a 3,000-seat theatre decorated in a flamboyant oriental style that would have appealed to Widow Twankey. Dan officially opened the new hall on 26 November 1900, introducing a bill that included his fellow Drury Lane performer Alexandra Dagmar, the 'coster' comedienne Kate Carney and Fred Karno's sketch company performing 'The New Woman's Club'. Of the consortium's music halls only the Grand survives, its austere red-stucco frontage dominating the skyline above Clapham Junction Station. The success of the four halls, each a limited company, was monitored with some concern by the directors and managers of other London variety theatres. Almost immediately plans were hatched to bring about their downfall.

Meanwhile Dan had taken on a new theatrical challenge. Not content with his variety and pantomime engagements and the directorship of four music halls, he had accepted an offer to appear in a musical comedy. He had been approached in 1896 by the theatre owner and entrepreneur Milton Bode, but his agent had explained that his client had no free engagements until 1898. Determined to secure the prize comedian, Bode expressed himself willing to wait for two years. A limited window of six weeks was also readily accepted. Finally, an agreement to pay £125 a week secured the deal, although, impressed by Bode's doggedness, Dan vetoed his agent's demand for a £500 deposit.

26 Poster for *Orlando Dando, c.* 1898

Orlando Dando was written by Basil Hood, a recently retired Army captain who had already devised two highly successful musical comedies for the comedian Arthur Roberts. The music for the show was in the capable hands of Walter Slaughter, a long-serving orchestra conductor at many West End theatres, including Drury Lane. Limited by time and with a reluctance to 'over-cook' his part, Dan stipulated that he should only attend the last of four weeks of rehearsals. On the first morning Milton Bode and Captain Hood were anxious to hear his impressions. After a run through of the first act Dan was asked for his opinion. Jimmy Glover reported the ensuing conversation:

> LENO: I see, we have the opening chorus of fifty ladies and gentlemen in my barber's shop?
> CAPTAIN HOOD: Yes.
> LENO: Then the two lovers meet and arrange a love meeting, and sing a long love duet – in my barber's shop?
> MILTON BODE: Yes, quite right.
> LENO: Then we have the Four High-Kicking Flappers of Tillerland; they do their number, and get a well-deserved encore – in my barber's shop?
> BODE: Yes.
> LENO: Then we have three or four more choruses, a rollicking quartette, a patriotic song, and, in fact, everybody who is anybody comes on, does what they like – make appointments, do

what they like with the till, dance, sing songs, do break downs – *all in my shop?*
BODE: Yes, Dan, that's quite right, and it all only lasts one hour, this act.
LENO: But don't you think it about time that I shaved some-body?[3]

Orlando was joined in his crowded barber's shop by one Thomas Turn-bull, a lovesick hairdresser portrayed by Johnny Danvers. After opening in Newcastle on 31 October 1898 the show toured Liverpool, Glasgow, Birmingham and Manchester before closing at Deptford, in South East London, on 10 December.

Dan's second musical comedy, produced in the following year, brought him into contact with one of the Victorian era's most colourful authors, George R. Sims. For the last 20 years of the nineteenth century the prolific Sims, also known under his pen name 'Dagonet', had been re-sponsible for a flood of plays, verse, burlesques, novels and factual works that enthralled readers from all social backgrounds. Several volumes of 'parlour poetry', such as 'The Lifeboat', 'Ostler Joe' and 'Christmas Day in the Workhouse' had reduced the nation to tears, while the stage melo-dramas *The Lights o' London*, *The Romany Rye* and *In the Ranks* became frequently repeated theatrical standards. In 1897, inspired by the suc-cess of Arthur Conan Doyle's Sherlock Holmes stories, Sims invented his own detective, an ex-actress named Dorcus Dene.

It was as a detective, Aubrey Honeybun, that Dan was cast in the musical comedy *In Gay Piccadilly*. Poking fun at his own convoluted melodramas, Sims created a plot in which a penniless younger son, Guy Brabazon, was thwarted in his love for the beautiful Lady Molly Wildgoose by her father's plan to marry her off to a wealthy business-man, Montague Miggs. As with all great sleuths, Honeybun had a faith-ful assistant, one Ebenezer Tinkletop, played by Johnny Danvers. Both detectives spent much of their time spying on wives for their husbands, and alternatively on husbands for their wives, a precarious pursuit that involved adopting many strange disguises. The show opened at the The-atre Royal, Glasgow, on 9 October 1899, went on to Edinburgh, New-castle, Sheffield, Birmingham, Manchester and Liverpool, and was first seen in London at the Alexandra Theatre, Stoke Newington.

There was no slackening in Dan's relentless pace. The musical com-edies involved him being on stage for up to three hours on six consecutive evenings, while appearances at provincial music halls usually involved an extended version of his act, with up to ten songs at a time. Even with less dancing his London 'turn' continued to be physically demanding:

Last month Dan Leno's exclusive West End appearance was at
the London Pavilion. For four and twenty minutes or so each
night he held the stage with Dan Leno and strong pieces of low life.

About his work there is a bouquet of a London back street. The
hopes, joys, sorrows and aspirations of his creations are well within the mental horizon of a cab-driver. His funniest song is about a
Robber Chief. The fighting of this chieftain is a series of four-ale
bar scuffles; his most heroic encounters are a collection of chuck-
ings-out; the foreign element is based on a popular view of the Italian ice-cream purveyor of the street corner. With this are streaks
of what can only be called Dan Leno – there is no other name for
it. To what form of art can you refer the following incident? The
robber carries a fearful musical instrument secured to him with a
strap. As soon as he appears before the audience he is nearly
strangled by this strap; then it winds round one foot and blinds
him. In an instant he is on the floor, and drawing a trusty dagger,
stabs the musical instrument fiercely and vindictively. The audience laughs until it is tired of laughing, and to give it time to get
its breath Dan Leno quavers to it, in a nonchalant way, something
he has forgotten for the last five minutes – his song.[4]

Any spare time that he might have was committed to business affairs
and charity work. J. Hickory Wood described a day – established as 6
May 1903 – which, if not typical, gives a good impression of Dan's frantic
schedule. In the morning he travelled the 130 miles to Dudley, in the
Midlands, to preside over the opening of the New Empire Palace Music
Hall. Returning home in the afternoon, he appeared at a charity concert
held at St James's Hall, Piccadilly. Having performed six songs, he made
the short journey to Joseph Lyon's palatial Trocadero Restaurant, in
Shaftesbury Avenue, where he gave a pre-dinner speech. It was then
time to walk, or run, the few yards to the Pavilion, where he presented
his variety act, after which he returned to the Trocadero to finish dinner.
It was by no means the end of his day for on reaching home he was
confronted with his usual heap of letters to be read and, more often than
not, answered.
    At pantomime rehearsals he was at his least animated while engaged
in the mundane task of reading through his lines. At other times he was
continually active, both on and off the stage. Hickory Wood remembered him as being always 'on the go', chatting and joking, devising impromptu dances to amuse groups of stage hands and entertaining the
child performers with riddles. Sometimes he disappeared from the stage
and auditorium completely, only to be discovered entertaining the occupants of the Drury Lane 'saloon', 'singing a mock pathetic ballad, ac-

companying himself the while on the piano, in some mysterious and inharmonious manner known to himself alone.'[5]

As Dan demonstrated at the Trocadero dinner, the solution to a critical shortage of time was to be in two places at once. In the *Era Annual* for 1902 he described a less than successful attempt at simultaneous appearance. The constable who eventually escorted him to Bow Street Police Station must have been one of the very few people in the capital unable to recognise the Drury Lane star. Dan provided a typically whimsical account of the incident:

> It happened like this, more or less; anyhow, it happened somehow.
> I was playing a Widow at the Lane in a certain pantomime in an uncertain year – uncertain to me only, because it certainly was a year or some date or other, but it has escaped me, like so many good things in this life. However, to go back and resume. I was a Widow once again, and an old friend was having a benefit at a music hall not a hundred miles from the Strand. I had promised to do something – to go on and sing at the last moment, and so clear the house for him, or something like it. I was anxious to oblige him and keep my word at the same time, but could not see how I could get away from my part in the pantomime and to be back again in time to pick up the cue. However, I had a fairly long wait for a change in one scene, so I determined to risk it, and it was arranged that directly I got to the hall I should go on in my turn or out of my turn. So I chartered a four-wheeler and started on my perilous journey dressed as a lady. All went well on the way there. I went on and made the audience weep, and then I started back for Old Drury somewhat nervous, as I don't think many people in the theatre knew that I had slipped out, and I had visions of the hubbub that would occur if I was found wanting when the call-boy went his merry rounds.
>
> The Jehu was faithful, however, and into the cab I tumbled, and began to make certain changes in my raiment in order to save time. I began to alter my bodice (ahem! Don't make me nervous, please) when the end of the world seemed to have arrived in a hurry after a most terrible earthquake, and I found myself all of a heap with my legs in the air and the cab completely toppled over.
>
> Here was a predicament. Everybody went to the assistance of the cabman and his horse, but the fare, not to say the fair – inside, as usual, was left to take care of itself. However, I screamed for help just as they were trying to right the cab with me inside, and after many struggles and tugs I was hauled on to the pavement by my

legs, amid sympathetic expressions from the public, such as 'Poor old lady!' 'What a tart!' and so on, which touched me deeply.

At this time I was trying to do up my bodice, which I had undone to change, when an enormous policeman spotted me and said, 'Hullo, what's this? Undressing yourself in a public thoroughfare! Come along o' me.' Fortunately I was able to persuade the Bobby to let me go to Bow Street in a cab – a hansom this time, and, as I knew it was useless arguing with a policeman who seemed new to the Strand, I waited until we got to the station, where in a very short time I was able to explain to the Inspector that I was not committing any offence against the law, and that I really was Dan Leno, and was then, at that moment, due at the Lane. To make sure, however, I was escorted in another cab by a Guardian of the Law to the Stage door, and as I dashed in I heard the dulcet voice of the call-boy screaming and bawling out: 'Mr Leno! Mr Leno! the stage is waiting!'

I had finished my toilet at this time, and was on the boards in a jiffy, flurried, distressed, and excited, but O.K. as usual. And there you are, it only shows that a Widow's life is not always a happy one.[6]

27   The Grand Theatre of Varieties

17

GRIMALDI'S SCISSORS

In November 1898 the directors of the Theatre Royal announced that they had secured Dan's services until Christmas 1935. Despite the longevity of some performers few expected that Dan would be able to fulfil his part of the agreement. It was clear to all that his body was frequently pushed to the point of exhaustion and that his mind was haunted by a nightmare past and an uncertain future. There were other, less obvious, demons at work – concerns about meeting the social and cultural demands of a widely varying public, a growing feeling of isolation and alienation, and an increasing reliance on alcohol.

The very nature of his stage performance was a cause of tension. On the halls he had always been free to improvise, but at Drury Lane he was expected to play a part in a carefully organised plot and to make the most of comic scenes in which he sometimes had little confidence. As he appeared more frequently at West End music halls he was forced to alter his act, abandoning much of his early subject matter in favour of material accessible to fashionable audiences. When playing proletarian London or provincial halls he once again had to adjust the balance.

Dan's attitude toward his working-class songs was equivocal. His early days on the lower levels of Victorian society, if not forgotten, had been put behind him, and he now lived the life of a prosperous middle-class gentleman. His personal interests were varied – water-colour painting, a passion for history, and an enthusiasm for the legitimate theatre, particularly the acting of Sir Henry Irving. He must have questioned whether he still needed to sing about the tally man, moonlight flits and cuts of meat known only to the poorest members of society. It would have been far easier to follow the example of Harry Liston, Arthur Lloyd and 'Jolly' John Nash, and become a society entertainer. But Dan could as little ignore his early inspiration as he could expunge the misery of his early life. Whilst he introduced a number of more socially neutral characters and generalised themes, working-class studies with their edge of cynicism and satire still remained a crucial part of his act.

28   Dan, Lydia and children

Two new character songs featured working-class men facing disquieting social transition. In 'The Huntsman' (1900) he played a humble tradesman who was explaining the embarrassment caused when he spent a week-end in the country with the Duchess of Piccadilly Circus. 'Well, I had never done any real hunting before,' Dan explained 'I am a tripe-dresser by persuasion.' He had been at a loss to understand such phrases as 'now we will go to the meet', which he took to be a cold platter, and, when finally mounted, his horse had bolted, depositing him in a ditch which had 'a kind of blancmange at the bottom and a verdigris at the top'. 'The Diamond Ring' (1899) told the unfortunate story of a manual worker, who, like George Bernard Shaw's Alfred Doolittle, had been forced to adopt a different lifestyle following an unexpected legacy:

Your soul is not your own
When a diamond ring you've got,
You can't enjoy your half and half
In a good old pewter pot.
You have to smoke cigars,
You cannot smoke a pipe;
And as for stewed eels, fish and chips,
And saveloys and tripe –

You can't have 'em. There's nothing I like more than steeled eels. People say a diamond ring is the most beautiful thing in the world. Is it? It may have a splendid lustre and brillianceness, but have you ever taken a basin of stewed eels down a dark passage and struck a match all of a sudden? That's when you get the lustre and brillianceness. You know I never ought to have had this diamond ring. I keep my hand in my pocket to hide it, but then I have to do everything with my left hand, and I can't use my left hand. When I went to drink a glass of beer this morning I poured it in my ear. I drive a water cart. This morning the manager of the water company gave me the sack, and accused me of stealing the water and selling it.

At home, amid the high-Victorian pomp of bronze statues, potted palms and gilded furniture, an element of self-mockery was seldom far from the surface. A tiger-skin hearth rug was apt to trip unwary visitors – 'They mostly does that' Dan observed.[1] A curio cabinet crammed with unusual artefacts sent to him by admirers from all parts of the world also contained an odd selection of rusty knives and nails. On one occasion he handed Hickory Wood a pair of broken scissors. Presenting himself in the guise of a learned antiquarian, he explained that 'these scissors are the identical pair with which the first clown's dress that Grimaldi ever wore was cut out.' Then, leaving his bemused guest no time to respond, Dan suddenly readjusted the historical perspective: 'and that's the biggest lie I ever told because I've just found them in the garden.'[2] Grimaldi's scissors were then reverentially replaced in the cabinet to resume their role as unique items of theatrical-tailoring history.

29   Dan Leno and family

In response to his changing audience Dan increasingly performed songs with a more abstract theme. 'The Jap' portrayed the Land of the Rising Sun not so much as a place but a series of contradictions ('We cut a slice of bread and put the butter on the top; they don't, they cut the bread, put the butter underneath, and turn it over.') Sentimental drawing-room ballads were slyly deconstructed in 'Listen to the Mocking Bird' and 'The Red Poppies', their poetic repetition subjected to apparently wide-eyed incredulity ('Well do I remember, remember, remember, Well do I remember ... He'd got a memory, hadn't he?'). There were distorted echoes of Sir Walter Scott's minstrelsy in a number where a kilted performer desperately tried to remember the last name in a litany of Highland clans:

There were McGregor's men,
And McPherson's men,
And McTullach's men
And Mc –

Eventually, the ballad singer decided to admit defeat and to extricate himself from the predicament by performing a Highland fling. It was a change of approach that freed the mental block, for the dance concluded in mid-step as he came out with 'McFarlane's men!'

Dan himself wrote a mock love ballad, 'The Wasp and the Hard-Boiled Egg', which he performed throughout the run of the 1902/03 pantomime *Mother Goose*. It was a tearful tale of unrequited love, perhaps inspired by Ellaline Terriss's famous 1901 musical comedy song 'The Honeysuckle and the Bee':

> But not one word said the hard-boiled egg,
> The hard-boiled egg,
> The hard-boiled egg,
> And what a silly insect was the wasp to beg!
> For you can't get any sense out of a hard-boiled egg.

The impossibility of communicating with eggs had already been discussed in 'Our Stores' (1897). Dan was portrayed on the cover of the sheet music wearing a white apron and brandishing a plucked chicken by its scrawny neck. Behind him was a typical grocer's shop crammed with hams, cheeses and trays of eggs. The chorus, with its listing of items for sale, reinforces the song as being typical of the shop genre popularised by Grimaldi and later by Herbert Campbell:

> Our Stores! Our Stores!
> Our nineteenth-century stores!
> There's mutton and lamb,
> And beef and ham;
> Sugar and spice,
> Everything nice.
> Our Stores! Our Stores!
> Our nineteenth-century stores!
> There's eggs overlaid,
> And new marmalade
> In our nineteenth-century stores.

With Dan, however, such stock subjects were inevitably presented with a new twist. Much of the song's patter was devoted to a philosophical discussion of the egg:

> Where is there an article that will compel you to tell more lies than an egg? Do you know, I don't think we properly grasp eggs. There is something awfully artful about an egg – there is a mystery in it. Of course, there are three kinds of eggs – there is the new-laid egg

(which is nearly extinct) – then there is the fresh egg, which is almost the same as the new-laid but with an additional something about it that makes all the difference. Then comes *The* Egg; that is the egg I am talking about. That is the egg that causes all the trouble. It's only a little round white thing, but you can't tell what it's thinking about. You daren't kick it, and you daren't drop it. It has got no face. You can't get it to laugh. You simply look at it and say 'Egg!'

Examples of Dan's own humour revealed in letters and notebooks give some idea how he influenced the stage material written for him. In the song 'The Beefeater' (1898) he impersonated an elderly Yeoman of the Guard who attempted to guide tourists away from the Tower of London's historic features towards a more enticing, beer-serving Refreshment Room:

There's no place on the face of the world like the Tower of London. If you've never been there, go again. It's a glorious place, and supplies a long felt want. Everything old. And the first ancient item you meet is the man that takes your money at the door. Then you pass through the Refreshment Room, which is the oldest Refreshment Room in the Tower, and the only one. And there's some very ancient items in the Refreshment Room, such as the buns, and the ginger beer, and the barmaids and whatnots.
Good-day, ladies! Do you want to see the Tower? Splendid day to see the Tower – nice and gloomy! Now – er – in the first place, this is the Refreshment Room. We – of course, if you want anything in the Refreshment Room, now is the time. You don't care for anything? No? Thank you! Only as we go along, there's no oranges or ginger-beer to be had, and of course, if you feel faint, you have to come back to the Refreshment Room. You … No … you don't care? No … Don't anything? No … I do! Still – we'll proceed. Standing with your back to the Refreshment Room, you get a lovely view of the Tower. Follow me, ladies. Standing with your back to the Tower, you get a lovely view of … er … the Refreshment Room. Now you see that man there? That's the sentry. He stands there night and day with his gun fixed, bayonet fixed and his eyes always on one spot … and this is – er – the Refreshment Room.

Dan's own jokey writings about the Tower might easily have formed part of the song's patter, even sharing the opening descriptive phrase:

It supplies a long-felt want; because at that time there was no music-hall nearer than Oldham.

It was built before Regent's Park was invented, and cost between eighteen shillings and sixpence. This may seem an exorbitant price; but in those days, money was money, and an ordinary cow fetched as much as three – three farthings. The first tower constructed was the White Tower, after which other towers were made and stuck on to it, as various people thought proper.

The chief 'turns' at this Ancient Palace of Varieties were – knife throwing and catching in the chest.

Slow roasting by ladies and gentlemen on a mixed grill; and

Head shifting in all its branches.[3]

Dan's manuscript went on to describe the murder of the two young princes in the Tower, and the subsequent discovery of their bodies many years later. In an illustration he depicted two white-bearded old men lying beneath a large tub with the explanation: 'The children's bodies were buried under the ash-barrel in the back-yard; but children no longer, for during the space of time, they had grown into hoary-headed men.'

From his drawings and watercolours and his skilful stage make-up it appears that he had a strong visual perception of his stage material. His ability to define and convey to an audience both the character that he was portraying and people that they themselves discussed was remarkable. At the conclusion of the third verse of another 1898 success, he casually introduced a character who was soon to become recognised as his greatest creation. Mrs Kelly hardly qualified to be described as a creation, for she was a shadowy figure represented only by a handful of words. She may well have been inspired by the Lenos' landlady of the same name from the 1860s, but she was also the distillation of Dan's memories of countless lodging-house owners, small shop-keepers and street-corner gossips encountered over the previous 30 years.

The song 'I'll Marry Him' resounded with Dan's working-class themes of the 1880s and early 1890s. Sung in the character of a middle-aged woman, it recounted the epic battle to bring Jim Johnson to the altar:

For twenty-five years I've been doing my best
To make with Jim Johnson a match;
I've done everything accept ask him point-blank,

But he won't come up to the scratch.
I really think Jim's very partial to me,
Though never a word has he said:
But this morning I passed where he's building a house,
And he threw half a brick at my head.

Just to call my attention. You know we've been courting a long
time – at least, I've done the courting; Jim's so slow. You see, I do
very well in my business. I'm a dressmaker's labourer. I think
Jim's awfully fond of me. I'm very fond of Jim, but I can't stand
his sister, she's so mean. Oh! she is a mean woman. She's so mean
that she'll buy half-a-dozen oysters and eat them in front of a
looking-glass to make them look like a dozen. But she sharn't turn
me against Jim:

My mind's made up, I'm going to marry him;
He'll have to come to church; if he won't I'll carry him.
Five and twenty years I've had my eye on Jim,
If he won't marry me, I'll marry him.

You see, we had a row once, and it was all through Mrs Kelly. You
know Mrs Kelly, of *course* – Mrs Kelly – *Mrs Kelly*!! *You* know Mrs
Kelly? Oh, you *must* know Mrs Kelly! Good life a-mighty! Don't
look so simple. She's a cousin of Mrs Nipletts', and her husband
keeps the little what-not shop at the – oh! you must know Mrs
Kelly. Everybody knows Mrs Kelly.

Dan's incredulous appeal 'you *must* know Mrs Kelly!' applied not only to
the notorious trouble-maker, but to an entire locality and its many
inhabitants. On stage he created the impression of a neighbourhood
where people lived in close proximity and were well acquainted with each
other's business. The working-class nature of the area was indicated by
the occupations of the song's characters. The narrator was a humble
'dressmaker's labourer' (a joke that Dan had used as far back as 1888);
Jim was a manual worker; while Mr Kelly was the proprietor of a small
shop.

Although unfamiliar territory to some of his audience, others would
have found the landscape of the song easy to imagine. A public house
was not mentioned, but any district that boasted a 'what-not' shop must
surely have had at least one 'local', to which Mrs Kelly and other house-
wives trooped to collect their evening beer. Like the Adam and Eve at
the entrance to Eve Place, such ornate establishments often stood on
corner sites, functioning as meeting places and entertainment venues.
Next to the pub there almost certainly stood a shell-fish stall, piled high

with glistening black winkles, curly-shelled whelks and Jim's sister's favourite oysters. A fried-fish shop would also have been a likelihood, with Friday-night queues waiting to purchase fish and chips cooked in a tank of sizzling lard. Housing in the area would have consisted of tenement blocks or rows of small, back-to-back houses, with scrappy back yards and outside lavatories. Like pubs, laundries were ubiquitous in such areas, their tall chimneys adding a steaming vapour to an atmosphere already heavy with the smell of stale beer and horse dung. And settling upon everything was the sooty fallout from household coal fires.

Mrs Kelly was probably not Mrs Nipletts's only cousin. Large families increased exponentially, populating the area with a multitude of relatives by birth and marriage. Marriages within the extended family were common and a high mortality rate meant that remarriages often occurred, a situation leading to complex and confusing inter-relationships. There was a probability that Mr Kelly and his wife were of Irish extraction – poverty and famine had driven many of the Irish poor to seek, at the least, a basic standard of living in the USA and British colonies. Many made the shorter journey across the Irish Sea to join economic migrants from all parts of Britain searching for employment in the larger industrial and commercial centres. The streets of London, Liverpool and Manchester may not have been paved with gold, but they offered occasional comforts and the rough and ready support of friends and family.

Dan's unseen characters were impressionistic creations, composed with a few subtle strokes that engaged the imagination of his audience. Although Hickory Wood considered that when Dan first came across Mrs Kelly 'he formed a vivid picture of her in his own mind', his allusions to her on stage provided only enough information for his audience to grasp the *type* of woman that she was. Over the period that Dan performed the number Mrs Kelly's character underwent certain changes. That the published versions of his songs only represented a base on which he gradually built is demonstrated by his 1903 recording of 'I'll Marry Him'. Jim Johnson now lodges with the infamous Mrs Kelly. His sister's gluttonous delight in consuming bi-valvular molluscs has been reassigned to his landlady, who has acquired a son, a 'little boy, who's got the sore eyes'. Mr Kelly is additionally described as 'that little stout man, always at the corner of the street in a greasy waistcoat'.

Such a flexible and adaptive approach was not ideally suited to the requirements of Drury Lane pantomime. Jimmy Glover had difficulty in appreciating Dan's eccentric talents:

It is the general impression that Leno 'improvised' everything at Drury Lane. Never was there a greater error. Leno was a 'builder', but without an 'architect' he could do nothing. Nearly everything in which he succeeded at the Lane he was 'written for'. Every song he worked was supplied to him by his own pet poet, Herbert Darnley. I don't say this in detriment to Harris, but Leno's successes with Harris were as nothing compared to his triumphs with Collins. Harris let him come on and simply 'be Dan Leno'. Collins thought out the Leno style and gave him the Leno material for the Leno triumph. Every funny situation or scene, first by the producer, and then written round by the librettist. He had the least iniative sense of humour of anyone I ever met; once provided with the material he had the best contributory and constructive power.[4]

A different assessment of Dan's pantomime performances was provided by Max Beerbohm. To him the specially written situations and carefully choreographed scenes detracted from Dan's comedy:

> For my part, I prefer Mr Leno in a music hall, which I take to be his natural element. Drury Lane is too vast for his peculiar method; he does not, as does Mr Herbert Campbell, 'carry' enough. Moreover, being by dint of long practice and inherent genius, supremely able to make his effects without aid from anyone else, he does not blend rightly with the other characters on the stage. He is alone and yet not alone, an element disturbing and disturbed. Nor is his heart in the buffooneries which he must perform. His is essentially a psychological humour.[5]

The final and most important arbiters of Dan's success, the public, were delighted by every aspect of his performance in the last three Drury Lane pantomimes of the nineteenth century. *Babes in the Wood* (1897/98) featured Dan and Herbert as Reggie and Chrissie, the babes grown to adulthood and attempting to make their way in fashionable London society. Wherever set, the action of Drury Lane pantomimes usually found its way to London. In *The Forty Thieves* (1898/99) Ali Baba fled from Baghdad with the brigands' treasure, finally settling in a Regent's Park pub. It was not long before Dan as Abdallah, the Captain of the Forty Thieves, caught up with the fugitive, a frantic and acrobatic sword fight ensuing. The combat should have had contained much additional fun, for Ali was played by Johnny Danvers, making the first of several Drury Lane appearances. But fun was at a premium the following year, when the 1899/1900 production of *Jack and the Beanstalk* was overshadowed by an international crisis that was to shake the British Empire to its core.

30 Herbert Campbell, Johnny Danvers and Dan Leno

Hostilities had broken out in South Africa after the Transvaal Republic and Orange Free State, fearing British military intervention, had invaded Natal. A surge of patriotic posturing soon ebbed away as an informally organised force of Dutch settlers inflicted a series of catastrophic defeats on the British army. Many young men whom Dan had entertained over the previous decade fell victim to Boer sharpshooters or died from disease. Almost immediately Dan became a symbol of home for the troops struggling to survive the harsh conditions on the veldt. Many letters and souvenirs were directed toward him: pieces of cannon shell said to have been collected at the Siege of Mafeking, a scrap of hair claiming to be a piece of General Cronje's whiskers, a pair of clogs that had apparently belonged to the Boer president's wife. Each artefact was carefully placed alongside Grimaldi's scissors and a cheerful letter despatched to its donor.

Jack and the Beanstalk was calculated to lift the prevailing air of pessimism and doom. Even those who did not witness the pantomime would have read of its spectacular scenes – 'The Roofs of the City' populated by chorus girls dressed as Louis Wain's famous cartoon cats, and 'The Road to the Market', in which flowers and vegetables were represented by 'the loveliest ladies in the loveliest of costumes'.[6] As the Dame, temporarily renamed Mrs Kelly, Dan was frequently compelled to chastise his oversize offspring Little Bobbie, portrayed, of course, by Herbert. Bobbie's unlikely brother, Jack, was played by Nellie Stewart, an Australian performer whose presence reminded the audience that colonial soldiers were currently fighting alongside British troops. The production's most overt reference to hostilities was the toppling of Giant Blunderbore When the ogre, who had been represented throughout the pantomime by an enormous pair of feet, was finally toppled, it was revealed to have the face of Paul Kruger, the Boer leader. The David and Goliath metaphor had been strangely inverted. An oppressive giant represented the makeshift Boer army, while the mighty British Empire became a heroic but poorly armed adolescent.

By the end of *Jack and the Beanstalk* superior British firepower had begun to retrieve the situation in South Africa. When the besieged township of Ladysmith was relieved on 27 February 1900 news of the victory did not reach London until after the Drury Lane audience were settled in their seats. To avoid disruption and to maximise the effect of the pantomime's finale Dan and Herbert decided to reveal the good tidings at the end of the show, but they were immediately upstaged by a junior members of the cast who joyfully announced the lifting of the siege in the first scene. 'I have never heard such an uproar in a theatre before,' reported Jimmy Glover. A few months later, on 18 May, Dan was on stage at the Pavilion when the audience heard about the relief of Mafeking. Amid scenes of jubilation Dan, who had been performing a number about an anatomy lecturer, threw his prop blackboard to the floor and danced a hornpipe upon it.

The Victorian era was coming to an end amid national feelings of confusion and doubt. Scientific progress was suddenly seen to have a destructive counter-side in the form of vastly improved weaponry – armoured trains, high explosives, mass-produced barbed wire, rapid-firing rifles and 'Long Tom' field guns which could accurately deliver heavy shells over a distance of 10,000 yards. Even that 'wonder of the age' the motion picture exchanged marvel for horror as it brought home images of heavily laden ambulances and bloodied troops returning from the front. News of British concentration camps and a brutal scorched-earth policy not only destroyed the concept of a gentleman's war, but provided a future glimpse of a much anticipated European conflict. Over a longer period leading figures in the new sciences of statistics and sociology had demonstrated the extent to which poverty and exploitation underpinned the functioning of contemporary society. It was a time for re-examination and re-evaluation.

Dan too struggled to come to terms with the changes that he had experienced in his lifetime. Having temporarily forsaken the music hall to appear in musical comedy, he stood outside the Malakoff Music Hall, in Cleveland Square, Liverpool, still decorated with a statue of Dan Lowrey. He reflected on his own career to the actor Herbert Shelley: 'Mother and father saw my start here, and watched me fight my way to Drury Lane. Now I have seen two lives, lived in two worlds, and made two names.'[7]

18

THE LIVING IMAGE

At the beginning of the twentieth century it was possible to pour a cup of 'G.P.' Government Tea, endorsed on the packet by Dan Leno, from the spout of a Dan Leno character teapot. One could tap out a pipe, its bowl decorated with Dan's distinctive features, into an aluminium ashtray impressed with the comedian's portrait. Dan's fictionalised exploits were recounted in a weekly comic and in a best-selling spoof autobiography that remained in print for many years. His voice could be heard at any time of the day by placing one of the new Gramophone discs on a turn-table, and his moving image could be conjured up by rotating the handle of a Kinora movie viewer. Dan had become a mass-marketing icon, his image represented in countless postcards, sheet-music covers, posters, cigarette cards and illustrations in the popular press.

Having loosed Mrs Kelly on the world, Dan now aided and abetted the creation of a far more fascinating fictional character – Dan Leno. A mythologised version of the comedian began to take shape with the publication on Tuesday 26 February 1898 of *Dan Leno's Comic Journal*, the first comic to present a real person as its central character. The comic, which ran until 2 December 1899, sold for a halfpenny and had eight tabloid pages containing a selection of stories, jokes and cartoon strips by Tom Browne (1870–1910). Published by the newspaper giant C. Arthur Pearson, the comic sold 350,000 copies of the first issue. Although broad in humour it was not primarily aimed at children, but at young adults who would recognise many of the music-hall performers alluded to in the text. As with Ally Sloper, Dan's exploits were often narrated by his offspring – not a beautiful daughter like Tootsie Sloper, but a cheeky, semi-literate son called Danny Junior. The cartoon version of Mrs Leno owed far more to Herbert than Lydia, being presented as a massive and intimidating presence, forever scowling and usually with arms folded menacingly across her ample bosom.

31 *Dan Leno: Hys Booke*, 1904 edition

The process of presenting Dan Leno as a comic character continued with the publication of *Dan Leno: Hys Booke. Written by Himself. A Volume of Frivolities. Autobiographical, Historical, Philosophical, Anecdotal, and Nonsensical.* The little book, first published at Christmas 1898, proved a valuable asset to the recently founded firm of Greening and Co, of 20 Cecil Court, Charing Cross Road. It had been announced in May 1897 under the provisional title *Leno's Larks*, but it is likely that delays were caused by Dan's busy schedule. Greening's owner, Arthur Collins, may have known Dan from earlier days, for he too had been a music-hall performer. Certainly the comedian and publisher formed a profitable partnership, with five large editions of the book being issued by June 1899. After Dan's death *Hys Booke* remained a bestseller, selling 152,000 copies by 1908.

The various editions of the book, available as a one-shilling paperback or a one-and-sixpenny hardback, contained different selections of illustrations, some of which were by Dan himself. A claim that Dan was not the author, and that the book was the work of a young ghost writer, T.C. Elder, is inconsequential.[1] It is possible that Elder had a hand in organising the rambling narrative, but much of the book was based on already published stage material that Dan was known to have influenced. Other passages have a style that is hardly separable from Dan's interviews, letters and notebooks. In *Hys Booke* Dan (or his ghost writer) discussed the supposed loss of his birthplace to St Pancras Station:

'Here' – you generally begin with 'Here' – 'here I spent my happy childhood hours. Ah! What is man? Wherefore does he why? Whence did he whence? Whither is he withering?'

Then the guard yelled out: 'Leicester, Derby, Nottingham, Manchester, Liverpool!' ...

So I decided to let my birthplace alone for that year. And on my next birthday I got connected with it by telephone and mused through that.

I said – you know how you get snappy at the telephone – 'Are you there? D'year? Are you there? What is man?'
'Who are you?' yelled the man at St Pancras.
'Who am I?' I said in a sad voice; 'Ah! Who is any of us?'
''Eh! What is it you want?'
''Tis now thirty-five long, weary years ago,' I soliloquised with my mouth against the box, 'since I first came into the world.'
'We didn't ring you up,' said the man at the other end; 'there must be some mistake.'

That makes me a little irritated.

'Aren't you St Pancras?' I demanded.

'Yes.'

'Very well then, you're covering up my birthplace, and I want to make some philosophical anniversary remarks. Why can't you go away instead of interrupting me when I'm musing with your in-sulting questions? What! Who's that? Miss Exchange? What have you cut me off Mr Pancras for? Oh! did they? Said it wasn't a solilophone did they? Well, but solilograms cost a halfpenny a word. Think they would? Let me send it cheaper as it's my birthday? Oh, don't go!'

But she does go, and I put the soliloquery shutters up.[2]

Dan wrote in a similar vein in a letter to a friend:

I am in Glasgow and I live near the docks. Opposite my window is a shipload of lime, at which I gaze affectionately day and night, because I seem to see your face in it.

It is raining; it has been raining; and it is going to rain. It has rained so much that it has washed all the figures off the Town Hall clock, and nobody in Glasgow knows what time it is.

When you say to a Glasgow man, 'I think we shall have some rain shortly,' he looks surprised, and says, 'Of course.'

He isn't surprised that we're going to have the rain, but he's as surprised as you would be if somebody said to you, 'I think the sun will rise to-morrow morning.'

It is also cold. In fact, it is so cold that when I sent my dresser out for beer last night, the publican cut it off in lengths, and he had to bring it back with him in a brown paper parcel.

In Glasgow they talk Scotch, and also do other things with it. They can't help talking Scotch, and they don't want to help the other things. When a Glasgow man is talking Scotch to you, don't swallow all he says, or you'll get drunk.

There is a river here called the Clyde, and I sailed on it as far as Greenock – once. They say nobody ever did it twice unless he was well paid for it. I said to the captain of the boat, 'The river's very high to-day, isn't it?' and he replied, 'Not at all. It's just the opposite.' So I said, 'Well, all I can say is that you must have a bad cold in your head.'

I fancy we meant different kinds of 'highness.'

Glasgow is the second city in the empire; I don't know what's the first, but when I find out I'll wire you to back it for a place.

We live in a flat entirely surrounded by human beings. The man who lives above us is a strong man, who juggles with mangles and grand pianos. He drops one occasionally, and if we're lucky before we leave, we shall have a grand piano to bring away with us.

The man next door is learning to be a brass band, and the steamers on the river all hoot at him as they pass.

When you go out into the streets for a rest, you find that they are paved with granite sets. This is done so that you can hear the traffic properly. Granite sets never wear out; they always wear you out first.[3]

The fullest expression of Dan as a comic character took place in the period running up to April Fool's Day, 1902. Horatio Bottomley, the colourful proprietor of *The Sun*, had decided to publish a light-hearted version of his evening paper to celebrate the forthcoming coronation of King Edward VII. A few days before the much-anticipated publication date, potential contributors received a gigantic postcard on which Dan had portrayed himself reclining in the rays of the setting sun with Herbert striding purposefully into the distance. Dan noted 'That's my sub-editor going to get a cup of tea', an in-joke that prompted Harry Furness to return his own version of the picture showing a tottering Herbert with the added comment 'That's your sub-editor returning from getting his cup of *tea*'. Despite Herbert's love of tea, *The Sun*, with its mixture of real news stories and joke items, was a tremendous success. Dan's editorial concluded with a tongue-in-cheek excuse:

I apologise to the public if there is anything they don't like in this number. Don't blame me. It is the fault of the sub-editor. There is a petty jealousy between us, but he has got the most of it.[4]

The most innovative aspect of *The Sun*'s well-organised publicity campaign was the making of a short film showing the two comedians in a supposed editorial office. It was hot work, for the one-minute comedy was photographed under a battery of powerful arc lights at one of the world's earliest indoor film-making facilities, the Biograph Studio at 107 Regent's Street. The story line of the now lost film can be recreated from a number of frame illustrations published at the time. Dan sat at the editorial desk in a swivel chair, his journalistic dedication demonstrated by the removal of his suit jacket. Herbert, also in his waistcoat, entered and tried to take possession of the coveted chair. Confusion ensued, during which a tray of copy was upset, its contents scattered around the painted set. Dan stood on the chair, Herbert tried to pull him off and, finally, the editor and his sub tried to resolve their differences by throttling each other. *Mr Dan Leno, Assisted by Mr Herbert Campbell, Editing The Sun* was shown by the British Mutoscope and Biograph Company as part of a programme of films at music halls, and was also available as a reel of flicked photographs on cast-iron 'What the Butler Saw' peepshow machines across the country.

Film makers had already been attracted by Dan's aptitude for impromptu clowning. On Sunday 23 June 1899 a 'Water Rats' excursion to the Surrey beauty spot of Box Hill was accompanied by the showman and cinematographer A.D. 'Edison' Thomas. It was a typically impressive gathering, with 130 Rats and their guests transported in ten four-horse coaches. As the convoy made its jovial progress through South London, Thomas positioned his movie camera by the roadside at Mitcham to film the approaching vehicles. Another sequence *Incidents on the Road to Box Hill* was taken before the Rats arrived at their destination. When the excursionists sat down for their picnic Thomas was again active with his camera, filming Dan and Herbert presiding over the open-air feast. A final scene, *The Rats at Play*, featured many of the leading music-hall performers of the day: Joe Elvin, Will Evans, George Robey, T.E. Dunville, Harry Randall and, of course, Dan and Herbert.[5] Within three days Thomas's Vitascope projected the films at the Royal Music Hall, Holborn, novelty being added by the presence of several of the Rats portrayed on screen.

The Rats reassembled on 4 July to participate in the Music Hall Sports held at the London County Athletic Ground, Herne Hill, South London. Interspersed between the track and field events were a number of comic set pieces intended to raise donations for the Music Hall Benevolent Fund. Early in the day Thomas filmed a comedy fox-hunt with an appropriately costumed Dan being chased out of the refreshment tent by a troop of huntsmen riding hobby-horses. Thomas's next film captured Dan 'in the character of Mrs Kelly, attempting to ride a bicycle and assaulting those who tender the dame doubtful assistance'. Finally, Thomas filmed several performers, including Dan and Herbert, acting out a scene borrowed from Buffalo Bill's famous Wild West Show. A band of bloodthirsty 'Red Indians' attacked and set fire to a settler's cabin, but were repulsed by cowboy Dan, who fought with a dummy and removed its scalp.[6]

Dan was also filmed at several charity cricket matches, in which scoring laughs took precedence over scoring runs. In the late summer of 1900 Birt Acres, who had photographed some of the first Kinetoscope subjects back in 1895, issued a number of scenes taken at a game between teams captained by Dan and T.R. Dewar. An advertisement described the 100-foot production:

This film shows the celebrated 'comique' at the wickets, also riding about the cricket ground on a bicycle. He is literally supported by nearly all the music hall 'stars' who are in the most grotesque costumes, and the whole film is full of the most ludicrous and comical incidents that ever transpired on a cricket ground. Through the courtesy of Mr Dan Leno, who, on one occasion came and played in front of the camera, we were able to secure a most excellent view of himself and his fellow artists and the facial expressions of these gentlemen is a study. Causes roars of laughter. Absolutely unique.[7]

A year later, in September 1901, the Warwick Trading Company issued two films taken at a charity match held at Stamford Bridge sports ground. Dan was depicted leading his team onto the field, returning to the Pavilion and bowing to the crowd, dressed as a Lancer, and then as a cowboy aiming his pistol at an umpire. He was also shown conducting the Metropolitan Police Band in a rendition of the music-hall song 'A Little Bit Off the Top.' A few weeks later, on 5 September, Dan performed some funny business before the giant Biograph camera at Kennington Oval, home of Surrey County Cricket Club. The highlight of *Dan Leno's Record Score* was the comedian's argument with the wicket-keeper, a dispute which led to the latter's top hat being trampled underfoot. The film was shown throughout September and October at the Palace Theatre of Varieties, in Charing Cross Road, extra humour being derived from its insertion between serious views of the Yorkshire cricket team, and the star players Ranjitsinhji and C.B. Fry.

32   Dan and Lydia on film, 1902

The large 70-mm gauge of Biograph films was designed to provide clear images that could be printed onto photographic paper and employed in the company's various flick-book devices. It was possible to view moving pictures of Dan in amusement arcades on the Mutoscope, at home on the smaller Kinora viewer, or even on a hand-flipped 'Bio-Gem' booklet. The Biograph Company issued two further films featuring Dan, charming domestic scenes taken in the gardens of his Clapham home early in 1902. In the first Dan and his family were seen enjoying an alfresco meal. The second depicted Dan and Lydia attempting to open a bottle of champagne, finally resorting to the use of an enormous property axe to unloose *The Obstinate Cork*. A single surviving Kinora reel of 600 photographs copied from the latter film is the only existing motion picture of Dan and Lydia.[8]

Dan died just as cinema pioneers were experimenting with the first extended fiction subjects. His only acted film performances were two brief sequences: *Editing The Sun*, and a scene from the 1901/02 Drury Lane pantomime in which he was seen exploring a dungeon in Bluebeard's castle. In the film, released by Warwick, Dan as Sister Ann was chatting to an enormous walking head, portrayed by his old Surrey Theatre colleague Arthur Conquest. Unlike Arthur, who was later to appear in several screen comedies, Dan had no further opportunities to test himself in the new medium.

Dan played a greater part in the development of another new form of entertainment, sound recordings. The films of the comedian were, of course, silent, but his voice was readily available on several one-sided shellac discs issued by the Gramophone and Typewriter Company. Cylinder recordings of Dan's songs, performed by a minor comedian, Harry Bluff, had been marketed by the Edison Bell Company of London as early as 1898, but it was some years before Dan himself was lured into a studio. When he finally arrived at the Gramophone Company headquarters in Maiden Lane, off the Strand, he was following in the footsteps of several other leading music-hall performers. Albert Chevalier had become one of the first stars to sign with the new company, his 1898 contact stipulating that he should be paid a royalty of one shilling per dozen on his four recordings. It had taken protracted negotiations to persuade Dan to record his first selection of songs in 1901 – he was used to the encouragement of a live audience and was apprehensive about singing into a gigantic horn with only a pianist to provide him with support.

Despite Dan's obvious discomfort in some of the recordings the Gramophone Company considered him to be one of their prestige artists, listing his name alongside such international celebrities as the actress Sarah Bernhardt, the violinist Joachim and the opera singers Emma Calve, Tamagno and Caruso. The cost of Dan's records, five shillings for a ten-inch disc of about three minutes' duration, would have restricted their purchase to a relatively well-off public. Contemporary advertising shows that the Gramophone was aimed at wealthy suburbanites:

> THE GRAMOPHONE is the out of doors instrument. Now is the time to buy a Gramophone. Everyone is fascinated and delighted with the Gramophone when played across the river or under the trees on the lawn. There is no need to stay in town and spend the evening in the heated air of the City when the Gramophone brings to you in your home the voices of the most popular singers …

> The Music Hall is hot and smoky. On the Gramophone Dan Leno will make your evening in the country a right merry one. He will sing to you 'Clever Mr Green', 'My Wife's Relations', 'The Mocking Bird', 'The Tower of London', 'Poppies', 'The Fireman', and many more of his most famous songs and patter. Now is the time to buy a Gramophone.[9]

Unlike his films, all Dan's recordings survive, providing the most comprehensive repertoire of a leading performer from his time. Sadly, he was never completely at ease before the recording apparatus. 'How the dickens can I patter and warble to that thing?' he was reported as asking. 'Can't a few of you come round and smile and clap a bit?'[10] But despite his reservations and the variable quality of his performances his records were immensely popular.

Dan's public, mindful of the transience of live performance, eagerly sought mementoes of their idol. He had become a much-loved but fragile treasure, an impermanent landmark that had erupted onto the theatrical scene, but one that was likely to disappear just as suddenly. Closely aligned to the array of souvenirs were the large numbers of caricatures produced to illustrate books and magazines. An artist did not have to take many liberties with Dan's appearance to create an amusing cartoon. A description written during his American engagement demonstrated his attraction to caricaturists of all abilities:

> Leno is short, thin and hatchet-faced. His costume consisted of odd garments, each several sizes too large for him. Semi circular black eyebrows lent a peculiar expressiveness to his features; his eyes he made seem tiny or large at will, and his mouth was all over the lower part of his face at different times, so extravagant were his grimaces …[11]

33   Dan as a dame, by Alfred Bryan

Most of the cartoonists who depicted Dan inhabited the same milieu as
music-hall performers, drinking in the same bars and relaxing in the
same clubs. Like the variety profession their lifestyle veered toward the
bohemian, and consequently their life expectancy was often short. Phil
May, once described as 'the Dan Leno of the Art World',[12] was the most
gifted and also the most reckless of his contemporaries. He had dragged
himself out of poverty by pursuing a range of occupations – office boy,
foundry worker, estate agent, jockey and actor. By the late 1890s he was

recognised as the foremost 'black and white' artist of his time. His severe economy of line was most often used to present humorous scenes of cockney life, although it was also well adapted to convey vivid impressions of theatrical performers. He sketched Dan on several occasions, his finest portrait being the *Punch* illustration entitled 'The Second Mrs Twankeray'. His death at the age of 37 was not unexpected.

Another artist who had triumphed over early adversity was Sidney H. Sime, several of whose caricatures were used in *Dan Leno: Hys Booke*. Having made a threadbare living in various trades Sime eventually became well known for his grotesque depictions of supernatural subjects. His simple, almost naïve, portrayal of Dan as Hamlet declaiming 'Alas, Poor Yorick' to a dead mouse was both eerie and poignant. Tom Browne depicted Dan as a more robust figure, a forerunner of his 'Father' series of postcards in which a larger-than-life paterfamilias became involved in countless scrapes. Other cartoonists to provide their own distinctive impressions of Dan were L. Raven Hill, J.W.T. Manuel, John Hassall, Bernard Partridge, Harry Furniss, Dudley Hardy and the incomparable Max Beerbohm.

The most perceptive of many caricatures were produced by Alfred Bryan, an artist with long experience of depicting stage celebrities. Most of his portraits of Dan were full-page pen and ink illustrations to *The Entr'acte* magazine, commencing with Dame Durden in the 1886 Surrey pantomime and continuing with a series of studies which seemed to reach straight to the heart of the comedian's performances. When Bryan died at the age of 47 in 1899, Dan joined with the theatrical luminaries Henry Irving, George Alexander and Herbert Beerbohm Tree on a committee organised to raise funds to support the artist's widow and children.

Perhaps the only works of art to attempt serious portraits of the comedian were an oil painting by J.W. Kent exhibited at the Tivoli in 1895 and a bronze bust by John Carter now displayed in the Theatre Royal. In an age whose heroes were frequently depicted as having imposing physical stature or striking dignity, Dan's features did not lend themselves to official portraiture. Or perhaps he chose not to lend his features, for he was as much a satirist of pomposity and self-esteem as any cartoonist. In March 1902 the *Punch* artist E.T. Reed employed Dan's comic appearance to deflate one of Britain's most august politicians, the Colonial Secretary Joseph Chamberlain. Following Dan's visit to the House of Commons Reed depicted Chamberlain – famous for his upright bearing, elegant suits and gardenia button-hole – gambolling around the stage in the comedian's baggy trousers and battered top hat. Chamberlain's likeness is preserved, with many other eminent Victorians, in the National Portrait Gallery, London. There are over 30 portraits of the noble statesman – oil paintings, drawings and photographs. Dan is represented by a single small-scale pen and ink sketch. Drawn in the same linear style as Phil May, the portrait shows the comedian with a quizzical, straightlipped expression. His eyes are shaded by the trademark top hat, his neck disappearing into an oversize collar. Though accomplished it is not the work of any of the professional artists who produced portraits of the comedian over the years. It is by Dan himself.

34   Dan portrayed by Phil May

19

THE APOTHEOSIS OF ST DANCRAS

'I can't. I'm appearing at Brixton!'[1] Dan was jokingly dismissive when notified that he had been commanded to perform before King Edward VII. In reality he was delighted by the honour, immensely proud that he had become the first music-hall performer to be asked to appear before a reigning monarch. The butter on Dan's bread had never been spread more thickly, but there were disturbing signs that it was beginning to lose its flavour. A lessening workload meant that he was able to spend more time with his family in a beautiful new home, whilst his high income guaranteed a standard of living hardly imaginable in earlier days. He was also gratified to see his daughter Georgie making her own way in their shared profession. But his perception of his own remarkable achievements was tainted by physical and psychological disorders.

The seeds of self destruction had begun to germinate early in Dan's London career. Johnny Danvers remembered his wild behaviour when his first son, John, was christened in May 1888. Shortly before the event Dan was nowhere to be found, forcing Johnny to search the local pubs 'in case he might be drinking the child's health (which he frequently did on small provocation with comparative strangers)'. Eventually Dan appeared, riding on the box seat of a four-horse coach. After the christening the party travelled to Carshalton, in Surrey, where they spent the rest of the day in a local tavern. Dan was hyper-active, managing to break an ornamental flower urn when he decided to perform a clog dance on its pedestal. His guests urged him to 'keep calm and cool', but he was intent on celebrating in the most flamboyant fashion. 'Finally,' Johnny recalled 'he concluded the entertainment by seizing a bottle of champagne, and this in hand, scrambling up the ivy on to the roof, where he drank his boy's health and delivered an address on the advantages and responsibilities of being the parent of a fine son.'[2]

It seems clear that Dan had become another of music hall's heavy drinkers. Will Leno's far from sober influence was gradually replaced by that of other performers, all merrily chinking their glasses on the road to ruin. There were also many acquaintances ready to feed Dan drinks in order to enjoy his never-ending performance or to bathe in his reflected celebrity. Chance Newton recalled:

> Indeed, Dan followed me about, and kept with me whenever practicable, with dog-like fidelity. As a matter of fact, the golden hearted little chap would do anything I asked him, even in the unhappy time when, thanks to well-meaning but foolish 'treating' friends he had become too fond of the often devastating 'another with me' habit.

> Many a time was I able – when other equally loyal friends had failed – to get Dan away from his 'bar' companions both of the well-meaning and ear-biting and slavering sort. Many a night, for months together, did I 'capture' Dan when he had finished his night's work, and carry him off straight away to his home.[3]

The acute perception of the external world that had contributed so much to his comedy grew increasingly confused. His memory became uncertain, and increasing forgetfulness often resulted in missed appointments. Deafness also became a problem, causing him to struggle to hear the music of his songs. On stage, in an attempt to keep time with his accompaniment he developed the habit of rhythmically bobbing his head and making a peculiar semi-circular movement with his right arm.[4] Sometimes his poor hearing created embarrassing misunderstandings. At the close of *Mother Goose* the directors of the Theatre Royal arranged a surprise presentation of a service of silver plate to both Herbert and Dan. Following an effusive speech by the chairman, Dan was asked to respond. He had heard nothing of the glowing account of his own career and wrongly assumed that the gift was intended for Arthur Collins. 'Governor,' he announced 'it's a magnificent present! I congratulate you, and you deserve it.'[5]

It may have been difficult to detect the first signs of an impending breakdown. Dan's cruel practical jokes were, after all, in line with the boisterous humour of the time; his detestation of plagiarism and sensitivity to criticism were perhaps only extreme manifestations of professional pride; and even the vast and totally unnecessary quantities of fried food regularly purchased from a Clapham fish-and-chip shop could be put down to the memory of a hungry past. But his compulsive behaviour was becoming more severe. At the Ottawa fire matinee, held at Drury Lane on 19 June 1900, he succeeded in angering his theatrical hero Sir Henry Irving. No-one in the theatre anticipated a straight dramatic performance, but Dan, who had become fixated with the idea of appearing as Shakespeare's Richard III, launched into an impassioned soliloquy. Although quick to take offence over infringements of his own act, he had failed to consider that Irving would be annoyed at being so unexpectedly upstaged. Eventually Dan sensed that he needed to curtail his theatrical experiment. Perhaps he had noticed Irving in the wings, 'white with anger'[6] according to Jimmy Glover, or possibly the audience had shown uncomfortable signs of confusion. He decided to make light of the performance, taking his exit with a jaunty hornpipe.

35 Dan, Lydia and baby May

Guilt too, troubled Dan's mind. He and his fellow directors had lost large amounts of money when their small chain of music halls came under sustained attack from the major London syndicates. In an attempt to crush their new rivals the proprietors of the leading halls redrew contracts with their star performers, preventing them from appearing at the Leno/Campbell halls. It was a dubious tactic, but one which performers dependent on the syndicates for employment could not resist. Six years later the music-hall profession was to strike against such arbitrary powers, but in 1901, when Dan announced his resignation as a director of the four halls, individual performers had few rights. Many of Dan's friends and colleagues lost money when the chain collapsed, a cause of sorrow and self-recrimination to the ever-generous comedian.

Despite such afflictions Dan and Lydia succeeded in creating a mini-paradise for their six children. The family had lived at a number of addresses in the Clapham and Brixton area, and in 1900 they moved to Springfield House, in Atkins Road, South London.[7] Their new home was situated on the Clapham Park estate, an exclusive residential area developed by the architect of Queen Victoria's Osborne House, Thomas Cubitt. Like many other Clapham Park villas, the house had extensive gardens, conservatories, greenhouses and stables. Dan quickly set to work to populate the three acres of land with assorted livestock: white rabbits, pigeons, hens, cows called Milk and Rum, three horses for his carriages and a donkey that continued to possess rights of habitation after the house had been sold. There were also ducks on a large pond 'until the family used it for paddling purposes'.[8] A wooden studio was constructed where Dan worked on a gigantic painted panorama depicting a tour around the world.[9] Inside the house Lydia had the assistance of two maids and a cook, while a coachman and his family occupied rooms above the stables. Sometimes Dan and Lydia escorted their children on bicycle excursions, riding through the tree-lined streets of Clapham Park to the open spaces of Clapham, Tooting and Wandsworth Commons. Other communal activities included theatrical entertainments, featuring Dan, family and friends, presented in a large room which was given the name 'the Duke's Royal Theatre'.

The King's command was delivered to Dan when he and Lydia were dining at the Trocadero Restaurant on the evening of Saturday 21 November 1901. There was little time to make arrangements, for the performance, planned as a birthday surprise for Princess Maud, was to take place five days later. Also commanded to appear at Sandringham House were Seymour Hicks and Ellaline Terriss, a highly successful husband-and-wife team who had starred in many of the 1890s' most popular musical comedies.

When the day arrived Dan did his best to defuse everybody's nerves with a succession of wisecracks. On entering the royal omnibus which had collected the party from Wolverton Junction, near the house in Norfolk, he surveyed his fellow passengers and enquired of a footman 'Night Charges?'[10] – a reference to the motley collection of wrongdoers transported every evening to Bow Street Police Court by 'Black Maria' prison van.

After the royal party had dined, several hundred guests gathered in the ballroom, which had been converted into a temporary theatre. Seymour Hicks and Ellaline Terriss were to present scenes from *Scrooge* and their latest production *Papa's Wife*, while Dan was asked to start the entertainment. Although only allocated ten minutes, his 'turn' was so successful that he remained on stage for over half an hour. The elite audience were kept in fits of laughter, particularly the King, who was observed guffawing as Dan pointed out the location of the Refreshment Room in the Tower of London.

Dan's ability to amuse his hosts continued after his stage performance had ended. Whether by accident or design he contrived to be presented to the royal party in a bizarre travesty of a dress suit. His dresser had forgotten to pack certain key elements of wardrobe, forcing him to borrow a shirt and tie from Seymour Hicks. After a fruitless hunt for a pair of dress trousers Dan returned to Hicks and borrowed the lower part of a blue serge suit. A considerable disparity in height meant that the trouser legs had to be turned up by about four inches. The performers remained at Sandringham until three o'clock the next morning, enjoying a lavish supper served in the conservatory by 12 liveried footmen. Ellaline and Seymour and then Dan were called to private audiences with the King. On his return to the conservatory Dan joked that his engagement had been terminated. 'Well boys', he shrugged 'I've got my notice.'[11] Some time later he was sent a souvenir of the occasion – a diamond tie-pin ornamented with the royal monogram 'E.R.'.

The party returned to London next morning. Dan's reflective mood on the journey was recalled by Ellaline Terriss:

> ... he talked without effort for a couple of hours and kept us all spellbound, telling us of the vicissitudes of his early life, painting comic pictures of places and people with a Balzac touch, and though they were all funny stories his sad little face brought tears to my eyes as he told us of how he had starved and been obliged to sleep for two nights in succession against the bronzed lions outside the Great Hall in Liverpool[12]

Quickly dubbed 'The King's Jester' by the popular press, Dan wore his present from the king with pride. He told an interviewer: 'Since my return I have done nothing but show the pin to all and sundry. And down Clapham way where I live the great saying is, "Show us the pin,

Dan!"[13] Despite its valued status the pin, or its absence, was turned into a piece of stage business. Soon after the command performance Dan made as if to show the royal gift to the Pavilion audience. Following prolonged fumbling in his pockets he was compelled to 'come clean'. 'Well, you know how things are, these days,' he quipped, a cheeky allusion to the supposed pawning of the precious pin.

Seven months after his command performance Dan was given the opportunity to combine the new role of 'King's Jester' with his longer-standing position as a hero of the working-class public. On a sunny July Saturday in 1902 half a million Londoners gathered in 400 makeshift restaurants to celebrate the impending coronation. 'The King's Dinner to the Poor' was provided free of charge, as was the entertainment given by an army of peripatetic performers. Dan was in his element as he drove from one engagement to the next, acknowledging the cheers of bystanders and, no doubt, deriving inner satisfaction from the copious amounts of pies, puddings and beer that were freely available.

Dan's music-hall engagements had become far less arduous after Whitsun 1901, when he accepted a three-year contract to appear exclusively at the London Pavilion, at a salary of £150 per week. Other theatres of variety may have claimed finer decorative features, better orchestras and a more refined clientele, but the 'Pav' remained the most atmospheric of the central London halls. It had been opened in 1861 as a small hall constructed over the stable yard of the Black Horse Inn. A far grander building had been erected in 1885, with a columned façade that still dominates Piccadilly Circus. By the early 1900s the stage had been enlarged, but essentially the hall remained as Dan had always known it.

From the start of the new century Dan was provided with pantomime scripts particularly well suited to his style. In his first pantomime for Drury Lane, *Sleeping Beauty and the Beast* (1901), J. Hickory Wood supplied Dan and Herbert with a passage of dialogue that touched on the frailties of the human mind:

QUEEN: Do you know I don't believe we're what you call really *asleep*.
KING: What are we then?
QUEEN: We're in a trance, that is strictly speaking in two trances. You're in one trance, and I'm in the other. You see a trance is a very small thing; it only holds one at a time.
KING: What is a trance?
QUEEN: Oh, a trance is a kind of – cataleptic distemper. You say things, you know, and you know what you mean all the time you don't know what you're talking about and you can't *do* anything at all but keep on doing it and you know you're doing it but you don't know why.
KING: It's like being a member of parliament.

36 'Mother Goose', 1902

37 'Sister Anne', 1901

Two further musical comedy tours punctuated Dan's Drury Lane
and Pavilion appearances. A revised version of *Orlando Dando* opened at
the Dalston Theatre on 15 July 1901, while *Mr Wix of Wickham*, written
and composed by Herbert Darnley, commenced its run at the Borough
Theatre, Stratford, on 21 July 1902. Mr Wix, played by Dan, was the
manager of a general stores and leading member of the town guard. The
plot, revolving around Mr Wix being mistaken for the heir of a dukedom,
provided Dan with an opportunity to reprise his clog dance and also to
appear with his daughter Georgina. Both Dando and Wix were male
roles, but the two greatest triumphs of his career, in the Drury Lane
pantomimes of 1901/02 and 1902/03, were scored as women.

Sister Anne in *Bluebeard* was described by her creator Wood as 'a
sprightly, somewhat below middle-aged person who was of a "coming
on" disposition and who had not yet abandoned hope'.[14] Dan was immediately taken with the character, but confessed that he was 'very much
afraid' after reading through the part. When asked if it was not to his
liking he had replied: 'Oh yes, I like it very much, that's what I mean. I
like it so much that I'm afraid I shall overdo it, and I don't want to do
that.'[15]

The comic subtext of the pantomime was that Sister Anne was determined to supplant her younger sister in the affections of Bluebeard,
a notorious wife-slayer. In terms of physical beauty Anne, with her simple plaid dress and thinning hair, could offer little competition to Julia
James's glamorous Fatima. But Anne explained that she possessed a
hypnotic charm:

> Men don't usually fall easily in love with me – not suddenly. I
> sort of grow on them. Then they generally fall quite gracefully in
> love with me. But when they're once there then they're there for
> ever. I'm a sort of female rattlesnake.

Critics noted a change in Dan's style which was not entirely attributable
to Wood's sympathetic scripts. *The Times* drama critic observed:

> It is a quite peculiar and original Sister Anne, who dances break-
> downs and sings strange ballads to a still stranger harp and plays
> ping-pong with a frying-pan and potatoes and burlesques Sherlock
> Holmes and wears the oddest of garments and dresses her hair like
> Miss Morleena Kenwigs, and speaks in a piping voice – in short, it
> is none other than Mr Dan Leno whom we all know. And yet it is
> not quite the Mr Dan Leno we all know, but a slightly novel Dan
> Leno, chastened in style, as he is, a Leno tending not only to droll-
> ery but to edification. It is as though Dan Leno had become a clas-

sic in his life time – like another classic ending on 'o', Victor Hugo
– and were 'assisting' with proper dignity, at his own apotheosis.[16]

The following year's pantomime, *Mother Goose*, provided Dan with a
challenging role that combined several different portrayals of the same
woman. Wood's simple moral, that neither riches nor beauty alone bring
happiness, was illustrated by a series of magic transformations. The original poor, plain and generally pugnacious Mother Goose became a
wealthy but tasteless parvenu, who in turn changed into a pretty but
penniless young woman searching vainly for a suitor. Eventually, after
visits to 'The Magic Pool' and 'The Wishing Gate', Mother Goose reverted to her natural, but now contented, state.

Dan brought all his experience to the three characterisations, but his
sympathies were, of course, with the careworn drudge who started and
finished the magical journey of self-discovery. With her tattered shawl,
crumpled apron and battered boots Mother Goose was the final sum-
mation of Dan's working-class female characters. Although in his mind
she probably occupied courts and alleys in any number of industrial
towns, her geographical background was specifically identified as London in the pantomime's opening scene. Mother Goose and her geese had
been sent flying by a speeding automobile, occupied by two fur-clad and
goggled men. Assuming that such strangely dressed and careless drivers
must be from foreign parts, the old woman cursed them in pigeon
French, German and Italian. Finally it was revealed that even Londoners were capable of driving badly. 'We ain't no foreigners!' asserted the
first motorist. 'I drove a Brixton 'bus for twenty years.' 'Yus!' chimed in
the second. 'And mine was a privileged keb in Euston Station.'

The production was one of Drury Lane's most successful pantomimes, running until 28 March 1903. However, Dan had already begun
to exhibit disturbing changes in character. After recovering from a minor
breakdown in September 1902 he suffered a second and more severe illness in June 1903. Harry Randall witnessed his volatile behaviour at
close hand:

> … he would make some strange remark to us, and then, in a flash,
> would come out with one of his humorous tales describing his ex-
> periences in the early struggling days. Later the symptoms be-
> came more acute. Suddenly he would 'go for' his closest pals, and
> then the next morning there would be a most apologetic letter full
> of self reproach and regret.[17]

It soon became obvious to his friends and acquaintances that he was in a
state of paranoia. When the song writers J.P. Harrington and George Le
Brunn visited him at Springfield House, they found his mood swinging

from anxiety to cheerfulness. After greeting them with a finger to his lips and a whispered 'Did you see a man as you came in? He's after me!' he produced a gigantic box of specially imported cigars which he insisted they share.[18] The situation came to a climax when his desire to become a respected Shakespearian actor resulted in a late-night visit to the apartments of actress Constance Collier. Sir Herbert Beerbohm Tree's leading lady had returned at about one in the morning to discover Dan waiting for her in a darkened room. Her initial delight in meeting a comedian whom she had seen many times in pantomime soon turned to concern when it became obvious that his mind was in a state of turmoil:

> He said he was the son of a Scottish marquis and that his mother had been a housemaid in his father's great mansion somewhere in the north. He was nine years old when he tramped up to London with her, and they walked all those miles in the bitter winter. He sang outside village public-houses for a few coppers to get food, and they ate snow to quench their thirst as they tramped along the frozen roads! It took them nearly a month to get down from Scotland walking all the way.[19]

While holding her hand in a painful grip he explained that his greatest ambition was to play in Shakespeare. He had studied Irving for years, and for the previous six months had watched her performances, sitting in the gallery or at the back of the pit 'with his collar turned up so few would recognise him'. Constance, who had heard of the debacle when he appeared as Richard III, realised that he was serious when he offered her a five-year contract to appear with him in Shakespearian productions. Recognising that he was 'very ill' she persuaded him to return to his carriage, recommending that he should meet with Herbert Beerbohm Tree the following day.

On her arrival at His Majesty's Theatre, Haymarket, the following morning the actress found a scene of absolute chaos. A crowd of newspaper boys had congregated outside, counting the coins that Dan had distributed to them on his way to the theatre. The stage-door keeper was also a beneficiary having been awarded the money to buy himself a silk top hat. Thinking that Dan was involving them in a gigantic practical joke a group of actors were laughing as he wrote out contracts on scraps of paper. A message was despatched to Beerbohm Tree who, on arriving, led Dan to a quiet area in the stalls. They spoke earnestly until Dan's manager and two helpers arrived to escort the comedian from the theatre. Tree was shaken and troubled by the experience. 'If this is madness,' he confided to his leading lady, 'what is the point of being sane? If ever he plays Richard III it will be the greatest performance of the part we have ever seen. Let's go back to work. How dull normal people are.'

Later the same day Dan returned to Constance Collier's apartment, bearing a diamond broach as a gift. He was mortified when she refused both the present and the offer to become his leading lady. 'You don't think that I can play Shakespeare then?' he asked with tears running down his cheeks. Two days later Dan was admitted to Peckham House Lunatic Asylum, but not before he had presented the diamonds to a friendly barmaid.

The elderly Dr Alonzo Henry Stocker had owned Peckham House for many years when Dan was confined there in June 1903. Occupying an eighteenth century mansion with several acres of gardens, the hospital was situated in Peckham Road, Camberwell. Stocker's prediction that there would be a six month period of 'recovery' implied that he had a clear understanding of the condition. Despite a family tradition that Dan had been suffering from a brain tumour, it is probable that Stocker considered that his patient was afflicted by neurosyphilis, a late onset condition that often manifested itself in memory loss, sudden rages, grandiose ideas and impairment of the senses. With no available blood test it is now impossible to establish the cause of Dan's final illness. But the euphemistic term 'general paralysis of the insane' employed on the death certificate appears to show that his doctors were satisfied that they were dealing with a late syphilitic disorder.

38 Water-colour painting by Dan Leno

Although he escaped and returned home at least once, he was relatively content at Peckham House, agreeing to appear as guest of honour
at the hospital's summer fete. Much of his time was devoted to writing
and producing paintings which, according to the comedian Arthur
Roberts, provided evidence of an 'abnormal and tortured mind'.[20] Humour, always a reflex to Dan, was evident soon after he arrived at the
asylum. On his second day at Peckham House he became involved in an
argument about the accuracy of a clock. 'No, sir, it's quite right,' re-
assured the attendant, setting himself up for Dan's punch line: 'Then if
it's quite right, what's it doing here?'[21]

When Herbert paid a visit Dan confided that he had been writing a
pantomime. Asked if it was intended for 'the Lane' Dan was amused:
'No, of course not. For this place. And I've written such a part for you
Herbert, old boy.' Herbert was sceptical of Dan being able to resume his
career, but did not rule it out: 'If they can get him to take a very long sea
voyage, say to Australia, on a sailing vessel, it might restore him to his
old vigour of mind.'[22]

Dan's state of health became a national preoccupation, with King
Edward himself enquiring after his favourite comedian. By the end of
August Dan was sufficiently 'restored' to leave Peckham House for a
period of recuperation at Boscombe on the Dorset coast, but when
Georgie married Percy Lubbock in September he was still not considered
fit enough to attend the wedding, his duties devolving upon Johnny
Danvers. At Drury Lane, Collins was thrown into uncertainty by the
possibility of his re-appearance. Exigency plans were put in place, with
Harry Randall being engaged as principal comedian, with or without
Dan. In December Dan was finally ruled fit to appear, a decision that
entailed re-writing much of the script. Dan worked hard to learn his
part, faltering only once when a group of music-hall colleagues lured him
to the bar of the London Hippodrome. Acting on a desperate phone call
from Arthur Collins, H. Chance Newton rescued the comedian as 'he was
just beginning to get "fresh" and, of course, was preparing for his old impersonation of the "drinks round" man.'[23]

There were concerns that Dan would not be able to cope with the
stress of the Drury Lane first night. He had always complained of the
coolness and formality of the occasion, but now he had to face an intense
emotional response from a public who had not expected to see him on
stage again. On the first night of *Humpty Dumpty* Randall carefully
studied Dan's reactions:

When his introductory music started and Dan emerged from the
castle gate, gorgeously dressed up as 'Queen', preparing to descend
the steps, the ovation he obtained was remarkable. The audience
stood up in their seats and roared themselves hoarse. Directly he

made a sign, as if about to speak, it would break out again. I am certain this enthusiasm must have lasted quite five minutes.[24]

After stumbling through his first few lines of dialogue Dan regained composure and appeared to be back to his normal self. He continued to turn in good performances throughout the pantomime's long run, coping well with the punishing schedule of two four-hour productions daily for six weeks, and a further six weeks of evening shows. Off stage his temporary recovery period was running out. Imaginary grievances would result in him causing acrimonious scenes and locking himself in his dressing room. Much of his anger was directed at Herbert, although his friend accepted such treatment stoically, explaining 'Dan's in his tantrums again.' At the conclusion of *Humpty Dumpty* Dan and Herbert re-affirmed their friendship with a touching duet:

In the panto of Old Drury Lane
We have both come together again,
And we hope to appear
For many a year
In the panto of Old Drury Lane.

Following the pantomime Dan drifted into a twilight world of performance, often accepting engagements at seaside towns in an attempt to combine work with convalescence. His unstable state of mind was widely recognised, and few were surprised by episodes of odd behaviour. Dan also learned to accommodate his own unsure grasp of everyday events. When the proprietor of a Folkestone hall explained that he had arrived a week early he decided to stay for a holiday, indulging his love of the sea by travelling back and forth across the Channel.

In July he was crushed by the most unexpected news. Herbert, who had seemed as solid and enduring as the Tower of London, died after bumping his leg against a carriage step. Blood poisoning set in, leading to a fatal apoplectic seizure. The day following Herbert's death Hickory Wood met Dan on a train returning to London, after appearing at the Kursaal, Harrogate, in Yorkshire. Throughout the journey Dan spoke about his old friend, at one time referring to his irritating habit of smoking in their shared dressing room. 'Dear old Herbert,' he grieved. 'I'd give a good deal to smell one of his cigars right now.'[25]

39 Dan Leno at the London Pavilion, 1904

There was one final voyage on the Irish Sea, in August, when Dan and his family took a holiday on the Isle of Man. In October he reappeared at the London Pavilion. He had a batch of new songs, including a female character-study 'The Widow with Memories of Friday Nights'. The performances were painful for audience and Dan alike. Sometimes he forgot the words of his songs and stood bemused on stage. Behind the scenes an incident involving a fellow performer, Maggie Duggan, forced him to issue an embarrassing apology: 'I hereby express my regret that anything in my conduct towards you on Thursday, 13th should have caused you any annoyance. I apologise to you, therefore, and undertake that I will never speak to you again unless spoken to by you.'[26] An old canker erupted with a supposed criticism leading to an angry and somewhat implausible note being added to his *Era* card:

Mr Dan Leno. Pavilion, where I am singing Two New Songs of my own, copied from no one. The 'Boy' Song, which an unkind critic compared to another, I beg to say I wrote and Sang in Glasgow Thirty-one years ago. Who is copying now? All my Thirty-four Minutes' Gags are copied from no one.[27]

Absent from the Pavilion on Monday 10th and Tuesday 11th, Dan's final appearance took place on Thursday, 20th October. Following the performance he was escorted home by his son John, and soon after was confined to bed. His condition rapidly deteriorated and he died, in Lydia's arms, shortly before 12 noon on the last day of the month. The spirit of St Pancras guided him to the very last. One of his final public acts was to call in at the Belgrave Hospital for Children, Kennington, to leave a donation. A year and a half later it was announced that £625 had been raised to dedicate a cot in the hospital to his memory. 'Everybody – mark this – everybody has to be born one way or another ... you have to go through this inconvenience.'

20

POSTSCRIPT

The newly established Gaumont Film Company was rapidly changing the face of popular entertainment. The film of Dan's funeral, probably taken by William Hough, was a straightforward newsreel, but the company's fiction productions had evolved from single-shot views to multi-scene narratives that told exciting and relatively complex stories. One of Gaumont's most innovative directors, Alfred Collins, was an actor and music-hall performer who had appeared with Dan in *Mother Goose*. Like Dan, whom he idolised, Alf had been born in a London slum and had worked hard to make his way in the theatrical profession. But unlike Dan he had channelled his experience into a new medium, combining slapstick elements of music hall and pantomime to create some of the first 'chase' movies.

Within a few years films had broken away from their music-hall background and were attracting huge audiences to purpose built 'electric palaces'. Gradually Dan's old haunts, The Foresters, Gatti's, the Tivoli, the Empire, the Alhambra and the Pavilion succumbed to cinema use. A dwindling number of music halls continued to provide live entertainment, although in an attempt to rival the exciting new medium they offered novelty and sensation rather than old-fashioned stand-up comedy. In 1911 the New Middlesex Theatre of Varieties opened on the site of the 'Old Mo', but its 3000-seat auditorium had none of the intimacy or atmosphere of the hall where Dan had made his London debut.

As the story-telling potential of films grew greater, several of Dan's music-hall contemporaries transferred their talents to the screen. The success of George Robey, Albert Chevalier, Arthur Conquest and Drury Lane's last great clown, 'Whimsical' Walker, suggests that Dan himself might have become a star of the early cinema. A younger generation of variety artists deserted the stage to start new careers in films. Fred Evans, the grandson of another popular Drury Lane clown, was transformed into 'Pimple', the anarchistic hero of over 100 comedies; Billy Merson, singer of 'The Spaniard that Blighted My Life', co-founded the Homeland Film Company to produce extended screen versions of his music-hall act; and the son of the ill-fated vocalist Charles Chaplin Senior abandoned his music-hall career to become the world's most famous movie star.

In an obituary Max Beerbohm regretted that Dan had been denied the possibility of a mechanical afterlife:

> Some day, no doubt, the phonograph and the bioscope will have been so adjusted to each other that we shall see and hear past actors and singers as well as though they were alive before us.

> I wish Dan Leno could have been thus immortalised. No actor of our time deserved immortality as much as he.[1]

Denied celluloid immortality, Dan lived on in the minds of his audiences and fellow performers. A famous Hamlet, Sir John Martin-Harvey, recalled that whenever he addressed the words 'a fellow of infinite jest of most excellent fancy' to the skull of the jester Yorick he inevitably thought of 'that gay and tragic genius, Dan Leno'.[2] With posthumous fame balanced against diminishing recollections of his performance, it was not long before Dan's name developed a powerful mystique. His was an increasingly obscure but still attractive cachet, ever-applicable to new generations of comedians. Parallels have often been drawn between his humour and the screen comedy of Charlie Chaplin and Stan Laurel, and the work of later performers such as Spike Milligan, the Goons and Monty Python's Flying Circus, but there is no clear line of development from Dan to modernity. Even the pantomime dames whom he had portrayed with sympathy and intelligence soon reverted to the grotesque stereotypes of earlier years. Occasionally there have been attempts to present his original material to a modern audience, although the dramatists who have woven his songs and patter into stage, TV and radio plays have inevitably discovered the difficulties in breathing new life into old comedy. Of all Dan's champions the most assiduous has been Roy Hudd, a comedian whose interest in his 'King Rat' predecessor was ignited by a mystical experience first recounted in his introduction to the 1968 reissue of *Hys Booke*. Perhaps the most unusual of Dan's post-mortem appearances was when the novelist Peter Ackroyd ceremoniously rearranged the details of his life and times for a blood-soaked tale of Victorian murder, *Dan Leno and the Limehouse Golem*.

It is not easy to separate Dan's amorphous reputation from his supernatural presence, a benign entity whose helpful intervention has been reported over the years by several struggling comedians. His spiritual form is said to have guided a number of actors, particularly young women, through difficult roles at the Theatre Royal. Sometimes he has appeared in his old dressing room flashing a reassuring smile and leaving a refreshing fragrance of lavender. A more extended visitation occurred when the film star Peter Sellers became convinced that Dan was assisting him with important career decisions. Over a period of years 'Dan' provided advice on film performances and on the publication of a biography in 1968. It was a situation that eventually resulted in Sellers forcing entrance into Dan's old home in Brixton, shouting 'Dan. It's me, Pete. I know you're here. Talk to me, Dan.'[3] Although Dan's ghostly collaborations were not always so dramatic, his enduring place in the imagination of many comedians is quite clear.

Had talking pictures been invented 25 years earlier, Dan's artistry might well have been preserved for future generations, but his material would have been rendered largely meaningless by the passage of time. The society that he so successfully represented on stage was in terminal decline, pushed like a vanquished tribe into out-of-the way and ill-favoured pockets of existence. One such enclave, a photographer's shop and studio, was situated at 221 Westminster Bridge Road, close to 'Poverty Corner' and the Waterloo Road venue for the painting 'Popularity'. Charles Chaplin called in at Edward Sharp's shop during his triumphant return visit to London in 1921; a framed portrait of Dan that he remembered was still displayed in the window. Encouraged by such a degree of continuity Charlie, the most recognisable man on earth, entered and enquired about his own portrait taken soon after he had started in the variety profession:

'My name is Chaplin. You photographed me fifteen years ago.
I want to buy some copies.'
'Oh, we destroyed the negatives long ago.'
'Have you destroyed Mr Leno's negatives?'
'No, but Mr Leno is a famous comedian.'[4]

In the course of time even the backward-looking assistant at Sharp's photographic emporium might have conceded that Charlie Chaplin had become a more famous comedian than Dan Leno. Memories of Dan faded as his family moved on with their lives. In 1907 Lydia married Charles F. Best, a variety performer known professionally as 'Serini the Contortionist'. She had inherited £10,994 and lived, presumably, in comfort until her death in Brighton in 1942. Georgie's first husband died at the early age of 24, and was buried with Dan in 1905. She remarried four years later and lived into old age. Perhaps inspired by his childhood bicycle-excursions, Dan's eldest son John set up his own motorcycle business during the early 1900s, later becoming sales manager for Hampton cars. Sidney adopted his father's name to appear as 'Dan Leno, Junior' in revue and pantomime during a long career which extended into the 1950s. Ernie and May also became performers, while Herbert lived long enough to assist Gyles Brandreth with his biography of Dan which appeared in 1977. Johnny Danvers survived his 'uncle' by 35 years, dying in 1939 after a painful retirement forced upon him by chronic arthritis.

Far-reaching changes in society steadily deprived Dan's humour of its relevance. The horrors of two world wars stripped Sergeant Smirks' recruiting patter of what persuasiveness it might once have possessed, whilst the creation of a national health service completely undermined Dr McFarback's market for bottles of nerve medicine. Similarly, the relentless rise of consumerism meant that even the most menial of workers might possess a diamond ring without fear of arbitrary dismissal. The imaginary background of his songs also began to disappear as large areas of Victorian housing were demolished to make way for council estates and the first tower blocks. In 1971 the quaint little Granville, at Walham Green, was torn down overnight by property developers anxious to avoid a last-minute reprieve. Nearby, the local authority designated a nondescript terrace of new houses 'Dan Leno Walk'. It was an empty and belated gesture. The day had already dawned when nobody knew Mrs Kelly.

JOHNNY DANVERS·   DAN LENO·   HERBERT CAMPBELL·

8086

40   Johnny, Dan and Herbert take their leave

NOTES

AN INCONVENIENCE

1 Leno, Dan, *Dan Leno: Hys Booke*. London, 1899, p. 22.
2 Reynolds, G.W.M., *The Mysteries of the Court of London* (second series). London, n.d., p. 270.
3 Ibid., p. 270.
4 *The Quaver; or, Songster's Pocket Companion*. London, 1844, pp. 185–7.
5 Mayhew, Henry, *London Labour and the London Poor*, Vol. III. London, 2nd edn., 1862, p. 205.
6 Ibid., p. 205.
7 *The Era*, 9 March 1856.
8 Ibid., 1 June, 13 July 1857.
9 Hollingshead, John, *Ragged London in 1861*. London, 1861, p. 135.
10 Ibid., pp. 141–2.
11 *Dan Leno: Hys Booke*, p. 25.
12 Hardy, Thomas, *Selected Poems*. London, 1998, p.20.
13 *The Era*, 29 June, 7 September, 14 September 1862.
14 Ibid., 12 April 1863.

THE INFANT WONDER

1 Newton, H. Chance, *Idols of the 'Halls'*. London, 1928, p.53.
2 Leno, Dan, *Dan Leno: Hys Booke*. London, 1899, pp. 28–9.
3 Ibid., p. 32
4 Wood, J. Hickory, *Dan Leno*. London, 1905, p. 34.
5 *The Era*, 12 February 1860, records William Leno appearing as Clown in *Harlequin and the Yellow Dwarf* at the Theatre Royal, South Shields.
6 *Liverpool Mercury*, 19 December 1865.
7 Ibid.
8 Broadbent, R.J., *Annals of the Liverpool Stage*. Liverpool, 1908, p. 339.
9 Bowers, Judith, *Stan Laurel and Other Star Turns of the Pantopticon*. Edinburgh, 2007, p. 32.
10 *The Era*, 23 December 1866.
11 Broadbent, *Annals of the Liverpool Stage*, p. 350.
12 *Liverpool Mercury*, 21 May 1867.

13 *The Era*, 11 October 1868.
14 Ibid., 5 January 1867.
15 Ibid., 23 February 1868.
16 Ibid., 1 November 1868.
17 Ibid., 15 November 1868.
18 Ibid., 29 November 1868.
19 Ibid., 10 January 1869.
20 Wood, *Dan Leno*, p. 68. Bransby Williams gives a fuller account of the meeting in *An Actor's Story*. London, Methuen, 1909.
21 Williams, Bransby, *Bransby Williams by Himself*. London, 1954, p. 195.
22 Wood, *Dan Leno*, p. 6.
23 *The Era*, 14 November 1869.
24 Ibid., 26 December 1869.
25 *The Porcupine*, 24 December 1869.
26 *The Era*, 9 January 1870.
27 Ibid., 26 October 1901.
28 Wood, *Dan Leno*, p. 7.
29 Sims, George R., *My Life. Sixty Years of Bohemian London*. London, 1917, pp. 116–17.

NIGHTMARE YEARS

1   'A Chat with Dan Leno', *The Era*, 26 October 1901.
2   'In the Days of My Youth, Chapters of Autobiography. CLXV – Dan Leno', *M. A. P.*, 10 August 1901.
3   *The Era*, 17 March, 14 April 1872.
4   *Freeman's Journal and Daily Advertiser*, 21 August 1872.
5   Baker, Richard Anthony, *British Music Hall. An Illustrated History*. Thrupp, Stroud, 2005, p. 35.
6   Wood, J. Hickory, *Dan Leno*. London, 1905, pp. 82–3.
7   Chirgwin, G.H., *Chirgwin's Chirrup*. London, 1912.
8   *The Football News*, Nottingham, 5 November 1904.
9   Coborn, Charles, *The Man Who Broke the Bank*. London, 1928, p. 142.
10 *The Era*, 6 October 1878.
11 *Bristol Mercury and Daily Post*, 3 June 1879.
12 'Leno on Clogs', *The Encore*, 10 March 1904.
13 Wood, *Dan Leno*, pp. 83–4.
14 Johnny's paternal grandparents were James Harold and Mary Danvers.
15 John Danvers Harold died on 26 October 1868 leaving a wife and four children. He had at least one child, Charles Edward Harold, by an earlier marriage or relationship. An appeal on behalf of his family was issued by E. T. Rossborough, Manager of the Britannia Music Hall, Glasgow, in *The Era*, 1 November 1868.
16 Wood, *Dan Leno*, pp. 54–6.
17 Ibid., p.15.

MONARCH IN WOODEN SHOES

1 'In the Days of My Youth, Chapters of Autobiography. CLXV – Dan Leno', *M. A. P.*, 10 August 1901.
2 *The Era*, 4 January 1880.
3 *The Entr'acte*, 24 August 1889.
4 'A Peep into Belmont's Scrap Book', *The Variety Theatre*, 29 September 1905.
5 Mellor, G.J., *The Northern Music Hall*. Newcastle upon Tyne, 1970, p. 77.
6 *The Era*, 30 May 1880.
7 Ibid.
8 Ibid., 27 June 1880.
9 Wood, J. Hickory, *Dan Leno*. London, 1905, p. 87.
10 Ibid.
11 *The Era*, 18 June 1881.
12 Ibid., 25 June 1881.
13 Ibid., 23 July 1881.
14 Ibid., 30 July 1881.
15 Ibid., 7 January 1882.
16 Ibid., 22 April 1882.
17 Ibid., 29 April 1882.
18 Coburn, Charles, *The Man Who Broke the Bank*. London, 1928, p. 150.
19 Wood, *Dan Leno*, p. 67.
20 *The Era*, 26 May 1883.
21 Ibid., 26 May 1883.
22 Ibid., 26 May 1883.
23 *The Stage*, 20 May 1881.
24 Ibid., 13 January 1882.
25 *The Era*, 29 December 1883.
26 Ibid., 18 February 1884.
27 Ibid., December 1883.

LENO'S GRAND VARIETIES

1 *Evening Telegraph and Star*, Sheffield, 30 May 1893.
2 Farson, Daniel, *Marie Lloyd and Music Hall*. London, 1972, p. 75.
3 Wood, J. Hickory, *Dan Leno*. London, 1905, pp. 60–1.
4 Ibid., pp. 30–5.
5 *The Era*, 5 November 1904.
6 Wood, *Dan Leno*, p. 90.
7 Ibid., p. 91.
8 Ibid., p. 75.

THE TALK OF LONDON

1 *The Era*, 14 February 1885.
2 Randall, Harry, *Harry Randall: Old Time Comedian*. London [1932], p. 38.

3   *The Era*, 21 February 1885.
4   Anstey, F., 'London Music Halls', *Harper's New Monthly Magazine*. New York, 1891.
5   Ibid.
6   Ibid.
7   Randall, *Harry Randall: Old Time Comedian*, p. 48.
8   Newton, H. Chance, *Idols of the 'Halls'*. London, 1928, pp. 66–7.
9   *The Entr'acte*, 26 October 1885.
10 Furniss, Harry, *Some Victorian Men*. London, 1924, pp. 157–8.
11 Wood, *Dan Leno*, p. 117.

DAME DURDEN AND MR TAMBO
1   *Dan Leno: Hys Booke*, pp. 42–6.
2   Wood, J. Hickory, *Dan Leno*. London, 1905, p. 52.
3   Ibid., p. 88.
4   *The Era*, 20 February 1886.
5   Wood, *Dan Leno*, p. 88.
6   Ibid., pp. 56–7.
7   *The Era*, 20 February 1886.
8   Ibid., 27 November 1886.
9   *Punch*, 27 March 1886.
10 *The Era*, 26 June 1886.
11 'Dan Leno: His Life', *English Illustrated Magazine*, January 1902.
12 Robey, George, *Looking Back on Life*. London, 1933, p. 59.
13 Desmond, Shaw, *The Days That Were*. London, 1927, p. 168.
14 Williams, Bransby, *Bransby Williams by Himself*. London, 1954, p. 98.

THE WAR BETWEEN THE SEXES
1   Anstey, F., 'London Music Halls', *Harper's New Monthly Magazine*. New York, 1891.
2   'The Middlesex Music Hall', *Pick-Me-Up*, 25 July 1891.
3   Booth, J.B., *The Days We Knew*. London, 1943, p. 53.
4   *The Era*, 12 March 1887.
5   Williams, Bransby, *An Actor's Story*. London, 1909, p. 178.
6   *The Era*, 30 December 1887.
7   *The Stage*, 30 December 1887.
8   *The Era*, 7 April 1888.
9   *The Entr'acte*, 14 April 1888.
10 Booth, *The Days We Knew*, p. 54.
11 *The Era*, 9 June 1888.
12 Ibid., 8 September 1888.
13 Ibid., 29 September 1888
14 Ibid., 10 November 1888.

15 Ibid., 'A Chat With Dan Leno', 26 October 1901.
16 *The Dramatic Peerage*. London, 1892, p. 192.
17 Glover, James M., *Jimmy Glover: His Book*. London, 1911, p. 158.

THE REIGN OF AUGUSTUS

1 Glover, James M., *Jimmy Glover: His Book*. London, 1911, pp. 158–9.
2 *Penny Illustrated Paper*, 5 January 1887.
3 *The Era*, 1 June 1889.
4 *The Times*, 10 May 1889.
5 Wood, J. Hickory, *Dan Leno*. London, 1905, p. 99.
6 Ibid., p. 125.
7 *Penny Illustrated Paper*, 3 January 1891.
8 Wood, *Dan Leno*, p. 126.

CRUFFINS AND MUMPETS FOR TEA

1 Booth, J.B., *The Days We Knew*. London, 1943, p. 53
2 Harrington, J.P., quoted in *Music Hall*, May 2003.

A LARGE, GENIAL GENTLEMAN

1 *The London Magazine*, quoted in *The Era*, 23 July 1904.
2 Lucas, E.V., *A Little of Everything*. London, 1912, p. 25.
3 Beerbohm, Max, *The Morning Leader*, 21 July 1904.
4 *The Era*, 23 July 1904.
5 *Penny Illustrated Paper*, 2 January 1888.
6 *The Times*, 1 April 1892.
7 *Illustrated London News*, 31 December 1892.
8 Ibid.
9 Archer, William, *The Theatrical 'World' of 1894*. London, 1895, pp. 7–8.

POPULARITY

1 Chaplin, Charles, *My Early Years*. London, 1979, p. 7.
2 Burke, Thomas, *City of Encounters*. London, 1932, pp. 153–4.
3 *Penny Illustrated Paper*, 16 August 1884.
4 Chaplin, *My Early Years*. pp. 52–3.
5 Wood, J. Hickory, *Dan Leno*. London, 1905, p. 277.
6 Ibid, pp. 140–1.
7 Roberts, Arthur, *Fifty Years of Spoof London*. 1927, pp. 142–4.
8 *New Era*, 28 January 1888
9 Randall, Harry, *Harry Randall: Old Time Comedian*. London, 1930, pp. 146–7.
10 'Dan Leno: His Life', *English Illustrated Magazine*, January 1902.

11 Beerbohm, Max, *Around Theatres*. London, 1953, p. 350.
12 Williams, Bransby, *An Actor's Story*. London, 1909, p. 184.
13 Wood, *Dan Leno*, p. 227.
14 Hotten, J.C., introduction to Sala, George Augustus, *Robson*. London, 1864, p. 21.
15 Scott, Clement, introduction to *Dan Leno: Hys Booke*, p. 19.
16 *The Bristol Times and Mirror*, 17 November 1897.
17 Wood, *Dan Leno*, p. 121.
18 Ibid., p. 229.
19 Randall, *Harry Randall*, p. 155.
20 Newton, H. Chance, *Idols of the 'Halls'*. London, 1928, pp. 68–9.
21 Williams, Bransby, *Bransby Williams by Himself*. London, 1954, pp. 56–8.

REGIME CHANGE IN DRURY LANE

1 *Punch*, 12 January 1895.
2 *The Sketch*, 2 January 1895.
3 *Penny Illustrated Paper*, 28 December 1895.
4 Ibid., 30 July 1898.
5 *The Era*, 27 May 1899.
6 Barnes, John, *The Beginnings of the Cinema in England*, Vol. 1. Newton Abbot, 1976, pp. 95–6.
7 Warwick Trading Company catalogue, quoted in Barnes, *The Beginnings of the Cinema in England*, Vol. V. Exeter, 1997, pp. 273.
8 *The Idler*, March 1896.
9 Wood, J. Hickory, *Dan Leno*. London, 1905, p. 128.
10 Glover, James M., *Jimmy Glover: His Book*, London, 1911, pp. 75–6.
11 Ibid., p. 76.

THE FUNNIEST MAN ON EARTH

1 'Dan Leno: His Life', *English Illustrated Magazine*, January 1902.
2 Wood, J. Hickory, *Dan Leno*. London, 1905, p. 175.
3 Ibid., p. 38.
4 *The Times*, 27 January 1894, p. 3.
5 Furniss, Harry, *Some Victorian Men*. London, 1924, pp. 158–9.
6 Payne, Teddy, 'Musical Comedy and Me', *The Penny Illustrated Paper*, 3 April 1909.
7 Disraeli, Benjamin, *Sybil*, Book 2. London, 1845, ch. 5.
8 *The Encore*, 3 June 1897.
9 Williams, Bransby, *Bransby Williams by Himself*. London, 1954, pp. 197.
10 'Music-Hall Celebrities: Mr Dan Leno', *The Encore*, 3 June 1897.
11 For a full description of Dan's New York debut, see 'Dan Leno in America', *The Era*, 24 April 1897.
12 Report quoted in Wood, *Dan Leno*. p. 165.

13 *New York Times*, 18 April 1897.
14 Wood, *Dan Leno*. p. 172.

ORLANDO DANDO

1 *The Era*, 3 September 1898.
2 Public Record Office, BT 31/31529/52795.
3 Glover, James M., *Jimmy Glover: His Book*. London, 1911, p. 157.
4 *The Playgoer*, June 1906.
5 Wood, J. Hickory, *Dan Leno*. London, 1905, pp. 149–50.
6 Leno, Dan, 'When I Was a Widow', *Era Annual*, 1902. Reprinted in *Music Hall*, June 1980.

GRIMALDI'S SCISSORS

1 Hibbert, H.G., *Fifty Years of a Londoner's Life*. London, 1916, p. 57.
2 Wood, J. Hickory, *Dan Leno*. London, 1905, p. 266.
3 Ibid., p. 50
4 Glover, James M., *Jimmy Glover: His Book*. London, 1911, pp. 153–4.
5 Beerbohm, Max, *More Theatres*. London, 1969, p. 528.
6 *The Sketch*, 27 December 1899.
7 *The Era*, 5 November 1904.

THE LIVING IMAGE

1 The claim that Thomas Coates Elder ghost-wrote *Dan Leno: Hys Booke* surfaced many years after its publication. By a curious coincidence, information on Collins/Greening's subsequent career in Australia was provided by one David Elder.
2 Leno, Dan, *Dan Leno:Hys Booke*. London, 1899, pp. 25–7.
3 Wood, J. Hickory, *Dan Leno*. London, 1905, p. 200.
4 Ibid., p. 216.
5 *The Era*, 1 July 1899.
6 Ibid., 22 July 1899.
7 Ibid., 22 September 1900.
8 Anthony, Barry, 'A "Kinora" Discovery: Thirty Seconds of Dan Leno on Film'. *Sight and Sound*, Winter 1989/90.
9 *Pearson's Magazine*, July 1903.
10 'Voice Reproduction', *The Playgoer*, April 1903.
11 Wood, *Dan Leno*. pp. 165–6.
12 *The Penny Illustrated Paper*, 20 December 1897.

THE APOTHEOSIS OF ST DANCRAS

1 'Dan Leno: His Life', *The English Illustrated Magazine*, January 1902.
2 Wood, J. Hickory, *Dan Leno*. London, 1905, pp. 252–4.
3 Newton, H. Chance, *Idols of the 'Halls'*. London, 1928, p. 68.
4 Wood, *Dan Leno*. p. 153
5 Ibid., p. 136.
6 Glover, James M., *Jimmy Glover: His Book*. London, 1911, p. 155.
7 Dan and Lydia lived at 278 Kennington Cross in 1888, 27 Cavendish Road, Clapham, in 1891, 345 Clapham Road in 1894–97 and 46 Akerman Road, Brixton, from 1898.
8 'Favourite Entertainers: No. 4, Mr Dan Leno', *The Playgoer*, April 1902.
9 Originally intended for Will Leno to use in a new theatrical venture, the panorama was offered for sale by Lydia in *The Stage*, 13 April 1905.
10 Wood, *Dan Leno*. p. 208.
11 Ibid., p. 248.
12 Terriss, Ellaline, *Ellaline Terriss: By Herself and With Others*. London, 1928, pp. 34–5.
13 'Dan Leno: His Life'.
14 Wood, *Dan Leno*. p. 133.
15 Ibid., p. 120
16 *The Times*, 27 December 1901.
17 Randall, Harry, *Harry Randall: Old Time Comedian*. London, 1930, p. 158.
18 Harrington, J.P., quoted in *Music Hall*, May 2003.
19 Collier, Constance, *Harlequinade*. London, 1929.
20 Roberts, Arthur, *Fifty Years of Spoof*. London, 1927, p. 95.
21 Wood, *Dan Leno*. p. 278.
22 'Stars of Stageland: Mr Herbert Campbell', unidentified cutting in the Tony Barker Collection.
23 Newton, *Idols of the 'Halls'*, p. 72.
24 Randall, *Harry Randall*, pp. 168–9.
25 Wood, *Dan Leno*, p. 280.
26 *The Era*, 22 October 1904.
27 Ibid., 1 October 1904.

POSTSCRIPT

1 Beerbohm, Max, *Around Theatres*. London, 1953, p. 352.
2 Martin Harvey, Sir John, *The Autobiography of Sir John Martin-Harvey*. London, 1933, p. 313.
3 Evans, Peter, 'Woooooooooh!', *The Independent*, 19 August 2002.
4 Chaplin, Charlie, *My Wonderful Visit*. London, 1922, pp. 101–2.

SELECT BIBLIOGRAPHY

Books

Brandreth, Gyles, *The Funniest Man on Earth. The Story of Dan Leno*. London, 1977.
Coborn, Charles, *The Man Who Broke the Bank*. London, 1928.
Glover, James, *Jimmy Glover: His Book*. London, 1911.
Leno, Dan, *Dan Leno: Hys Book*. London, 1899.
Newton, H. Chance, *Idols of the 'Halls'*. London, 1928.
Randall, Harry, *Harry Randall, Old Time Comedian*. London, 1930.
Williams, Bransby, *An Actor's Story*. London, 1909.
Williams, Bransby *Bransby Williams by Himself*. London, 1954.
Wood, J. Hickory, *Dan Leno*. London, 1905.

Articles by or about Dan Leno

'A Chat with Dan Leno', *The Era*, 26 October 1901.
'Dan Leno. His Life', *English Illustrated Magazine*, January 1902.
'Dan Leno at Home', *The Era*, 7 January 1893.
'Dan Leno in America', *The Era*, 24 April 1897.
'Empire Celebrities. Dan Leno Interviewed', *Western Mail* (Cardiff), 5 December 1893.
'Favourite Entertainers. No. 4. Mr. Dan Leno', *The Playgoer*, April 1902.
Leno, Dan, 'I Remember'', *The Era Annual*, 1904.
Leno, Dan, 'In the Days of My Youth. Chapters of Autobiography. CLXV', *M. A. P.*, 10 August 1901.
Leno, Dan, 'When I Was a Widow', *The Era Annual*, 1902.
'Leno on Clogs', *The Encore*, 10 March 1904.
'Music-Hall Celebrities. Mr Dan Leno', *The Encore*, 29 September 1893.
'Music-Hall Celebrities. Mr Dan Leno', *The Encore*, 3 June 1897.
'Music-Hall Celebrities. Mr Dan Leno', *The Encore*, 11 May 1899.
'The People's Dan', *Eureka*, Christmas 1897.

For general bibliographies of music hall see Laurence Senelick, David F. Cheshire and Ulrich Schneider, *British Music Hall 1840–1923*, Hamden, Conn.:, 1981, and Richard Anthony Baker, *British Music Hall: An Illustrated History*, Thrupp, 2005. A vast amount of day to day information about Leno and his music hall contemporaries is to be found in the theatrical periodicals *The Era* (1838-1939); *The Entr'acte* (1869–1907); *The Stage* (1880-); *The Music Hall and Theatre Review* (1889–1912); and *The Encore* (1892–1930). In more recent years *Music Hall* (1978–) and *Music Hall Studies* (2008–) have set new standards for research into the history of the subject.

INDEX